The MEANING
of the
NEW TESTAMENT

Barclay M. Newman

BROADMAN PRESS
Nashville, Tennessee

DEWEY DECIMAL CLASSIFICATION NUMBER: 225
Library of Congress catalog card number: 66-19906
Printed in the United States of America
3.5MH6613

To my wife,
Jean
and our daughters two,
Tina *and* Dana

Preface

The Meaning of the New Testament was written both as a textbook for students taking their first course of study in the New Testament and for pastors, Sunday School teachers, and others interested in exploring the meaning of the New Testament. Since the New Testament cannot be understood apart from its Jewish heritage, the theme has been followed of continuity-discontinuity between the faith of Israel and the faith of the Church, between the Old Wine and the New Wine.

The central core of the book consists of a background study and interpretation of each New Testament writing, while the initial division draws attention to the religious life and thought of Judaism in light of its historical setting. Contained in the final section are a brief history of the New Testament canon and a discussion of the inspiration and authority of the New Testament. Maps, photographs, and other helps have been provided so as to make the book as serviceable as possible.

At least two factors have suggested the need for a selected Bibliography of important and readily accessible works in English to be provided at the end of the book. (1) As a general rule bibliographical references are given in the footnotes only where there is a conscious and direct dependence upon a specific source. Sometimes these sources are neither in English nor immediately accessible to the college student or to the general reader. (2) Although an attempt has been made to present both representative and diverse points of view throughout, this has not been possible at every place. The Bibliography includes the titles of books which supplement the material in the text and represent alternative viewpoints.

Much appreciation is due to many persons for their assistance in this undertaking. The advice of several readers has contributed toward making this a better volume than it otherwise would have been. In particular the detailed criticisms of my former colleague, Dr. Robert

S. Alley of the University of Richmond, have been most helpful. Another former colleague, Dr. Oscar S. Brooks of William Jewell College, made some helpful suggestions concerning the earlier chapters.

Although my teaching load remained constant during the time that I was working on this manuscript, I am grateful to William Jewell College for typing assistance in the person of Miss Mary Sprankle, who, along with my wife, typed the manuscript from my handwritten draft. Dr. H. Guy Moore, President of William Jewell College, was always a source of encouragement to me. Nor can I fail to thank my former professors at Union University and the Southern Baptist Theological Seminary, whose influence is evident in numerous ways. Finally, I am most grateful to my wife and family for their many sacrifices and constant understanding during the while that I was engaged in writing.

Most Scripture quotations are from the Revised Standard Version of the Bible, copyrighted 1946 and 1952, and from the Revised Standard Version of the Apocrypha, copyrighted 1957, by the Division of Christian Education, National Council of Churches, and are used by permission. Some translations are original, and the translation of the Apocrypha by Edgar J. Goodspeed has been used in a few places. Quotations from Irenaeus, Ignatius, Justin Martyr, and the Muratorian Canon are from Volumes I, VI, and VII of *The Ante-Nicene Fathers*, edited by Alexander Roberts and James Donaldson, and are used by permission of Wm. B. Eerdmans Publishing Company, Grand Rapids, Michigan. Quotations from Eusebius and Athanasius, except where otherwise indicated, are from Volumes I and IV of *The Nicene and Post-Nicene Fathers*, edited by Philip Schaff, and are used by permission of Wm. B. Eerdmans Publishing Company, Grand Rapids, Michigan. Quotations from the Psalms of Solomon, I Enoch, II Esdras (IV Ezra), and II Baruch are from Volume II of *The Apocrypha and Pseudepigrapha of the Old Testament*, edited by R. H. Charles, and are used by permission of the Clarendon Press, Oxford.

Contents

Maps and Illustrations

Part One
The Old Wine

The old [wine] is good (Luke 5:39)

Continuity . . . discontinuity: this delineates the relationship between the faith of Israel and that of the church, between the old wine and the new wine. Israel's faith and history are incomplete without their fulfilment in the faith and history of the Christian community. But, at the same moment, the latter cannot be understood apart from its continuation with, as well as cleavage from, the former. As the author of Hebrews suggests, the one God may be compared to the root of a vine from which flowed both the wine of Israel and the wine of the church (1:1-2). The church, however, is spirited and permeated by that which Irasel did not possess—God's final historical manifestation of himself in his Son.

The hope of Israel and the history of Israel are consummated in the church's encounter with the One whom she confesses to be her Lord. And, in a real sense, one must study the *entirety* of Israel's sacred history before he can appreciate in proper measure its fulfilment. But limitations are necessarily involved in any study, and a point of beginning must be selected. Herein the emphasis is upon the new wine rather than the old wine, and thereby the point of departure is determined.

The form of Israel's faith at the time of Christ may be termed Judaism. Although related to religion in Israel before the exile to Babylon (sixth century B.C.), some of its striking characteristics developed after the return from exile. Since this particular expression of faith served as the immediate matrix for the church, it is from here that we must proceed.

1

Origin and Development of Judaism

—THE VINE

Exiles in Babylon (586-538 B.C.)

Jew and Judaism.—As early as the fall of the Northern Kingdom, the term Judah could be used in connection with the relatively small segment of land surrounding Jerusalem, wherein the traditions of the entire people, formerly known as Israel, continued to be perpetuated. After the exile the people who settled in the province of Judah sharply distinguished themselves from their non-Israelite neighbors, so that it was natural that the term Jew (an inhabitant of Judah) came to refer to one who lived in the province of Judah and who adhered to the customs of that people. Thus it is, in the postexilic period, that either term, Israel or Judah, predicated at once both the *people* of that land and their *religious traditions.* However, Israelite and Jew were not at first used indiscriminately: Israel was the name by which the people chose to define themselves as the elect of God; while the title Jew was used, usually with defamatory connotations, by the non-Israelite world. Later the Jews also took up this term to qualify themselves in connection with their religious history and heritage.[1] It is in this final sense that Jew and Judaism will be used in what follows. The term Jew describes those "descendants of Abraham" who came out of the exile, while the unique cast of their religion and manner of life is designated Judaism.

Collapse of the nation.—Before entering into a discussion of the political, economic, social, and religious conditions of the exiles, it is necessary to take a historical orientation. Samaria, capital and last stronghold of the Northern Kingdom of Israel, fell in 722 B.C.,

---

[1]K. G. Kuhn, "Israel," *Theologische Wörterbuch zum Neuen Testament,* ed. Gerhard Kittel (6 vols.; Stuttgart: Verlag von W. Kohlhammer, 1933-19—), III, 360-61.

and many of her inhabitants were deported to other areas under the domination of Assyria.   For a while Judah exercised a vain struggle to exist, and did exist, until she irrevocably rebelled against Babylon, successor to Assyria.   Her people were then transported to Babylon in a series of three deportations, beginning in 597 B.C. and culminating in the final deportation of 586 B.C.

Political, economic, social conditions of the exiles.[2]—The primary blow sustained by the overthrow of Judah was the absolute loss of political self-existence.   Only for a few brief years during the Maccabean period did the Jews regain their independence, and even this was not as real as many felt at the moment.   Other than these political limitations, the life of the exiles was not so difficult as it is generally conceived to have been.   Jeremiah, in a letter to those deported, advises:

Build houses and live in them; plant gardens and eat their produce. Take wives and have sons and daughters; take wives for your sons, and give your daughters in marriage . . . ; multiply there, and do not decrease. But seek the welfare of the city where I have sent you into exile (Jer. 29:5-7).

No doubt some Israelites were put into slavery and others suffered assorted types of ill treatment, but the overall indications of Jeremiah and Ezekiel, as well as certain archaeological finds, would suggest that life for the exiles went on much as normal.   In fact, the policy of deportation was not so much to put the conquered to the task as it was to deprive them of their nationalistic hopes and aspirations.   People are much less likely to incite insurrection against their conquerors while living in a foreign land among strangers than if they are at home among their own people, with the camp of the foreign power in their midst.

At least two factors contributed to the Israelites' continuing sense of unity with their homeland, as well as to an abiding fellowship among themselves.   First, they were allowed to live in the same communities where others of their race dwelled, and second, they seem to have shared rather easy intercourse with those of their countrymen who had been left behind, as the frequent communications between Jeremiah and the exiles would lead one to believe.

---

[2]Observations in this section are indebted primarily to W. O. E. Oesterley, *A History of Israel* (Oxford: Clarendon Press, 1951), II, 42-59.

Evidently the Palestinian Jews suffered more than many of their kin who were transported to Babylon. Government in Palestine was difficult to administer with efficiency, and anarchy often interrupted the simulated order. Intrigue from within and harassment from without were constant plagues. Jeremiah characterized those left behind as "bad figs," signifying thereby that they were not artisans, tradesmen, nobles, landowners, or other persons of community status. These "bad figs" did not adjust so well to the basket of the new government, and the inevitable internal problems arose. Moreover, the surrounding neighbors, particularly the Edomites, interpreted the deprivation of Judah as a moment of opportunity for their own interests and frequently made raids on the now mortally crippled nation. To intensify these difficulties, immorality and superstition often crept into the religion of the "rejects."

Religion among the exiles.—More significant than the external events which transpired in conjunction with the Babylonian exile are certain components that became a permanent part of Judaism's religious life during this period. Especially prominent are three motifs that received initiation in Babylon: (1) the loss of prophetic consciousness, (2) the ever-expanding separatism, and (3) the three "pillars" of Judaism.

By the loss of prophetic consciousness is meant the encroaching feeling, especially among the later exiles, that God would no longer raise a prophet from among his people. Direct statements from later rabbis declare this and the indication of the historical events in conjuction with the rebuilding of the Temple attest to this. No longer was God to speak directly to his people through a prophet. There could be heard only the *bath qol,* which literally means "daughter of a voice" and was interpreted as merely an echo of God's voice. The rabbis compared the *bath qol* to the cooing of a dove, by which was made known God's will to those who were especially devout.

Recognition that God's Spirit had withdrawn from the people led them in the direction of a book religion, based on the Torah (first five books of the Bible). Along with the Torah developed the "oral law," which is referred to in the New Testament as the "tradition of the elders." The oral law served a double purpose: (1) It aided one in avoiding violation of the written Law; and (2) it served as

1. *Map (opposite page) showing cities mentioned in the New Testament*

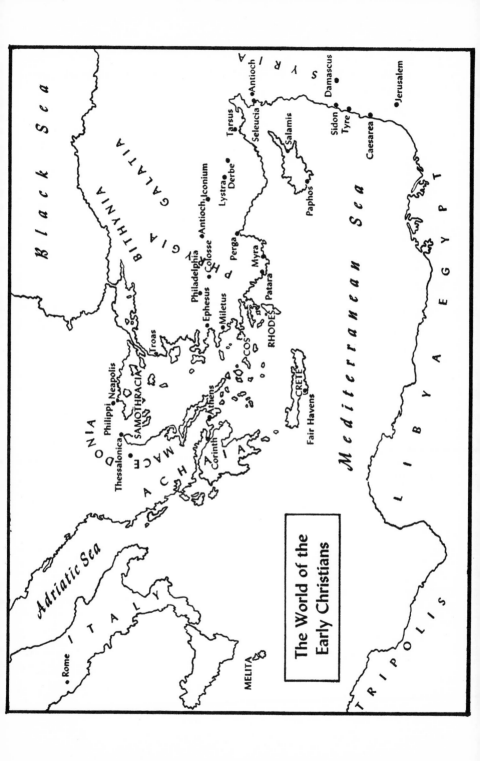

The World of the
Early Christians

an application of the written Law for present and immediate circumstances.

Originally the oral regulations attempted to serve a very practical purpose and were not intended to place extra burdens on people. For example, the Old Testament commands that the sabbath day must be kept holy. But what profanes the sabbath day, and how can one conduct himself so as not to incur guilt for its transgression? It was to such questions that oral tradition sought to give answers. Though the oral law was not finally codified until A.D. 220 by Judah ha-Nasi, many of the regulations go back into the period of the exile. The rabbis sought to give the oral law the same authority and origin as the Scriptures themselves. Danby summarizes a passage from the Mishnah:

At the same time that the Written Law was given from Sinai, the Oral Law, too, was delivered to Moses, and handed down (orally) in turn to the leaders of successive generations—to Joshua, to the Elders (Joshua 24:31), to the Prophets, to the "Men of the Great Synagogue" (the body of teachers who administered and taught the Law after the time of Ezra), to Simeon the Just (c. 280 or 200 B.C., one of "the remnants of the Great Synogogue"), to Antigonos of Soko; then, in turn, to the five "Pairs" of leaders. . . . Thus the chain of tradition was brought to the threshold of the Christian era.[3]

The Mishnah (from a root word signifying, "to teach by means of repetition") is the title given to the compilation and codification of these oral regulations concerning the interpretation of the Law. It is arranged into six sections and relates to all areas of Jewish life: (1) Zeraim (or seeds) dealing mainly with laws connected with agriculture; (2) Moed (festivals), relating to the observance of the secular and religious days, including the sabbath; (3) Nashim (women), pertaining to marriage laws, with two tractates dealing with vows in general; (4) Nezikin (damages), concerned primarily with civil and criminal law; (5) Kodashim (holy things), relating to the administration of sacrifices, also supplying a description of the Temple; and (6) Tohoroth (purifications), laws concerning personal and ritual purifications.

Finally, the Mishnah itself became the source of further juristic discussion and amplification, the result of which was the Talmud (meaning "teaching" or "doctrine"). One Talmudic tradition received

[3]Herbert Danby, *The Mishnah* (Oxford: University Press, 1958), p. xvii.

its written form in Palestine during the course of the fifth century, while the other was not edited and codified until the sixth century in Babylon. The language of the Talmuds is brief and frequently obscure, with no attempt at rhetoric; the discussions, in the form of dialogues, are tangled and often difficult to pursue. One might look upon these three—Torah, Mishnah, and Talmud—as three concentric circles, the second larger than the first and the third larger than the second, with each larger circle interpreting the one immediately smaller than itself. Both the Mishnah and the Talmud are characterized by two elements: Halakah and Haggadah. The former is the statement of a particular rule or regulation; the latter a practical illustration of its application in a specific situation, primarily through the medium of stories or legends about biblical and postbiblical saints.

"Our God has sent us into exile because we have disobeyed his laws; we have mixed ourselves with foreigners, and God intends to purify us!" This was the feeling of the Israelites with regard to their captivity. As a natural consequence of this line of thought the people determined to distinguish themselves radically from all other peoples. This movement is known as *separatism* and exposes itself in at least three avenues: (1) circumcision, (2) sabbath observance, and (3) laws that relate to clean and unclean.[4]

Originally circumcision was a puberty rite given either in connection with marriage or with the attainment of manhood, and was in no wise limited to the Israelites. In fact the Philistines appear to have been one of the few, if not the only, people in direct contact with Israel who did not circumcise. But the strictly religious connotation of circumcision "is a particular development amongst the Hebrews, whereby a puberty rite of admission to the tribe, becomes an infant rite of admission into the People of God."[5]

Similar is the story of the sabbath day. The sabbath day literally signifies the "seventh day." In both Canaan and Babylon the seventh day occupied a special place in the calendar.[6] Babylonian (and perhaps pre-Babylonian) tradition emphasized the sanctity of the number seven. Babylonian influence on the exiles magnified the observance of this day, even though the Israelites gave it a religious

[4]Werner Foerster, *From the Exile to Christ*, trans. Gordon E. Harris (Philadelphia: Fortress Press, 1964), p. 5.

[5]Norman H. Snaith, *The Jews from Cyrus to Herod* (Wellington: The Religious Education Press, 1949), p. 81.

[6]J. Morgenstern, "Sabbath," *Interpreter's Dictionary of the Bible*, IV, 135-36.

significance relating to their history. In this respect the history of
the sabbath day is not unlike the history of many other sacred seasons celebrated in Israel: an originally non-Israelite festival was taken
over and given a religious significance in light of Israel's past history.
From the exile on, the Jews' insistence on the sabbath made it a
sacred symbol by which they fervently differentiated themselves from
all other peoples.

Also in this period the Jewish way of life accentuated itself
through ornamentation with elaborate legalistic details, differentiating
between things clean and unclean, both in connection with the celebration of sacred seasons and with the concerns of everyday life. By
the keeping of these regulations the Jew at once sought to please his
God and separated himself from the "unclean" Gentiles, who did
not follow these traditions.   Ultimately, all this led to an emphasis on
externals in religion. The spirit in which these ordinances were begun
was forgotten or at least relegated to secondary status.

Three "pillars," upon which Judaism rests, came into focus during
this period: (1) the Scriptures (the Hebrew Bible, usually called the
Old Testament by Christians), (2) the synagogue, and (3) the office
of the scribe.[7]

[7]Foerster, *op cit.*, pp. 26-28.

**2. Part of colonnade in Samaria (Sebaste), erected
by Herod the Great before the birth of Christ**

The development of the Hebrew Scriptures involves many questions that cannot be dealt with here. This is a matter of Old Testament rather than of New Testament study. Undoubtedly, the people of Israel possessed and relied on written laws before the exile. One familiar biblical record of this is the reform carried on by King Josiah on the basis of a "book of the law."[8] There are good reasons for believing, however, that it was only after the exile that the Jews collected and arranged their books in the form that we now find in the Hebrew Bible. Along with this development came a growing emphasis on the importance of Law observance. After the exile there was a new insistence that every member of the community must know and keep the Law. Hence the Torah, the written Law, or the first five books of the Bible, gained an exalted authority.

Later in the postexilic period, some of the historical and prophetic books gained similar recognition. By the time of Christ, the poetic books and certain others, such as Chronicles and Daniel, were also counted as Scripture. Finally, in a meeting of Jewish rabbis at Jamnia, A.D. 90-100, there was official agreement that the 39 books of our present Old Testament would constitute the Bible of the Jews.

Law for the Jews was the way of life, and life apart from its knowledge was viewed as vanity. It was all important that one become familiar with the content of the Law; thus the synagogue gained its impetus. One cannot determine for certain when the synagogue came into existence, and there are various theories relevant to its date of origin. Yet, it seems fair to suggest that the synagogue may have come into being during the course of the exile. A necessary concomitant for a meaningful existence in Babylon would have been the gathering together of the people for recitation of the mighty acts of their God in times past and for the kindling of similar hopes for the future. In the experience of the exile the synagogue would also have served to meet a social need of these who were now far from familiar surroundings. But, whatever the origin, the synagogue developed as one of its primary goals the study and perpetuation of the Law.

One of the most important and earliest elements in the service of the synagogue was the reading of the Law. When Hebrew (the language of the Scriptures) was displaced as the common tongue, it

---

[8]See 2 Kings 22:8 to 23:25. Many scholars believe that the law book was at least part of the present book of Deuteronomy, perhaps chapters 12-26. Cf. Norman H. Snaith, *The Interpreter's Bible*, III, 317.

was necessary to speak in the language of the people. A translator (Targoman) stood beside the reader of Scripture and paraphrased the reading into the vernacular. For a while these translations were purely oral, but then they assumed a fixed form and were finally written, being known as Targums. Beyond its role as the custodian of the Scriptures, the synagogue also shared in such subsidiary functions as providing a center of fellowship for the adults and a school for the training of the young in the rudiments of education and religion, elements closely joined in Jewish life.

Law may determine life, but men determine the interpretation of the Law and make application of its truths. In the history of Judaism, these men were known as scribes. At the beginning, the duty of the scribe was only to propagate the Law through the copying of the text on fresh rolls of parchment, but later the scribes became the authoritarian interpreters of the letters of the Law. One does these men an injustice to assume that they were not meticulously zealous in this endeavor. The Law was God's will, the scribes were its custodians, and proper application depended upon their ability to grasp its truth. As a rule the scribes of the New Testament period belonged primarily, but not exclusively, to the Pharisaic party.

The Persian Period (538-331 B.C.)

Persian policy.—When the army of Cyrus marched into the city of Babylon in 538 B.C., a new era was begun for the Jews. Before the period of Persia's supremacy the policy of conquering armies was deportation, but Cyrus initiated a reform which was designed "to win friends and influence people." Under the conviction that peace within the kingdom could be maintained with much more facility through a policy of toleration than through deportation, Cyrus permitted the deportees to return to their homeland and reestablish their national religions. So welcome was the new policy of Cyrus that one of the Old Testament prophets called him "the anointed of the Lord" by whose fiat comfort had been conveyed to Israel (Isa. 40:1 and 45:1). Cambyses in 529 B.C. succeeded his father, and himself was followed by Darius I (520/18-486 B.C.), who is noted especially for his reorganization of the territories of Persia into twenty provinces, each controlled by a military governor directly responsible to the king. In such a situation peace was more certain than before, and the returned exiles sought to reestablish themselves and reconstruct their homeland.

Religious reforms.—There are some difficulties in interpreting the sources available,[9] but it appears quite likely that the reconstruction of the Temple was not begun until 520 B.C. and completed only in 516 B.C. It is probable also that the entire structure had not been demolished by the Babylonians and that the Palestinian Jews had used it, in a state of disrepair, during the period of the captivity. Furthermore, it was the "people of the land," that is, those Jews who were left in Palestine, who initiated the renovation of the Temple.

However, it was not until the time of Darius I that the real impetus that was needed to accomplish the task was received. This impetus came in the persons of the prophets Haggai and Zechariah, who were joined by Zerubbabel, the governor, and Joshua, the high priest. In this connection it should be noted that there was as yet no racial hostility among the people; opposition to the "people of the land" comes only as the strong separatist feelings of the returned Babylonian Jews are given vent. From this time on, until the destruction of Jerusalem in A.D. 70, the Temple served as the main symbol of Judaism. A description of the Temple and its ministry during the New Testament period will be presented in the next chapter.

In 444 B.C., the twentieth year of King Artaxerxes I, Nehemiah appeared on the scene. Nehemiah was originally from Jerusalem, and in the court of Artaxerxes he had come to occupy the important position of cupbearer to the king. The trouble in Jerusalem —primarily the fact that the walls were down—came to the ears of Nehemiah. Artaxerxes could not endure the sad countenance of his cupbearer and so commissioned him to go to Jerusalem and secure the necessary materials for the project.

Nehemiah, a devout separatist, intended to keep the "people of the land" from helping in the construction project because they were not anti-Samaritan. His actions aroused hostility from within the city itself. Sanballat, the governor of Samaria, who had political ambitions involved, also did his part to cause disquietude among those concerned with the building project. Nevertheless, the walls were completed in the remarkable period of only fifty-two days. Nehe-

---

[9]The chronology presented here follows the reconstruction of events offered by Oesterley, *op. cit.*, II, 71-158. For a different arrangement, especially with regard to Nehemiah-Ezra, cf. Solomon Zeitlin, *The Rise and Fall of the Judaean State* (Philadelphia: The Jewish Publication Society of America, 1962), I, 13-29.

miah stayed on in Jerusalem for twelve years before returning to the court of Artaxerxes.

Soon thereafter Nehemiah came again to Jerusalem, this time as a religious reformer. He refused the Ammonites and Moabites admission to the Temple, and he removed from the Temple chamber Tobiah, an Ammonite friend of Eliashib, the high priest. He forbade mixed marriages and restricted trading on the sabbath day. He also made certain reforms in the Temple services relevant to sacrifice and the tithe.

Ezra, a Jewish priest from Babylon, arrived in the seventh year of Artaxerxes II (397 B.C.) as a religious reformer. His intention was to continue and intensify the work of Nehemiah through making the Jews in Palestine conform to Babylonian Jewish practices. And this he did uncommonly well. He continued to speak out against mixed marriages and even encouraged Jews who had married foreigners to separate from them. He imposed an annual Temple tax on the people, and saw to it that the altar was properly maintained and that the tithe was paid. Most important, however, was his reading of "the law" before the people and making this law the basis of all his reforms. What this "law" was is not altogether evident, but it seems to have applied to all areas of the life of the people. In the judgment of many, such as Harrelson, it was the substance of the Torah.[10] Ezra cannot be called the founder of Judaism—it was practiced in Babylon before his time—but he was the one who imposed its strict regulations upon the Palestinian people, and in this sense might be called "the father of Judaism."

Greek Period and Divided Kingdoms (331-168 B.C.)

History.—Philip of Macedon, himself not strictly a Greek, achieved the unity of the Greek states and initiated the proceedings which ultimately led to the fall of Persia, a nation now weakened through internal disorder and intrigue. In 336 B.C. Philip was murdered but was succeeded by one more capable than himself, his nineteen-year-old son, Alexander the Great. At Issus (333 B.C.) the army of Darius III Codomannus was totally defeated, though it was not until 331 B.C. at Arbela (Gaugamela), which lies east of the Tigris River and south of Nineveh, that the doom of the Persian Empire was firmly fixed. When Alexander died (323 B.C.), the choice

---

[10]W. J. Harrelson, "Torah," *Interpreter's Dictionary,* IV, 673.

of successors was not easy. After a struggle of more than a decade, two rival powers emerge which from this time on play major roles in the history of Coele-Syria: the Seleucid regime in Syria and the Ptolemaic house in Egypt. As in times past, Palestine became a playing field upon which Syria and Egypt engaged. In general the period during which the Ptolemaic kings exercised major domination over Palestine was from 302-198 B.C. Antiochus III, king of Syria, managed to lay claim to this territory after the battle of Panion (Caesarea-Philippi in New Testament times) in 198 B.C. From this date on, until the direct intervention of Rome in 63 B.C., Palestine remained either directly or indirectly under the suzerainty of the Seleucids.

Hellenistic influences.—Hellenism is a label for that culture which was characterized by its adherence to the Greek ideals and way of life. Jewish-Hellenistic literature, that literature of Judaism which in varying degrees emerges from intercourse with elements of the Greek culture, will be discussed in the next chapter. Also in that chapter will be presented the unique religious concepts that emerged pursuant to and in conjunction with that literature. Here it is necessary only to point out that contact with the Greek way of life was not without its influence upon Judaism. Even before the time of Alexander, but most especially after the victories of Alexander, the influence of Hellenism was felt throughout the Near Eastern world.

The conquests of Alexander paved the way for the march of Hellenism which followed in his wake. Close upon the soldiers followed the merchants; and very soon Greek colonists arrived to settle down permanently in the newly conquered lands; and when once colonies of Greek-speaking people were founded they acted as centres from which Hellenism was disseminated.[11]

A direct effect of the decay of the Greek city-state, soon followed by the conquests of Alexander, "was paradoxically to give human life both a cosmopolitan and an individualistic aspect."[12] National cultures gradually lost their peculiar identities; there emerged one culture for *all men*. Society was concerned about the international as much as the national; and there was a common language, the Koiné or common Greek, spoken without the dialectical pecu-

---

[11]Oesterley, *op. cit.,* II, 177.
[12]R. H. Pfeiffer, *History of New Testament Times* (New York: Harper & Bros., 1949), p. 98.

liarities of the classical Greek. Many religions and philosophies affirmed the equality and oneness of all men. Social clubs, trade unions, and guilds were formed. Family life was elevated, and the role of the woman assumed greater dignity.

Prime centers of expression for these newly felt cosmopolitan and individualistic tenets were the stadiums and theaters. But most important were the gymnasiums, which "were as much of the essence of the Greek city-state as the public assemblies."[13] Not only were these places of bodily exercise, but they served as social and civic centers and tended to produce an esprit de corps wherever they appeared. Attached to the gymnasium were groups of young men known as the *epheboi,* who dressed in distinct garments and marched during certain festivals. Since these men trained in the nude, more than one Jew sought to cover his circumcision through surgery so as to appear more "Greek" to his comrades.

The Maccabean Revolt (168-134 B.C.)

Causes.—Factors leading to the Maccabean revolt may be classified as three, though it must be realized that among the Jews these could not be altogether distinguished from one another: (1) cultural, (2) political, and (3) religious.[14] The rising surge of Hellenism, especially by way of appeal to the young and the aristocratic, introduced certain cultural involvements that added their weight to the fracas. When Antiochus IV became king of Syria (175 B.C.), it is noted that certain Jerusalemites went to him with the request that he construct a gymnasium in their city. And this request was not an isolated phenomenon. Rather it was a symptom of an underlying feeling among many Palestinian Jews of their desire to engage more fully in the new and exciting offerings of the Greek way of life.

Not unrelated to the cultural factors were the political, since in Palestine at this time there were Jews of many diverse viewpoints: some were pro-Egyptian, others pro-Syrian; while others, still extremely conservative, desired to maintain at any cost the traditions of their fathers.

Yet the situation only fermented and did not erupt until a strange admixture of circumstances combined. Jason succeeded in having

---

[13]Edwyn Bevan, *Jerusalem Under the High-Priests* (London: Edward Arnold & Co., 1952), p. 35.

[14]Oesterley, *op. cit.,* II, 217-27, to whom is indebted the following interpretation of events.

3. *"Needle's Eye" entrance,*
Church of the Nativity, Bethlehem

himself appointed high priest (175 B.C.) by Antiochus IV, while
Onias III, the official high priest, was out of the city. It was not
uncustomary for a king to appoint whom he wanted, or who paid
the highest bribe, to an office in one of his subject nations. But the
orthodox Jews felt that God alone could designate a man to be high
priest.

Three years later Jason was outbid by Menelaus, a man of nonpriestly heritage. By a series of malicious deeds Menelaus made
himself even more despised among the orthodox, and Jerusalem
reached a boiling point. The mass of the people refused to acknowledge Menelaus as high priest, and consequently Antiochus IV
sent a Syrian official to Jerusalem to resolve the situation by any
means necessary. And this he seems to have done in conjunction
with the Hellenistic Jews in Jerusalem, who themselves had **made**
such a request of the king. First Maccabees depicts the outcome
quite vividly:

And they stationed there a sinful people, lawless men. These strengthened their position; they stored up arms and food, and collecting the spoils of Jerusalem they stored them there, and became a great snare. It became an ambush against the sanctuary,
> an evil adversary of Israel continually.
On every side of the sanctuary
> they shed innocent blood;
> they even defiled the sanctuary.
Because of them the residents of Jerusalem fled;
> she became a dwelling of strangers;
> she became strange to her offspring,
> and her children forsook her.
Her sanctuary became desolate as a desert;
> her feasts were turned into mourning,
> her sabbaths into a reproach,
> her honor into contempt.
Her dishonor now grew as great as her glory;
> her exaltation was turned into mourning.

Then the king wrote to his whole kingdom that all should be one people, and that each should give up his customs. All the Gentiles accepted the command of the king. Many even from Israel gladly adopted his religion; they sacrificed to idols and profaned the sabbath. And the king sent letters by messengers to Jerusalem and the cities of Judah; he directed them to follow customs strange to the land, to forbid burnt offerings and sacrifices and drink offerings in the sanctuary, to profane sabbaths and feasts, to defile the sanctuary and the priests, to build altars and sacred precincts and shrines for idols, to sacrifice swine and unclean animals, and to leave their sons uncircumcised. They were to make themselves abominable by everything unclean and profane, so that they should forget the Law and change all the ordinances. "And whoever does not obey the command of the king shall die" (1:34-50).

For Antiochus this was a political issue, involving his sovereign right as king, but from this point on the Jews interpreted the main issue as religious, a threat to the sovereignty of their God and his Law. No route but resistance was open to the orthodox Jews. Initially the refusal to cooperate was passive. Then in the village of Modein, about two-thirds of the distance between Jerusalem and Joppa, the first blow of active resistance was struck. Mattathias, a priest of the Hasmon house, when coerced to offer sacrifice upon a pagan altar, instead killed the renegade Jew under whose sponsorship the sacrifice was to be offered. This was the first blow; others were to follow. Soon after, when the elderly Mattathias had died, the revolt was continued by his five sons.

History.—It was the spring of 166-165 B.C. when Judas Maccaheel[15] assumed the role of captain for the Jewish forces. Antiochus IV apparently did not consider the situation critical, for simultaneously he undertook a campaign to the east against the Parthians. Judas' ability at guerilla warfare, in combination with an accumulation of other circumstances favorable to the Jews, enabled the Jewish party to regain access to the Temple in December, 164 B.C., three years after it had been desecrated by Antiochus Epiphanes.[16] The Feast of Dedication (also called Hanukkah or the Festival of Lights) was established as a memorial to this occasion, which was interpreted by the Jews as the attainment of their religious freedom. The taste of victory was sweet with the result that Judas now attempted to enlarge the realm of his domain and to seek political freedom. However, in April of 161 B.C. at Elasa, the exact location of which is not known,[17] Judas was killed in battle. His brother Jonathan was acclaimed leader of the Jewish revolutionary forces and later also assumed the role of high priest. Jonathan was more of a politician than a swordsman. If it is true that "those who live by the sword die by the sword," it is also true that those who live by intrigue perish by intrigue. This was the outcome of Jonathan in 142 B.C.

Last of the Maccabaean brothers to exercise leadership was Simon (142-135 B.C.). By the time of Simon the Jews had already acquired religious freedom, enlargement of their territory, predominance for their partisan group, and the high priesthood.[18] Simon was destined to gain for them "political freedom." This he did in 142 B.C. when he recognized Demetrius II as the legitimate claimant for the Syrian crown, and Demetrius in turn granted the Jews political freedom, for all it was worth. Actually the Jews enormously overestimated this freedom, which did not amount to much but freedom in name only. By popular vote the Jews appointed Simon to the high priesthood (140 B.C.) in order to express their gratitude for

---

[15]The nickname "Maccabee," literally means, "hammerhead" or "the hammerer." Whether Judas received this name because of his ability at guerilla warfare, whereby he would strike suddenly like a hammer, or because his head reminded one of a hammer, remains a question. Zeitlin, *op. cit.,* p. 96, suggests the latter theory.

[16]"Epiphanes," meaning the "illustrious one," was one of the titles that Antiochus gave to himself. The Jews referred to him as "Epimanes"—"the mad man."

[17]Oesterley, *op. cit.,* II, 240. But Zeitlin, *op. cit.,* p. 117, locates the region about ten miles north of Jerusalem.

[18]Oesterley, *op. cit.,* II, 263.

him and his family. Simon was murdered (134 B.C.) by his son-in-law, Ptolemy, who hoped to ascend to Simon's position. But John Hyrcanus, a son of Simon, forewarned of the treachery, managed to get to Jerusalem before Ptolemy, and there was acknowledged high priest.

The Hasmonaean High Priesthood (134-63 B.C.)

John Hyrcanus (134-104 B.C.), first of the Hasmonaean princes to issue coins in his own name, and apparently the first to be called "King of the Jews," entitled himself, "John the high priest and head of the Community of the Jews." This indicates that John felt himself to be basically the leader of a religious community. His religious interests were further indicated through his destruction of the Samaritan temple on Mount Gerizim in 129 B.C., and by his coercing the Idumaeans to accept Judaism. But he was not without other ambitions, and the internal difficulties in which Syria found itself at this time permitted him to enlarge the scope of Israel's territory.

The reign of John Hyrcanus is significant also because during his lifetime first mention is made of the existence of two opposing partisan groups within Judaism. These were the high-priestly party (Sadducean) and the Pharisaic, or more conservative group. Apparently, the Pharisees were remnants of those "pious ones" (Hasidim), who entered the fight for religious freedom but began to separate themselves from the conflict when they realized that their national leaders were developing political ambitions. Josephus, the Jewish historian, passes along a human interest story which indicates that initially John and the Pharisees were on friendly terms, but then he broke with them and linked himself with the Sadducees.

Aristobulus I (103 B.C.), oldest of Hyrcanus' five sons, inherited the high priesthood when Hyrcanus died, while Hyrcanus' wife took over the civil power. This young man was not unambitious. He placed three of his brothers in prison, later murdered the remaining one, and finally starved his mother to death. Much of his cruelty seems to have been encouraged by his wife, Alexandra Salome, who acceded to her husband's power when he died. She had no children by her first husband. Following his death she released his brothers from prison and married the oldest, Alexander Jannaeus, whom she designated king. When he became king, he naturally became high priest as well.

The hatred between the Jewish masses and Alexander Jannaeus (102-76 B.C.) is indicated by their pounding him with citrus fruits and palm branches when he officiated at the Feast of Tabernacles. He retaliated by having a number of them mercilessly slaughtered. In 88 B.C. he was engaged in a life-death struggle with the Syrians. So severe was the Jewish hatred of Jannaeus that a number of Jews had joined ranks with the Syrian forces. Suddenly these deserters decided it would be better to support the Jewish army in spite of their personal feelings towards the king. This turn-about enabled Jannaeus to win, and he expressed his appreciation—at his victory banquet he had several hundred Jews crucified and their wives and children put to death before their eyes. From this time on the Pharisees were quiescent. Before he died, Alexander Jannaeus had managed to spread his kingdom over a larger area than any other of the Hasmonaeans.

Alexandra (75-67 B.C.) outlived her husband. Alexander Jannaeus realized that no government in Palestine could endure peacefully without the cooperation of the Pharisees, so before his death he urged Alexandra to make peace with them. Then, too, Alexandra herself seems to have had a natural inclination in their direction. These two factors led Alexandra to place a certain amount of power in the hands of the Pharisees. Not satisfied with a little gain, they worked until they all but ran the government during the early years of Alexandra's power; but Alexandra was able to cope with the problem and ultimately managed to orient the situation in her favor. Of her two sons, she appointed the older, John Hyrcanus II. to the high priesthood, while she retained the civil authority. The appointment of Hyrcanus II to this office showed his mother's political shrewdness. Not only was he the older, but he was retiring and possessed no overt political ambitions as did his brother, Aristobulus II.

In 67 B.C. Alexandra died. John Hyrcanus II was the rightful heir to the throne, but even before the death of Alexandra, Aristobulus II had made plans of his own. Soon after his mother's death he defeated Hyrcanus II in battle and made arrangements for his older brother to retire into private life, while he himself became both high priest and king (66-63 B.C.). It is necessary to recall an event in the reign of Alexander Jannaeus before the later developments can be understood. When Alexander Jannaeus forced the Idumaeans into Judaism, he appointed Antipas, an Idumaean, as

governor of that region.   Antipas' son. Antipater, gained great influence in Jerusalem and later sought to stir up difficulties between
Hyrcanus and Aristobulus. He enrolled an army to support
Hyrcanus, and together they besieged Aristobulus in Jerusalem.   In
the meanwhile, a Roman army had been advancing south, and its
impact was felt by both sides.   Aristobulus and Hyrcanus each sent
messengers to Scarus, Pompey's general, seeking his favor.   Pompey
himself arrived in 63 B.C. and determined the outcome of events.
Judah was greatly reduced in size and annexed to the Roman province of Syria.   Aristobulus and his family were deported to Rome,
with the exception of one son who escaped from the ship.   Though
Hyrcanus was made ethnarch and granted the high priesthood, the
real power behind him was Antipater, who had confirmed himself
a friend of Rome.

Roman Period (After 63 B.C.)

History before Herod.—The Jewish people prospered as long as
Pompey lived, because of the loyalty that Pompey knew he had in
Antipater.   But in 48 B.C., after a year of conflict, Caesar managed
to conquer Pompey. Antipater acted with his usual swiftness and
perceptiveness. He convinced the new ruler that as he had been
faithful to Pompey, so now he would be faithful to Caesar.   As
evidence of this he furnished reinforcements for Caesar's army in
Egypt.   The contribution of Antipater was not forgotten by Caesar,
and a firm friendship was established between the two.   Caesar's
friendship for Antipater had positive consequences.   Hyrcanus II
was permitted to continue as high priest and received the position
of ethnarch. Antipater was made procurator of Judea, given Roman
citizenship, and no longer required to pay taxes.   As for the Palestinian Jews:

Caesar had, moreover, with wise political foresight, great favours to
bestow on the Jews and their land. All taxation was remitted; entire
religious liberty was confirmed, with full permission to exercise the laws
and customs of the race; the people were to be judged by their own
tribunals; they were relieved of military service in the legions; Roman
troops were withdrawn from the land, a welcome relief for more reasons
than one. The boundaries of the land were extended in Galilee, and, what
was far more important, the seaport of Joppa was given back.[19]

---

[19]*Ibid.*, 339. Josephus, *Antiquities*, XIV, X, contains the full text of Caesar's
decree.

These, and other advantages were shared by the Jews, and their new status was spread also to the Jews of the Diaspora—those who lived outside of Palestine.

Yet, despite all the gains that they had made through Antipater's bonds with Caesar, the Jews could not stand the presence of a semi-Jew with so much authority in their midst. Nor could they endure the emblem of a foreign power standing over them. Thus Antipater had to face many internal difficulties. Another problem arose when Caesar was murdered and Cassius moved into Syria. Cassius needed money for his military campaigns and the logical collector was Antipater, though Antipater did not want to act in this capacity. Antipater had to depend in large measure upon the aid of his two sons, Phaasel (in Jerusalem) and Herod (in Galilee), for the enforcing of Cassius' decree, which added further fuel to the fire of the Jewish hatred for Antipater and his family. But Antipater did not have to endure this situation long, for he was murdered in 43 B.C. In the next year, when Cassius pulled out his forces for a final encounter with Antony and Octavian, Judah was left with no semblance of order.

Meantime, Antigonus, the son of Aristobulus who had escaped being deported to Rome, made a plea for support among the Jews. He attempted to usurp the positions of both Hyrcanus and Herod. Previous to this, Herod and Hyrcanus had fallen out with each other, but now they felt it mutually beneficial to be reconciled. As a seal of their friendship, Herod became engaged to Mariamne, a granddaughter of Hyrcanus. The army of Antony and Octavian had downed the forces of Cassius and Brutus at Philippi in 42 B.C., which meant that the outcome in Palestine would be determined by Antony, now on his way to Syria. Antony gave the authority of tetrarch to both Herod and Phaasel and permitted Hyrcanus to maintain his status as ethnarch and high priest. However, Antony proceeded to Egypt, and there gave himself—with much more vigor—to Cleopatra, which left his Palestinian allies in a dilemma. Antigonus reasserted himself and gained a number of followers. Phaasel was compelled to commit suicide, and Hyrcanus was disfigured by Antigonus so that he would no longer qualify for high priest. Now Antigonus was both high priest and king. Herod was alone, unless he could find help in Rome.

As it happened, both Antony and Octavian were in Rome with their differences resolved. The outcome was more than Herod dared dream! Herod appealed for Rome to instate as king his wife's brother,

Aristobulus III, since Rome customarily granted a position of this type to persons in the royal house of a subject nation. Rome responded by appointing Herod himself king of Judah and by adding Samaria to his territory. Antigonus was soon put to death, and no more immediate claimants to the throne existed.

Herod and his successors.—At least four factors clouded Herod's beginning as king of the Jews. (1) His father was an Idumaean, of a race that were enemies par excellence of the Jews. (2) In 37 B.C.. the year Herod assumed office as king. he felt it politically necessary to put to death certain or his more influential enemies. Among these were some members of the Sanhedrin, the highest court of the Jews. (3) If Herod was to maintain himself as king, he had to depend upon the amiability of Rome; and in order to feed this friendship he was required to be constant in exacting from Judah a tax levy. (4) Though Herod had not originally intended to do so, he had, nevertheless, displaced the Hasmonaean dynasty, something even Antipater had not done.[20]

As though this were not enough, Herod had family problems. His mother-in-law, Alexandra, despised him because he had not secured the kingship for her son Aristobulus III, nor appointed him high priest. Alexandra managed to work her intrigue through a mutual enemy of Herod, Cleopatra. Cleopatra wanted Antony to give her control of Palestine, but Antony could not do this without losing the support of Herod, a thing he could not afford. On the other side, Herod's mother and sister had felt the pressure of the Idumaean-Jewish hatred. They sought to alienate Herod from Alexandra and Mariamne. Finally, Herod did appoint Aristobulus as high priest; but afterwards, believing that this appointment was being used by Alexandra to secure political advantages, Herod presumably gave the orders for Aristobulus to be drowned while swimming in Herod's resort pool at Jericho. Cleopatra then attempted have Antony put Herod to death for this deed, but Antony exonerated him instead. Meanwhile, Alexandra was seeking to interest Antony in the charms of Mariamne, which would be an indirect route of attack on Herod.

---

[20]*Ibid.*, 351-53.

4. Road leaving Nazareth toward Jerusalem

All these factors were brought to a climax soon after the defeat of Antony by Octavian at Actium in September of 31 B.C. Herod had fought on the side of Antony and so was summoned before Octavian to give answer. What Antipater had been able to achieve before Caesar, his son was able to accomplish before Octavian. Herod recounted his absolute support of Antony and promised Octavian the same, if Octavian would act propitiously towards him. The new emperor was convinced by the words of Herod; and when the vapor of battle finally settled, Herod was in a much better position than before, for Octavian had granted him all the possessions Cleopatra had previously held in Palestine, along with several other choice cities.

Now Herod was able to turn his attention to his family affairs. Mariamne, whom Herod actually appears to have loved very much, was put to death on trumped-up charges of adultery, and ultimately Alexandra herself met a similar fate. Apart from a few minor difficulties with the Jews, the remainder of Herod's life was characterized by extensive building campaigns, one outcome of which was the reconstruction of the Temple in Jerusalem.

5. Nazareth

When Herod died in 4 B.C., all was not well. Only a short while before his death Herod had to deal with three of his sons, who were found guilty of treason and put to death. Three other sons were named in the will of Herod. With the approval of Rome, Archaelaus was given the title of ethnarch and control of Judea, Samaria, and Idumaea; Herod Antipas was made tetrarch of Galilee and Perea; and Philip was established as tetrarch of the regions northeast of Palestine proper. With the exception of Archaelaus, these men were able to remain in their position for a long while. Philip, who of the three had the least amount of bearing on Jewish history, lived until A.D. 34. Antipas was well established until A.D. 39, when he became too ambitious and Rome had him banished to Gaul. Archaelaus expressed such extreme cruelty both to Jews and Samaritans that he was deposed A.D. 6. After this, his territory was assigned to procurators, the most noted of whom was Pontius Pilate (A.D. 26-36).

2
Jewish Religion

—THE FRUIT OF THE VINE

The literature of a people is an expression of their inner history. And if the external history of Israel may be compared to a vine, the literature produced by this people may be made analogous to the fruit of that vine. The present chapter is designed to introduce the reader to the more significant noncanonical compositions of the so-called "interbiblical" and New Testament periods. Following a survey of these writings, certain vital doctrines of Judaism that received a flowery growth during this era will be discussed. Finally, there will be a description of some of the more essential expressions of Israel's religious life as it existed in the days when the new wine began to flow.

Literature of Judaism

Apocrypha.— The designation Apocrypha has commonly been used in the limited sense of those books contained in the Greek version of the Old Testament but were never able to find their way into the Hebrew Bible. A companion term, Pseudepigrapha, has been used to refer to other extracanonical writings penned under an assumed name. A study of the Apocrypha and Pseudepigrapha is extremely important, for these writings have played, and continue to play, a vital role both in the history of Judaism and in the history of the church. Of particular concern for this study is the fact that this literature is indicative of Judaism's thought during that most fertile period immediately prior to, and simultaneous with, the earliest history of the church.

In the ensuing discussion an asterisk will mark each writing contained in the Old Testament Apocrypha. These books are included in Catholic versions of the Old Testament but are omitted from almost all printings of Protestant versions. Four categories of classification will be used: (1) historical, (2) poetic and sapiential, (3) hortatory and apologetic, and (4) apocalyptic. Related, but in a class of their own, are the works of Josephus and Philo, which will receive separate attention. The literature of the Dead Sea community will receive mention in connection with the discussion of the Essenes.

Historical.—First Maccabees* covers the period from the accession of Antiochus Epiphanes (175 B.C.) to the death of Simon (135 B.C.). It is our primary source of information about the Maccabean struggle. The author (rather, editor) patterned his work after the books of Kings in the Old Testament and wrote in Hebrew, though the only manuscripts now existent are in Greek. He was a native of Palestine and a devout patriot. Some scholars hold that he was of the Sadducean persuasion, though Pfeiffer believes instead that he wrote with a pro-Hasmonaean leaning.[1] "What is certain is that his book is permeated with an authentic and unmistakable piety," which acknowledges that all human undertakings are dependent upon divine providence.[2] First Maccabees must have been written after 135 B.C. and before 63 B.C., in light of the favorable attitude reflected toward Rome. Oesterley would narrow the date of composition to the decade between 100 and 90 B.C.[3]

In Protestant translations of the Apocrypha, the next work is called 1 Esdras.* Catholic translations call it 3 Esdras, designating Ezra and Nehemiah as 1 and 2 Esdras. The name "Esdras" is derived from the Greek spelling of the Hebrew name usually rendered as "Ezra" in English. The present work largely parallels 2 Chronicles 35-36, Ezra 1-10, and Nehemiah 3, and concerns the history of Israel from the initiation of Josiah's reform (621 B.C.) until the rebuilding of the Temple and the reaffirmation of the Law under Ezra, with the main interest on the latter two aspects. The Temple's reconstruction had arrived at a standstill and the author intends to relate how it was resumed.

Three guardsmen of Darius were debating what has the most strength in the world: wine, the king, woman, or truth. The king called upon each to defend his case; Zerubbabel, who had propounded

---

[1] *Op. cit.,* pp. 492-93.

[2] Bruce M. Metzger, *An Introduction to the Apocrypha* (New York: Oxford University Press, 1963), p. 131.

[3] W. O. E. Oesterley, *The Books of the Apocrypha* (New York: Fleming H. Revell & Co., 1914), pp. 413-15.

the cause of truth, won. The king then honored Zerubbabel's request, which was to lead in the rebuilding of the Temple in Jerusalem. The narrative is climaxed by allusion to Ezra's reforms among the returned exiles.

The primary significance of Greek Ezra (as 1 Esdras is sometimes called) is its value in helping to reconstruct the text of Chronicles and Ezra-Nehemiah. Torrey believes the original language to have been Semitic, "partly Hebrew, partly Aramaic,"[4] while Goodspeed affirms that the good Greek, along with certain non-Hebraic concepts, attests to Greek as its original language.[5] A date somewhere around 150 B.C. is generally accepted.

The Septuagint, or Greek translation of the Old Testament, has certain additions to Esther* that are lacking in the Hebrew edition. One view is that certain devout Jews, upset because the Hebrew Esther omits reference to the name of God, made additions to the original in order to enhance its air of piety. This would have taken place around 100 B.C.,[6] or perhaps during the Maccabaean revolt.[7] On the other hand, Torrey has developed the thesis that the original Esther (in Aramaic) was longer than the Hebrew version. He holds that the Greek translation (made from the original Aramaic in 114 B.C.) more accurately represents the archetype.[8]

Poetic and sapiential.—Wisdom (or sapiential) literature had a wide and colorful development prior to its appearance in Israel. An abundant number of parallels, which antedate the wisdom literature of Israel, appear in the literature of other cultures. Originally, wisdom literature was written from a purely utilitarian and practical angle with the intention of offering guides for successful and happy living, and was confined to no one particular area of life. Later, especially in Israel, wisdom was identified with God's intention and purpose for mankind as it is embodied in his Law. At this point the wisdom literature of Israel makes its unique contribution. Because of the similarity in form and, at many places, in content, the poetic and sapiential literature of Judaism will be discussed jointly.

Ecclesiasticus* or the Wisdom of Jesus, the Son of Sirach is, like

---

[4]Charles Cutler Torrey, *The Apocryphal Literature* (New Haven: Yale University Press, 1948), p. 48.

[5]Edgar J. Goodspeed, *The Story of the Apocrypha* (Chicago: The University of Chicago Press, 1952), pp. 41-42.

[6]*Ibid.*, p. 57.

[7]Oesterley, *Apocrypha*, p. 403.

[8]*Op. cit.*, pp. 58-59. Cf. Pfeiffer, *op. cit.*, pp. 309-10.

Proverbs, a collection of wisdom sayings related to many different areas of life. Somewhere between 200 and 180 B.C., a wise man of Jerusalem, Ben Sira (Sirach) by name, composed this work in Hebrew, and in 132 B.C. it was taken to Egypt and there translated by his grandson. No situation in life is left without comment, but the most permanent contribution to the thought of Judaism is its unlimited praise of wisdom:

> Wisdom will praise herself,
>   and will glory in the midst of her people.
> In the assembly of the Most High she will open her mouth,
>   and in the presence of his host she will glory:
> "I came forth from the mouth of the Most High,
>   and covered the earth like a mist . . .
> Then the Creator of all things gave me a commandment,
>   and the one who created me assigned a place for my tent.
> And he said, 'Make your dwelling in Jacob,
>   and in Israel receive your inheritance.'
> From eternity, in the beginning, he created me,
>   and for eternity I shall not cease to exist . . .
> Just as the first man did not know her perfectly,
>   the last man has not fathomed her;
>   for her thought is more abundant than the sea,
>   and her counsel deeper than the great abyss (24:1-29).

The Wisdom of Solomon,* also known as the Book of Wisdom, represents the apex in the Jewish development of the concept of wisdom. Evidently the author of Hebrews, as well as Paul, and perhaps even the author of the Fourth Gospel, were influenced by the concept of wisdom presented in this work. The Wisdom of Solomon falls easily into two divisions (1-5 and 6-19), and the best solution appears to be the suggestion that the book was originally of composite authorship, though the final editor has carried throughout the exalted position of wisdom. An Egyptian Jew (most likely in Alexandria), devoted to the Law, is responsible for the book in its present form. Theories concerning the date range anywhere from 150 B.C. to A.D. 40. Torrey, who places the date in the last quarter of the second century B.C., concludes, "The doctrines of the book are not new because they embody late concepts, but because they fuse Jewish orthodoxy with Greek ideas of long standing."[9] The heart of this composition is the unqualified praise of wisdom:

---

[9]*Op. cit.*, pp. 102-3.

I learned what is secret and what is manifest,
for wisdom, the fashioner of all things, taught me . . .
For she is a breath of the power of God,
and a pure emanation of the glory of the Almighty;
therefore nothing defiled gains entrance into her.
For she is the reflection of eternal light,
a spotless mirror of the working of God,
and an image of his goodness.
Though she is but one, she can do all things . . .
in kinship with wisdom there is immortality,
and in friendship with her, pure delight . . .
and with my whole heart I said:
"O God of my fathers and Lord of mercy,
who hast made all things by thy word,
and by thy wisdom hast formed man . . .
give me the wisdom that sits by thy throne" (7:21 to 9:4).

The Psalms of Solomon, eighteen in number, are, in respect to form and content, much like the book of Psalms in the Old Testament. A unique aspect of several of these psalms is their connection with a specific political situation, whereas many of the Old Testament psalms are "characteristically timeless."[10] Psalms 17 and 18 are of basic importance for depicting the nationalistic proportions of the Messiah as they had developed by the first century B.C. A general consensus of opinion is that these psalms represent the late Hasmonaean period, especially between 63 B.C. and 48 B.C., the dates of Pompey's arrival in Jerusalem and his death, for these two events are believed to be alluded to. It is interesting to note that the Sadducees are depicted as sinners and man-pleasers, whereas the Pharisees are upright, pleasers of God. The present recensions of the psalms are only in Greek and Syriac, though the language of original composition was Hebrew.

Hortatory and apologetic.—The hortatory literature of Judaism was intended to call the faithful Jew to a firmer faithfulness and the unfaithful Jew to faithfulness. Apologetic writings were designed to speak to the pagan world concerning the superiority of Israel's faith in comparison to other religions. Therefore, these two types of literature are closely aligned and may be studied jointly. As a rule, the author will accomplish his purpose through the recitation either of legends concerning famous Jewish heroes of faith or events in Israel's sacred history.

---

[10]*Ibid.,* p. 107.

Tobit* is one of the best told short stories in all literature. The author has at his disposal a number of sources which he has woven together into a unified tale. Among the Jewish sources reflected in his composition are the Law and the Prophets, Psalms, Proverbs, and Job.[11] Other than these, the most widely utilized source would appear to be the originally non-Jewish tale of Achikar the Wise. Evidently the traditions concerning Achikar were widespread and popular and entered Jewish realms as early as the fifth century B.C.[12] The author assumes that his readers are familiar with the story of Achikar and its moral: "To him that doeth good, what is good shall be recompensed; and to him that doeth evil, what is evil shall be rewarded. And he that diggeth a pit for his neighbour, filleth it with his own stature."[13]

[11]Pfeiffer, *op. cit.*, pp. 266-67.
[12]Oesterley, *Apocrypha*, pp. 349-50.
[13]*Ibid.*, pp. 352-53.

Tobit was written after 200 B.C., and the limits of 190-170 B.C. are most probable.[14] The author writes "to dissuade his co-religionists from apostasy, and convert if possible any pagan who might read it."[15]　Primary values of Tobit are the reflections it casts upon the ascending role of angels in the thought of Judaism and the exalted position of the Law among Pharisaic Judaism.　The story itself concerns Tobit, a devout Jew, who remains faithful to the Law in the midst of many difficulties and discovers, like Job and Achikar, that righteousness ultimately prevails.　Tobit's blindness, caused by obedience to the Law, is healed; his son (Tobias) marries the beautiful Sarah and overcomes the demon, Asmodaeus, who himself desires Sarah; and Tobit's fortune is recovered from the friend with whom he had left it years before.

Judith,* meaning "Jewess," was certainly intended to suggest the representative significance of the central character,[16] who is the author's ideal embodiment of Judaism.　The story of Judith is not unlike that of Esther, for both women, through their beauty and wisdom, cause the Jews to be victorious over their would-be annihilators.　The teaching and purpose of Judith must be undertaken together.　"The teaching is that of the rigidly orthodox Pharisaic type; observance of the Law is the one thing needful . . . The main purpose of the book is, therefore, clearly to inculcate and to forward Pharisaic Judaism."[17]

The Judaism depicted in Judith is aggressively warlike, so that it seems best to date the composition somewhere after the middle of the second century B.C., and perhaps as late as the end of that century.　A number of historical inaccuracies are present, but these are intended by the author for the amusement of his readers.

The story itself concerns Judith, a beautiful widow, scrupulously devoted to the Law, "for she feared God with all her heart," who was able to deceive and behead Holofernes, the general of the Assyrian army.　Throughout the story are emphasized such Pharisaic teachings as the importance of fasting and prayer, obedience to dietary laws, ritual purification, and the foolishness of idolatry. There is a balance between determinism and free will, and an emphasis

---

[14]Pfeiffer, *op. cit.*, pp. 273-74.

[15]R. H. Charles (ed.), *The Apocrypha and Pseudepigrapha of the Old Testament* (Oxford: The Clarendon Press, 1913), I, 186.

[16]Torrey, *op. cit.*, p. 88, fn. 80.

[17]Oesterley, *Apocrypha*, p. 381.

upon the doctrine that "the end justifies the means." Judith prays, "By the deceit of my lips strike down the slave with the prince and the prince with his servant; crush their arrogance by the hand of a woman" (9:10). And after her victory she gives thanks, "It was my face that tricked him to his destruction, and yet he committed no sin with me, to defile and shame me" (13:16).

Baruch* falls naturally into two major divisions, the first of which is in prose and the second in poetry. The second division in turn consists of two parts that differ in content. Thus Baruch may be outlined: (1) *The Book of Confessions* (1:1 to 3:8); (2) *A Sage's Words of Wisdom* (3:9 to 4:4); and (3) *A Message of Good Cheer* (4:5 to 5:9).[18] The first section purports to be the lament of Baruch, the scribe of Jeremiah, five years after the destruction of Jerusalem in 586 B.C. The remaining two sections praise God for his faithfulness toward Israel and offer hope and encouragement to the people upon the basis of God's help in times past. The actual composition of the book is believed to have taken place sometime between the middle of the second century B.C. and the middle of the first century B.C. Of particular significance is the identification, made in 3:9 to 4:4, between Wisdom and the Law, a further insight into the progressive elevation of the Law in Pharisaic Judaism.

In conjunction with Baruch the Epistle of Jeremiah* should be examined. In the Latin Vulgate this forms the sixth chapter of Baruch but in the Septuagint is a separate writing, following Lamentations. The content is a polemic against idolatry, reminding the reader of Isaiah 40. Dates from 317 B.C. to 100 B.C. have been assigned to this brief leaflet.

The Greek and Latin Bibles contain additions to the book of Daniel that are not in the Hebrew Old Testament. In the present editions of the English Bibles these stories have been relegated to the apocryphal collection. These narratives are generally divided into three parts, though some of these are also composite works.

The first of these narratives concerns Susanna,* a faithful and pure Jewish wife, with whom two men desired to commit adultery. When she rejected their advances, they vowed to avenge themselves by testifying in court that they had seen her being unfaithful to her husband. As the verdict of the jury was about to be carried out against Susanna, Daniel appeared and proved that the witnesses were

---

[18]*Ibid.*, pp. 495-506.

false, whereupon they themselves were stoned, the fate that had awaited Susanna. Perhaps this story at first was told merely for the sake of interest, but then was given a moral and the name of Daniel ("God is my judge") attached to the hero. The purpose would have been to reform Jewish court procedures through requiring a more thorough interrogation of the witnesses. If this is the case, a date in the last century B.C. is consistent with its incorporation into the Septuagint.

Goodspeed is concise in his description of the second addition to Daniel:

The Song of the Three Children [*] is the second of the additions made in the Greek form of the Book of Daniel. The Song, with the accompanying Prayer of Azariah, is associated with the deliverance of Daniel's three friends from the fiery furnace and follows 3:23 in the Greek Daniel. Both are pieces of Jewish liturgy—the prayer from the dark days just before the Maccabean uprising, or about 170 B.C.; the Song, a splendid hymn of thanksgiving, from the days of the Maccabean triumph, about 150 B.C.[19]

The person of Daniel and a stringent tirade against idolatry are the two unifying factors in the narratives of Bel and the Dragon.* The Dragon (a serpent) was proved to be no real god when he was slain in the course of eating Daniel's mixture of tar, fat, and hair. As a consequence, Daniel was cast into the den of lions, but was miraculously preserved and his own God vindicated. In the story of Bel (an idol), Daniel demonstrated that the idol did not consume the food offerings made to him. Instead, the priests, along with their families, would sneak in each night and have a feast upon the generous offerings. Each of these accounts grows out of the idealization of Daniel's virtues and would seem to have originated during the first century B.C.

Jubilees, known also as "little Genesis," is a "treatise with an apologetic purpose thoroughly accomplished. It aims to show that the Judaism of its day had existed as normative from the beginning of human history."[20] The author's plan is accomplished by means of recounting the events surrounding Moses' reception of the law, oral as well as written. In conjunction with the law given to Moses

---

[19]Edgar J. Goodspeed, *The Apocrypha: An American Translation* (Chicago: The University of Chicago Press, 1956), p. 355.

[20]Torrey, *op. cit.*, pp. 126-27.

is an outline of world history from the time of creation to the crossing of the sea. Other emphases of the author pertain to sin, demons, angels, and the future life. Dates anywhere from the fourth century B.C. until the last part of the first century B.C. have been suggested for the period of composition.

Second Maccabees,* more of a "hortatory history" than its companion volume, 1 Maccabees, is the summary of an earlier work by Jason of Cyrene and covers the Maccabean period to 161 B.C. Beyond this, it possesses the value of lending insight into the status of certain Pharisaic doctrines of that same era. Second Maccabees is included in this present section rather than in the "historical" section because its author has intentionally designed his work to emphasize religious teaching. His main intent was to encourage faith in the God of history, who might at any moment intervene in the affairs of mankind. Indications suggest the last quarter of the second century B.C. as the time of writing.

Third Maccabees, even more than 2 Maccabees, uses history as an attestation to the omnipotence of Israel's deity. Ptolemy IV, Philopator, is depicted as being thwarted in his attempt to annihilate the Jewish element in Egypt and finally as being "converted" to Judaism. Of course, the narrative is not strictly factual, but the author combines fact with fancy for the accomplishment of his purpose. Perhaps 3 Maccabees should be placed about a century later than 2 Maccabees, and, in all probability, was written by an Alexandrian Jew.

The Martyrdom of Isaiah and the Prayer of Manasseh* are two examples of the pseudepigraphical literature that must have flourished abundantly in the course of the several centuries before and after the dawn of the Christian era. Each of these pamphlets, in its own way, purposed to exhort men to worship the God of Jacob, who alone is worthy of man's devotion.

Apocalyptic.—Since the nature of apocalyptic literature is often misunderstood, special care must be given to defining it. "Apocalyptic" comes from a Greek noun whose meaning is "disclosure"—the dramatic uncovering of something important that had been hidden. "Apocalypse" is the English equivalent of the noun, which is the opening word and part of the Greek title of the book of Revelation in the New Testament. Both "apocalyptic" and "apocalypse" are used with reference to literature which, like the book of Revelation, shows certain definite characteristics in both form and content.

Several observations are relevant to the form of apocalyptic literature:

(1) It is always written rather than oral in origin. This immediately differentiates apocalyptic from prophetic works. In the main, the prophet's words were first spoken, passed along by word of mouth for a while, and then written by a "disciple" of the original prophet. On the other hand, apocalyptic is a conscious literary product, intended from the beginning to be read.

(2) Apocalyptic always developed out of a particular historical situation and was intended to instruct and reassure readers in that situation. The apocalyptic author may have chosen to use figures and symbols that strike the modern reader as somewhat bizarre and foreign, but his original readers understood his message and received encouragement from it for facing their problems.

(3) Authorship of the non-Christian apocalyptic writings is either anonymous or pseudonymous. Perhaps some earlier apocalyptic passages originally circulated without any author's name attached, but most were from the first intentionally pseudonymous. By adopting the name of some ancient noteworthy, the author felt that he was speaking in the spirit of the person whose name he had attached to his writing. He did not intend to deceive his readers, nor were they deceived, for they understood and accepted this literary technique.

(4) A constant use of symbolism was chosen to express the content of the message. No language is more vivid than that of myth or symbol to delineate the demonic proportions of the present evil age, the finality of God's judgment, and the glorious rewards of the future golden age. Animals are kingdoms, while their horns are kings; all the elements of nature dance in the author's pageantry.

(5) Finally, the apocalyptist utilized and reinterpreted similar literature that had preceded him. The book of Daniel reinterprets portions from Jeremiah and Ezekiel; the book of Revelation uses not only Daniel but Daniel's sources and sources later than Daniel.

More striking than the form of apocalyptic literature is its theological content.

(1) Most generally the apocalyptic writers were extremely nationalistic in their outlook. The Gentiles would either be destroyed

or else subordinated to Israel. Sometimes a touch of universalism is detected in that the Gentiles would be permitted to worship the true God; but, when this transpires, it is only as the Gentiles approach God through the medium of Israel.

(2) The writers appealed to history for the sake of verifying the outcome of the future. They traced the past history of the nation, always with the conclusion that God was victorious, and interpreted this to signify that in a similar fashion history would reach its goal or climax either in the present or else in the immediate future.

(3) A type of determinism permeates the apocalyptic view of history, which is extremely pessimistic toward the present. God has established certain periods of time, and man cannot change these. Immediately prior to the coming glorious future lies the climax for the present age of evil in which evil will reach proportions it never before has attained. This means that the faithful must endure extreme hardships for the present and await the moment of God's intervention, which will surely come before his holy nation and his elect people are utterly consumed.

(4) God has a purpose in history, and a glorious future awaits those who are faithful in this life to the will of God. This future may be depicted as an earthly golden age similar to the Garden of Eden, or as a heavenly kingdom, or as a combination of the two, whereby the golden age on earth becomes translated into a heavenly and spiritual kingdom. In conjunction with this concept of a glorious future are developed doctrines of resurrection, final judgment, and real heavenly existence that has meaning—indeed, more meaning than one's present existence.

Two examples of apocalyptic literature will be presented. Second Esdras* (4 Esdras in the Catholic Bible) is a composite work, with the first two chapters and the last two forming an introduction and an appendix, while chapters 3-14 constitute the main core of the book. Oesterley thus outlines the book:

I. *The Salathiel Apocalypse* (3-9, divided into four visions)
II. *The Eagle Vision* (11-12:39, excluding 12:40-51)
III. *The Vision of the Man Rising from the Sea* (13)
IV. *An Ezra Legend* (14)[21]

The Salathiel Apocalypse consists of a series of four dialogues be-

_____
[21]*Apocrypha*, p. 513.

tween Salathiel (who is Ezra or Esdras) and an angel. Primarily the dialogues concern the problem of sin and suffering. Why does the righteous man suffer and the wicked prosper? The solution is found in the immortal life which is the reward of the righteous. Evidently the author was a devout Jew, but one who was extremely pessimistic and not so fervently nationalistic, because he sees no hope for the sinful nature of mankind, and even Israel has gone too far from God to find restoration in this world.

Chapters 11 and 12 describe an eagle with twelve wings and three heads emerging from the sea. The eagle settles, increases the number of his wings, and rules the entire earth. Suddenly a lion roars from the forest and destroys the monstrous bird. There is a common consensus of opinion that the eagle represents the Roman Empire under Domitian (A.D. 81-96) and the lion is the Messiah from Israel.

The third section depicts a man rising from the sea. A great host gathers against him, but he destroys them with a fiery breath. This man, the preexistent Messiah, whom God speaks of as his Son, gathers together the ten lost tribes and they become his people. This section dates from the era of the Jewish war (A.D. 66-70) and may reflect editing by Christians.

The Ezra legend may also be referred to as "the Writing of the Books." Ezra is addressed by God from out of a bush and is commissioned to write ninety-four books, which he does in forty days. Twenty-four (representing the Jewish Old Testament canon) of these books are made public, but the others are given to certain wise men who will deal equably with their contents. This legend was composed around the turn of the first century A.D.

Most significant of the noncanonical apocalypses is 1 Enoch, which again is a composite work dating from different periods, but all within the last two centuries B.C. and the first century A.D. One intimation of the role that this apocalypse held for the early church is the fact that it is the only apocryphal apocalypse directly quoted in the New Testament (Jude 15). The outline below is adapted from Torrey.[22]

I. *Introduction* (1-5). Enoch introduces himself and surveys the religious instruction to follow.

II. *Angels and the Universe* (6-36). Herein is focused attention upon

[22]*Op. cit.,* pp. 111-12.

the highly elaborate angelology occurring throughout the remainder of the book.

III. *The Parables of Enoch* (37-71). This is the most important section and will be discussed below.

IV. *Astronomy* (72-82). This division gives insight into the Jewish world-view and to the importance of the calendar in Jewish thought.

V. *Dream Visions* (83-90). Enoch relates the dreams he has experienced, one dealing with his foreknowledge of the flood and a second with a symbolic description of the history of mankind.

VI. *Religious Instruction* (91-108). With his children gathered around him, Enoch offers instructions of various sorts, but primarily his teachings concern the end of time.

The doctrine of the Son of man as contained within 1 Enoch, especially within the parables (or "similitudes"), is the most important contribution made by any apocryphal writing, for this doctrine sheds light upon the enigmatic phrase used in the New Testament with reference to Jesus. Erick Sjöberg[23] has produced what at pres-

---

[23]*Der Menschensohn im Äthiopischen Henochbuch* (Lund: C. W. K. Gleerup, 1946).

8. Traditional mount of temptation

ent is the most comprehensive and definitive work on 1 Enoch, and it is to the results of his careful study that attention will now be directed. Sjöberg feels that, taken as a whole, the parables form a unity written by Jewish rather than Christian hands. A date around the beginning of the procurators in Palestine appears to be the most probable period for their composition, although a Hasmonaean date is not excluded. What can one affirm with respect to the Son of man in 1 Enoch?

First of all, Sjöberg points out that this apparently was not a messianic title as such, even though in the apocalyptic circles where 1 Enoch originated, one could speak of the "Son of man," and everyone would know the "heavenly man" was indicated. There is an evident difference between the Son of man and the messianic King, even though there are certain similarities. The Son of man is not depicted as an earthly Messiah, as a king from the tribe of David. Rather, the Son of man is a being who descends from the heavens, a preexistent figure, whose appearance indicates the inbreak of the new age and the dissolution of the old. This Son of man has an eschatological function; that is, a function dealing with the final events. God grants him the role of the eschatological judge who affirms the cause of the righteous and condemns the wicked.

It must be mentioned in this connection, however, that the Son of man never acts in the capacity of forgiving sins. The Son of man belongs to the heavenly world, which in this age is hidden from the eyes of sinful men; whereas, the great privilege of the righteous is that they may learn these divine mysteries and know the Son of man. To the question whether or not the Son of man is a "suffering Son of man," as in the New Testament, one must conclude that neither the idea of suffering nor death is involved for him either in 1 Enoch or in 4 Esdras.

Josephus.—Flavius Josephus was born A.D. 37, the same year that Caligula was pronounced emperor of Rome. Although the exact date of his death is not known, he did outlive Herod Agrippa II, who died A.D. 100. As a youth, he was deeply influenced by the piety of Banus, the hermit, and spent three years in the desert in imitation of this man's way of life. At the age of nineteen, he began to conduct himself according to the rules of the Pharisees.

A visit to Rome (at age twenty-six) convinced Josephus of the Roman power, and from that moment on he was an ardent advocate of peace with the conquerors. When once introduced firmly to the

Greco-Roman culture, he apparently attempted to appropriate from it whatever he felt valuable for himself. Upon the inception of the Jewish-Roman war, he was placed as a leader in Galilee, but he gladly submitted to the Roman authority without a skirmish. Wherein lies the greatness of Josephus?

No hero, nor a man of sensitive honour; but whilst we cannot admire his character, and are at liberty to question his merits as an historian, it is impossible to deny the greatness of the debt posterity owes him for having given an invaluable record of events, which, but for him, would have been buried in oblivion.[24]

In his writings Josephus utilizes every means possible to depict Judaism in a light favorable to Rome. He intentionally avoids the inclusion of anything that would intimate the strong Jewish nationalistic hopes and their avowed hatred for Rome.

Josephus' primary works are four. (1) *The Antiquities,* his magnum opus, surveying Jewish history from creation to A.D. 66, was completed before A.D. 95. For his sources he utilized the Old Testament, especially in the first half of *The Antiquities,* as well as legends, other histories, and his own memory. (2) *The Life,* Josephus' autobiography, was attached to *The Antiquities,* and dates after A.D. 100. In this most illustrious self-portrait, the author was unhindered by humility. (3) *The Jewish War,* which incorporates Jewish history from the ascendancy of Antiochus IV in 175 B.C. to the aftermath of the war of A.D. 67-70, focuses attention mainly upon the events of the Jewish-Roman conflict, much of which Josephus had experienced firsthand as an eyewitness. This was published between A.D. 75 and 79. (4) *Against Apion* represents Josephus' apology for Judaism in connection with the anti-Jewish envoys who were sent to Rome during the riots in Alexandria. The date of this last effort was approximately A.D. 100.

Philo of Alexandria.[25]—One can affirm without any degree of reservation that Philo Judaeus (*ca.* 25 B.C. to A.D. 45/50) stands as the

---

[24]F. J. Foakes-Jackson, *Josephus and the Jews* (New York: Richard R. Smith, 1930), p. 18.

[25]For the following discussion acknowledgment is due to Erwin R. Goodenough, *An Introduction to Philo Judaeus* (New York: Yale University Press, 1940); Harry Austryn Wolfson, *Philo* (2 vols.; Cambridge: Harvard University Press, 1948); and C. H. Dodd, *The Interpretation of the Fourth Gospel* (Cambridge: The University Press, 1954), pp. 54-73.

best single representative of Hellenistic Judaism. Born into an aristocratic Alexandrian family, Philo was destined to produce a voluminous amount of material, related to a multiplicity of subjects. All is intended to demonstrate the originality and reasonableness of his Jewish faith. Philo's position in Judaism is not unique, for there existed a long line of predecessors as well as successors to what he attempted. His work, however, stands out in both quality and quantity. As one reads Philo, it must never be forgotten that he considered himself to be a devout Jew who sought to observe the Jewish way of life as it was defined in the Law. Philo was extremely faithful to the Jewish God, Law, and people; he was a deep-dyed monotheist, he hated idolatry and despised the secret rites of the mystery religions.

An outstanding feature of Philo's monographs is his "allegorical method" of interpretation. Through this medium he was able to find hidden meanings in any portion of the Old Testament and to make the Jewish Scriptures speak to his contemporary world. *On the Life of Moses,* an apology for nonhostile pagans, presents Moses as the ideal sage, the perfect priest and prophet, who embodied the essence of the universal law which the Gentiles had sought in ignorance. *On the Creation of the World,* designed for those who had read the previous work, reads into the Genesis account a great amount of Greek cosmology and metaphysics. In particular, it embodies the Platonic concept of creation as understood in the popular mind of Philo's day. *On Abraham* allegorizes Abraham as the unwritten law which was united with wisdom (Sarah). *On Joseph* delineates Joseph as the ideal ruler, who was, of course, a Jew.

Philo's major contribution, as far as New Testament background is concerned, is embodied in his concept of "Logos." The Greek word "Logos," usually translated as "word," contains a wider range of connotations than its English counterpart. In using the term, Philo apparently brought together the Stoic idea of Logos and the Jewish concept of Wisdom. For the Stoics, the Logos was the essence of the universe, and the existence of the Logos within each man was the rationale that gave meaning and unity to the world. Thus each man was a part of the total universe (Logos) and could find meaning in life only as he was obedient to that reason (Logos) residing within himself. Ultimately, therefore, *Logos* (or reason) was an impersonal "deity," which found individual expression through the divine "Logos spark" abiding in each man. In Hebrew thought Wisdom was at once the first created entity and the medium through which God fashioned the universe; but Wisdom was never identified either with God or with the universe, as was the Logos in Greek thought.

Philo remained ever loyal to his Jewish heritage when he adopted the term "Logos." Indeed, it was the Greek Old Testament that served as the background for Philo's Logos concept. The psalmist declared, "By the *word* of the Lord the heavens were made" (33:6); while Genesis reiterates, "and God *said,*" throughout the course of the creative process. Prophets testify that the *word* of the Lord came to them. Thus Greek-speaking Jews were already familiar with the Logos of God.

The task of Philo was thus to relate the Greek and Hebrew concepts of Logos, to connect these with the Jewish concept of Wisdom, and to add a few facets of his own. First of all, the Logos became for him the "thought" or "idea" existing in the mind of God; it was the *content* of what God willed. Secondly, Logos was the *medium* through which God accomplished or brought about his will or thought, the artificer of all things. Again, as in Stoicism, the Logos was the cohesive force within the universe, so for Philo it became the *means of divine government* and orderliness within the universe. Finally, the Logos was the means through which *God revealed his will* to man, and the way whereby one might respond intelligently to God.

Theology

The literature of Judaism is like a fertile garden, filled with variegated flowers, each displaying its own beauty to the eye. To gather all the "flowers" from this vast garden would be impossible. Certain "blossoms," however, are so important for an appreciation of the New Testament environment that they must be "picked" and "arranged" for viewing by those who have never visited the garden. One must not expect absolute consistency within such a "floral arrangement." Each flower must be accepted for its own sake and evaluated for its particular contribution to the total bouquet in which it appears.

Eschatology.—As the reader will recall, "eschatology" is the technical term for religious beliefs about the "last days" or "the end of the world." Eschatological beliefs ultimately developed from Israel's faith in God as the Lord of history. Since God is Lord of history, history must have a purpose and a goal; and this purpose is controlled by the will of him who is at once Creator and Redeemer.

Apart from a vital faith in a creative and redemptive God there can be no meaningful eschatology. Eschatology, then, is an inclusive term referring to beliefs about the end of history based on the axiom of God's lordship over the entire created order.

A colorful array of teachings about life after death comes to fruition within the apocryphal literature. To appreciate this, it is necessary to notice that the Old Testament is severely limited in its views concerning life after death. Men of that era believed that death brought the cessation of meaningful existence; were life to have fulfilment, it must be realized on this side of the grave. When one was "gathered to his fathers," he passed into oblivion and his life could have continuation only through his sons and daughters, to whom he had transmitted life. Thus children were for him a heritage from the Lord and an indication that his name would not be forgotten in the city gate.

In the Old Testament, Sheol (the grave) was one's final resting place. Here, the rich and the poor, the mighty and the weak, the good and the evil shared the same lot. Any existence in Sheol was but a shadow of the former life; and in Sheol one's self was no more real than a distorted reflection produced in a muddy pool.

Yet, certain elements of Israel's faith were eventually combined with other factors in such a manner that thoughts of an afterlife emerged.

(1) Implicit in the affirmation of God's lordship over the created order was his sovereignty over Sheol. Already the psalmist (139:8), as Amos (9:2), had declared that Sheol could not shield one from the presence of God. Thus was opened the possibility of God's intervention into Sheol for recompense to those who in life had not received their due.

(2) Before Jeremiah and Ezekiel, the primary emphasis in Israel was upon the person as a member of the corporate society rather than upon him as an individual. With the ascending recognition and acknowledgment of individual responsibility, the significance of the individual within the group tended to be elevated. This developing emphasis upon the individual's role in society implied that there ought to be some differentiation between persons in the afterlife.

(3) Furthermore, if life is without significance except in the present world, the only rewards for goodness or retribution for evil is that reaped during one's earthly sojourn. As illustrated by the story of

Job, the suffering of the righteous and the prosperity of the wicked caused serious minds to reconsider this philosophy and to think in terms of rewards after death as compensation for the inequities of this life.

(4) Finally, fellowship with God surely involves more than the imperfect communion shared amidst the perplexities of daily struggle for existence. Men of faith perceived that fellowship with God must be the determinitive factor in life. There must be possibilities that transcend the frustrations of the "now" and transform the "then" into a glorious reality.

Eschatology in the apocryphal literature is not uniform; delineations regarding the end of the world order and what shall transpire thereafter most often disagree in detail. Indeed, one sometimes discovers that a given book is not consistent within itself. Attention will now be directed toward some of the manifold doctrines of the afterlife as they appear in several apocryphal sources. Within the context of the apocalyptic writings, teachings of this nature germinated more frequently than elsewhere. These teachings often are linked with a doctrine of resurrection in one form or another.

Before a survey of these sources is undertaken, several reasons should be pointed out why the Jewish doctrine of an afterlife went in the direction of a belief in bodily resurrection rather than immortality of a nonmaterial soul.

(1) The Jews thought in concrete terms, and they could not conceive of a person as a complete entity unless he was in possession of a "body." In Greek thought, one's body might be looked upon as the "prison house of the soul." For the Jew, the body gave reality and actuality to existence, and life was not real without it. In the Hebrew language there was no word equivalent to the overtones conveyed by the Greek word "soul"; a person was a total *being*, "body" and "soul," an inseparable unity. Thus, if one is to live after death, he must possess a body of some kind.

(2) Man was a creature made by God, and his continuing existence depended on God's grace. This meant that each person came into being only through a creative fiat of God. Unless God re-created him and granted him a new "body," after death he ceased to be. On the other hand, the Greek concept of the soul's immortality was related to the belief in a preexistent and uncreated soul, which, when it left the body, went back into the world above, from which it had come.

Galilee

IN THE TIME OF

Christ

Scale of Miles

0 2 4 6 8 10

CHORAZIN

CAPERNAUM •BETH-SAIDA

Sea of Galilee

•CANA

GERGASA

TIBERIAS

HIPPOS

G A L I L E E

•NAZARETH

+ Mount Tabor

Jordan R.

GADARA

D E C A P O L I S

SCYTHOPOLIS

S A M A R I A

•PELLA

(3) The entire created order, including one's body of flesh, was within the creative purpose of God, and, therefore, was "good." No stigma was attached to the flesh, which was as much a part of God's created order as the remainder of man's being. Indeed, as noted above, a person could not be conceived of except in terms of an inseparable unity with his body of flesh. In diametric contrast stood the remainder of the Hellenistic world, where the body was subordinated and secondary in status to the "soul." Therefore, where the emphasis upon immortality, with its various facets, receives precedence over the emphasis on resurrection, one may feel certain that the Hellenistic world has left its mark upon Judaism.

Ecclesiasticus and Baruch offer substantially the classic Old Testament concept concerning the necessary end of life, while 1 Maccabees offers no suggestion at all in this direction. Tobit and Judith make allusions to a possible life after death, but in each instance the reference is poetic and perhaps not expressive of theological beliefs. In 2 Maccabees there is a rather developed doctrine of resurrection. Those who suffered for righteousness would be restored (7:10 ff., 23, 29; 14:46), but not the wicked (7:14, 36). Prayer was offered for those killed in battle, who, it was feared, might have died outside God's grace (12:43-45). The Wisdom of Solomon, through the influence of Greek thought, subdues the doctrine of resurrection and, in its stead, presents a modified immortality:

> But the souls of the righteous are in the hand of God,
>   and no torment will ever touch them.
> In the eyes of the foolish they seemed to have died, . . .
>   but they are at peace. . . .
>   their hope is full of immortality (3:1-4).

The Testaments of the Twelve Patriarchs[26] describe first a resurrection of the Old Testament patriarchs (Testament of Benjamin, 10:6-8), then a resurrection of the righteous, followed by a resurrection of the wicked, including Gentiles as well as Jews (10:8).

First Enoch, most flamboyant of the apocalypses, presents a threefold division of Sheol, consisting of the place of the righteous (paradise), the sinners who were not judged on earth (torment), and the sinners already judged on earth (remain in Sheol). Later the angels who overgave judgment to Israel are condemned to fire and flame, as are the apostate Jews (83-90). After the judgment, a new Jerusalem appears; the non-Jewish nations will be converted and serve Israel; only the righteous are raised to a kingdom on earth and then transformed to members of a heavenly kingdom (90:28-42). In the section 91-104 there comes a new heaven from above, but no notion of a renewed earthly reign (91:16). Sometimes the righteous dead are raised with a spirit (100:5; 103:3-4); elsewhere, Sheol is looked upon as the final resting place of the wicked (103:7-8). In the "parables" Sheol is the same as Gehenna or hell (56:8; 63:10); there is a spiritual body for the righteous (62:15-16).

In the Assumption of Moses[27] the righteous (i.e., the faithful Israelites) will be elevated to heaven and watch their enemies being tortured in Gehenna (10:8-10). The Baruch Apocalypse[28] depicts a

---

[26]An apocalypse dating from the end of the first century B.C. or the beginning of the first century A.D.

[27]A Palestinian apocalypse written between A.D. 6 and 30.

[28]Written in the last quarter of the first century A.D.

resurrection of the dead with no change from their previous earthly form (49:1 to 50:4).

Messiah and the messianic age —The basic notion involved in the classic Jewish concept of the "messianic age" was that of an earthly kingdom in which Israel would bask in the full glory of God's suzerainty. Sometimes, though not always, this age was conceived of in conjunction with a designated figure known as the "Messiah." "Messiah" is the transliteration of a Hebrew participle meaning "an anointed one." In ancient Israel anointing was the means whereby one was set aside to a specific task for God, and, accordingly, prophets, priests, and kings could be called "anointed ones." Even a foreigner, should he be confirmed as a chosen instrument of God, could be addressed, "his anointed one" (Isa. 45:1).

Finally, the term "Messiah" came to be used with such a connotation that it became more closely identified with the king than with any other person; therefore, in a unique sense, the king was among his people the anointed representative of God. Even before the day of Amos, Israel had looked forward to the "day of the Lord," which was interpreted by them as the day of exaltation for Israel and judgment for her foes. After the time of David's reign, which was memorialized by Israel as her "golden age," many began to reinterpret the future "day of the Lord" as a revivification of the Davidic era. In those circles of thought David himself became the ideal pattern for the coming "anointed one" (Messiah) who would act as God's co-regent, not only over Israel, but over the other nations as well, during the "golden age" (messianic age). Consequently, at its roots, the messianic idea was a *nationalitic hope related to an earthly kingdom* in which Israel, the elect nation of God, would be elevated over all other peoples.

Messianic motifs, as they occur in the apocryphal literature, germinated from these basic presuppositions. The actual significance of the Messiah himself was dependent upon the extent to which the role of the kingship was emphasized in the framework of the future government, and there were some strands of tradition, especially the apocalyptic, wherein the figure of the Messiah had no function whatsoever. But whenever a Messiah did appear in the tradition, he always appeared in conjunction with a nationalistic earthly reign, and his fate at the end of the age was the same as the remainder of his contemporaries. Either he would die and go to Sheol, or else he would be translated and taken to a heavenly kingdom. Although

a militant messianism appears elsewhere in the apocryphal sources (e.g., 1 Enoch 89-90), the most classical example of this strong nationalistic tint, as it existed at the beginning of the first Christian century, is to be discovered in the Psalms of Solomon, especially 17 and 18:

> Behold, O Lord, and raise up unto them their king, the son of David,
> At the time in which Thou seest, O God, that he may reign over Israel Thy servant.
> And gird him with strength, that he may shatter unrighteous rulers,
> And that he may purge Jerusalem from nations that trample [her] down to destruction . . .
> He shall destroy the godless nations . . .
> And he shall have the heathen nations to serve him under his yoke . . . (17:23-32).

Angels and demons.—The earliest traditions in the Old Testament suggest no need for a doctrine of angels or demons. Yahweh, the God of Israel, was directly responsible for all phenomena. Whatever happened, natural or supernatural, good or evil, was ascribed to the immediate intervention of God into the affairs of the world. Not until the exile did angels and demons acquire real importance and receive definite functions in Jewish thought. Both Babylonian and Persian influences were primary elements in the development of Judaism's angelology. Although opinion is divided regarding the exact degree that either of these cultures left its imprint upon Israel, the important thing is to realize that Judaism did not develop in a vacuum without foreign influence upon its life and thought. On the other hand, one should keep in mind that a unique trait of Judaism was its ability to absorb foreign elements without producing contradictions within the *essential core* of its confession.

A second factor contributory to this growing angelology was later Judaism's concept of a transcendent God. As was pointed out in the initial chapter, this idea of God's transcendence had effects upon Judaism's concept of prophecy in that it caused them no longer to believe that God would communicate directly with his people through a prophet. Another outcome of this doctrine was the appearance of a series of intermediaries (angels) who were mediators between the world of God above and the world of men below. These angels

10. North end, Sea of Galilee

were increased in number, given specialized functions, and arranged in a hierarchy with special privileges. The functions of these angels varied. (1) They brought men's prayers and petitions up before God. (2) God used them as messengers to do his bidding, in the sphere of nature as in the realm of human history. (3) Each nation possessed its own guardian angel, and later even individuals felt they had angels that watched over their affairs. (4) Finally, one's heavenly counterpart was represented as an angel who acted out in heaven what one did on earth, so that God needed only to look upon the angel in order to judge the individual whom the angel represented. First Enoch indicates the proportions that the angelic hierarchy had attained in certain areas of Judaism:

> And these are the names of the holy angels who watch. Uriel, one of the holy angels, who is over the world and over Tartarus. Raphael, one of the holy angels, who is over the spirits of men. Raguel, one of the holy angels who takes vengeance upon the world of the luminaries. Michael, one of the holy angels, to wit, he that is over the best part of mankind and over chaos. Saraqael, one of the holy angels, who is set over the spirits, who sin in spirit. Gabriel, one of the holy angels, who is over Paradise and the serpents and the Cherubim. Remiel, one of the holy angels, whom God set over those who rise (20:1-8).

Primitive peoples in all parts of the world appear to have believed in some sort of animism; that is, the feeling that everything, animate or inanimate, possesses some sort of power to be feared. Evidently this notion existed even among the Israelites, since there are at least a few Old Testament indications that suggest a belief in demons, especially such as were partial to the desert regions and to nocturnal hours. Yet no mature demonology appears in Judaism until the time of the exile and after. Foreign influences in combination with logical deductions of their own compelled the Jews to realize that God could not be the immediate cause for good and evil alike.

As a practical answer to this dilemma Judaism adopted a modified dualism. Dualism, in its absolute form, is the theory that two powers, Good and Evil, have eternally coexisted. Absolute dualism could offer no appeal to the Jew, for Yahweh, Israel's God, was the only eternal and sovereign deity. Any other power must ultimately owe both its origin and continuation to the will of this one God.

Consequently, Judaism accepted a modified dualism. Demonic powers were thought to exist, but in some manner their existence served the purpose of God. What finally ensued was the creation of an elaborate system of demonic beings with a leader of their own, known most frequently in New Testament times as Satan. These demonic creatures possessed power to induce physical and mental illness and to tempt men away from God. But their authority was ever a delegated one, and there would come a day when God would judge these demons and the men whom they had seduced.

The origin and nature of sin.—The exile served as a period of transition in Judaism's concept of the origin and nature of sin. Basically, the Old Testament idea of the nature of sin was either rebellion against God or against the moral law which God had established for mankind. When a devout Israelite transgressed against one of those laws, he felt, as the psalmist: "Against thee, thee only, have I sinned, and done that which is evil in thy sight" (51:4).

Theoretically, sin was still rebellion against God, but in actual practice it was "breaking the Law," understood in terms of a failure to comply with the multiplicity of juristic regulations perpetuated in the written Law and the oral tradition. This led in the direction of a differentiation between good and evil acts, with the outcome that the *basic emphasis* was placed upon the *deed* as sinful rather than upon the person as a sinner.

11. Synagog at Capernaum, built after the time of Christ

Consonant with this concept of sin were the various avenues through which it was thought forgiveness and atonement might be secured. Ecclesiasticus presents works of charity as a means of forgiveness:

Whoever honors his father atones for sins . . .
For kindness to a father will not be forgotten,
    and against your sins it will be credited to you . . .
Water extinguishes a blazing fire:
    so almsgiving atones for sin. (3:3-30).

Tobit suggests a similar array of effectual deeds:

Do good, and evil will not overtake you. Prayer is good when accompanied by fasting, almsgiving, and righteousness. A little with righteousness is better than much with wrongdoing. It is better to give alms than to treasure up gold. For almsgiving delivers from death, and it will purge away every sin (12:7-9).

Second Maccabees teaches that it is feasible to offer sacrifices as an "atonement for the dead, so that they might be set free from their sins" (12:45); while Ecclesiasticus will even submit that one's own suffering and death are effectual acts of atonement:

Before judgment, examine yourself,
    and in the hour of visitation you will find happiness.
Before falling ill, humble yourself,
    and when you are on the point of sinning, turn back.
Let nothing hinder you from paying a vow promptly,
    and do not wait until death to be released from it (18:20-22).

For many minds the Old Testament was too vague with respect to the enigma of sin's origin, so imaginative persons reached picturesque conclusions. These conclusions fall into one of two camps, according to whether they interpreted the origin of sin as coming upon man from without or as lying within man. Ecclesiasticus (15:11-13) warns against accusing God, "for he will not do things that he hates," and God does despise sin. Passages in 1 Enoch and Jubilees lay the burden of guilt either upon the "fallen angels" or else upon demonic spirits. The Wisdom of Solomon traces sin to the envy of the devil, while the "parables" of 1 Enoch in places suggest the "satans." Second Esdras, on the one hand, states, "A grain of evil was sown in the heart of Adam from the beginning" (4:30); while elsewhere a contrary view is given by the same source:

"For the first Adam, clothing himself with an evil heart, transgressed and was overcome; and likewise all who were born of him" (3:21).

The noted passage from 2 Baruch exonerates no man from guilt: "Adam is therefore not the cause, save only of his own soul. But each of us has been the Adam of his own soul" (54:19).

Cult

Cult (or cultus) is a comprehensive term utilized to characterize the religious life and the way of worship of a group of people. The Jewish cult of the New Testament period found expression through a holy people (the Jews) whose worship was centralized in a holy place (the Jerusalem Temple) and whose manner of life was governed by a holy tradition (the Law). Since the Law has already been touched upon, it is requisite to survey only the first two areas.

The holy people.—Israel are the chosen people of God; to them belong the history of the sacred past, as well as the promises of the glorious future. At the heart of the nation were the so-called "people of the land" (*Am ha-aretz*). These were the working class of people whose daily struggle for existence prevented them the opportunity of formal training in any rabbinic tradition. Though there seem to have been moments when they were despised by the Pharisees for their lack of knowledge of the Law, their beliefs would possibly have been very closely akin to those of the Pharisees. Among these untrained multitudes were many pious souls who anxiously awaited the "consolation of Israel," which God had long since promised to the fathers through the prophets.

"Pharisee" comes from a root word meaning "separated one" and was possibly first attached to this specific group of people because of their desire to separate themselves from any unclean deed or situation that would defile them and keep them from being holy unto God. The Pharisees were more influential among the common people than any other of the Jewish sects, because they were the recognized authorities in the interpretation both of Scripture and of tradition. Through combining the evidence of the New Testament with that of Josephus, the following reconstruction of the essential Pharisaic doctrines emerges.[30] (1) Of basic concern to the Pharisee was his religion revealed in the Law of God; and all other areas of life

[30]Emil Schürer, *A History of the Jewish People* (Edinburgh: T. & T. Clark, 1885), Division II, II, 4-43.

had monument only as they affected those sacred religious traditions. (2) The Pharisees believed in an afterlife with rewards and punishments in direct ratio to one's acceptance or rejection of the Law. (3) They acknowledged that all human actions and choices, whether good or evil, were made possible only through the providence of God. (4) In accord with the general viewpoints of later Judaism, they affirmed the existence of angels and demons.

The Zealots were the extreme left wing of the Pharisees. Both groups believed in the ultimate triumph of Israel's God. But, whereas, most of the Pharisees seem to have been quietists who waited for God to act in his own time, the Zealots felt they must actively initiate hostile proceedings against the foes of God and Israel. Thereby the Zealots became ardent messianists who would zealously follow anyone they were convinced might be the promised Messiah. Through their instigation war was made against Rome in A.D. 67-70 and again in A.D. 132-35, with the result that their nation was overrun on each occasion.

The origin of the name Sadducee is not altogether certain, but generally one of three alternatives is pursued. (1) "Sadducee" may be derived from a Hebrew word signifying "the righteous ones." However, this suggestion is at present not so widely accepted because of certain etymological problems involved. (2) A second, more probable alternative is that the name was derived from Zadok, whose family had been in charge of the priestly affairs since the days of Solomon. (3) Finally, it is not unlikely that this designation originated from connection with some unknown Zadok who had been the founder of this Sadducaean movement.

The Sadducees represented the aristocracy of the priestly class, and, as such, were concerned that the status quo remain unchanged so they could continue to enjoy the favors of Rome, to whom they were indebted for the security of their position. The high-priestly family belonged to the Sadducees, which meant that oversight of the Temple services and leadership of the Sanhedrin, the highest Jewish court, were under Saducean persuasion.

With respect to their Jewish religious heritage, the Sadducees accepted only the written Law as binding and rejected the later additions to the canon, along with the oral traditions of the Pharisees. Consequently, they did not accept those concepts that developed in conjunction with the later Jewish literature; they denied the reality of a life after death and rejected the possibility of angels and spirits.

All this meant that the Sadducees were primarily concerned for the affairs of the present life and were most susceptible to accumulating whatever elements of the Hellenistic world they felt advantageous to themselves.

So much has been learned in the last decade and a half about the people of the Dead Sea community that one is tempted to discuss them out of proportion to the remaining Jewish sects of the New Testament era. There were four major periods of occupancy for this small region near the Qumran stream at the northwest edge of the Dead Sea. The initial settlement by the Essene group appears to have come about during the reign of John Hyrcanus I (134-104 B.C.) and would have continued until around 31 B.C., when the buildings were destroyed by an earthquake.

At the beginning of the first century A.D. the earthquake damage was repaired, new assembly halls added, and the water system enlarged. This occupancy lasted until A.D. 68, at which time the community met a cataclysmic fate at the hands of the Tenth Roman Legion. From this time on until A.D. 100 the remaining structures were occupied by the Roman forces as a military outpost overlooking the Dead Sea. The latest occupation was during the Jewish Revolt of A.D. 132-35 by a small group of Jewish rebels. The Essene community itself flourished in this region from about 134 B.C. (110 B.C. may be more accurate) until A.D. 68.

Isaiah 40:3 summarizes the purpose adopted by the Essenes: "In the wilderness prepare the way of the Lord, make straight in the desert a highway for our God." Evidently they felt that the Jerusalem cultus had fallen into corruption through the influence of the outside world; they, therefore, would avoid this contamination by withdrawing into the desert and there "prepare the way of the Lord."

The Essenes were highly organized with a designated procedure for entrance into their group, and the requirements for remaining in fellowship with the community were as stringent as those for entrance. Among their religious practices were a variety of lustrations, a daily sacred meal, and strict worship, especially on the sabbath. These people anticipated the coming of a Messiah (perhaps two Messiahs: a kingly and a priestly), believed in angels and demons, affirmed the immortality of the soul, and placed a strong emphasis upon a divinely ordained fatalism.

Included in their curriculum were the copying of sacred manuscripts and the composition of other literature unique to themselves, some of which gave rules and regulations for their common life, while other compositions were interpretations of biblical texts or discourses and reflections upon theological and devotional subjects. A primary contribution for the study of the New Testament, made through the discovery of this Dead Sea community and their scrolls, is the new light shed upon an hitherto dark facet of Jewish life, and, consequently, another light reflected upon the background in which the early church had its inception and earliest development.

The holy place.—From the rededication of the Temple in 164 B.C. until the few years before the acquisition of Palestine by Herod the Great, the Temple suffered no significant damage. But immediately prior to Herod's reign the Temple became in a state of disrepair, and in the eighteenth year of his reign Herod is quoted as saying:

I will do my endeavour to correct that imperfection, which hath arisen from the necessity of our affairs, and the slavery we have been under formerly, and to make a thankful return, after the most pious manner, to God, for what blessings I have received from him, by giving me this kingdom, and that by rendering his temple as complete as I am able.[31]

The completion of the Temple proper required only a year and six months, during which time "the people were full of joy"; yet the remainder of the construction was not entirely finished before the catastrophic events of A.D. 70.

The Temple proper was located in the northwest sector of the large open area known as the Court of the Gentiles, which was marked off on all four sides by a series of porticoes, wherein were provided entrance ways into the Temple complex. Solomon's Porch was the name given the eastern portico, while the southernmost portico, which was also the widest, was designated the Royal Porch. Gentiles could congregate in the enclosed court area but could not proceed farther without risking their lives. Leading into the Court of the Women was the Corinthian Gate (or Beautiful Gate).

Adjunct to the Court of the Women, beyond which the Jewish women were not allowed, was the Court of Israel, the farthest destination that nonpriestly personnel could enter. From here the Israelite men could see the sacrifices offered upon the altar in the

---

[31] *Antiquities,* XV, XI, 1. Translation by William Whiston, *The Works of Flavius Josephus* (New York: Leavitt & Allen, 1853), p. 429.

12. The Jordan River as it leaves the Sea of Galilee

Court of the Priests, which was separated from the Court of Israel by the Nicanor Gate. Beyond the Court of the Priests lay the holy place and then the holy of holies. Priests on duty entered the holy place in the course of their ministering, but the high priest alone could enter the holy place, and this only once a year, on the Day of Atonement.

Although the Temple liturgy varied somewhat, according to what holy day or sacred season was in progress, there was a standard procedure followed daily in the Temple which must have left significant impressions upon the routine of life in Jerusalem and the surrounding territory. This daily offering, known as the *Tamid* (meaning "continuous" or "continued"), had its basis in a command of the Old Testament: "Now this is what you shall offer upon the altar: two lambs a year old day by day continually. One lamb you shall offer in the morning, and the other you shall offer in the evening" (Ex. 29:38-39).

Actual preparations for the perpetual morning sacrifice, requiring the services of nine to twelve priests, began before daylight. Each participating priest diligently kept himself ceremonially clean before engaging in the activities of sacrifice. One of the priests went to remove the ashes of the previous sacrifice from the altar, while others went to make the "baken cakes." After the altar was cleared, several of the priests joined together in setting the fire in order. The officer who was "over the lots" cast lots to determine who would trim the lamps, slaughter the lamb, sprinkle the blood, and take the necessary portions of the sacrifice up the ramp to the altar. At dawn, when "the whole east was alight," the lamb was taken from the chamber of lambs, given a final inspection while drinking from a golden bowl, and was then led away to be slaughtered.

Opening the "great gate" produced a noise which became the signal for slaying the lamb. Simultaneous with the slaying of the lamb the Levites, assistants to the priests, made music with flutes, cymbals, and singing; a priest blew three blasts upon the shofar, a trumpet made from a ram's horn. According to the Mishnah, these sounds could be heard as far as Jericho:

From Jericho they could hear the sound of the flute; from Jericho they could hear the noise of the cymbal; from Jericho they could hear the sound of the singing; from Jericho they could hear the sound of the *Shofar;* and some say, even the voice of the High Priest when he pronounced the Name on the Day of Atonement (*Tamid* 3:8).[32]

The lamb's blood was sprinkled upon each of the four sides of the altar, with the residue of the blood poured out at the base of the altar; the animal was then cleaned and his carcass borne up the ramp in position to be offered.

With all preparations now completed, the priests withdrew to the Hall of Hewn Stone where they led the people in reciting, among other things, a benediction, the Ten Commandments, and the Shema (Deut. 6:4-5). After this ceremony, confessions were made and requests for prayer were received. These were brought symbolically before the throne of God through the incense offering. Then, with outstretched arm, the same priest imparted to the people the Aaronic blessing in the forecourt from the platform over the fifteen steps in the Court of the Priests.

At this juncture the high priest went forward to the altar where he burned all the offering, except the drink offering, which he poured out at the foot of the altar. During the course of these events priests blew blasts on the trumpets and the people prostrated themselves. The so-called Week Psalm, which gave thanks to God for his creation and gracious leading of Israel, concluded the ceremonies. The evening sacrifice was accomplished in essentially the same manner as the morning sacrifice.

---

[32]Translation by Herbert Danby, *op. cit.,* p. 585.

Part Two
New Wine and Old Skins

No one places new wine in old skins (Mark 2:22).

The Judaism of Jesus' day had become stereotyped in its demands upon society. One could not approach God apart from the mediation of the institutionalized religion. Any attempt to discover God outside these designated forms immediately affixed one either as an overt sinner or else as a despised person who "knew not the Law." The skins into which the old wine had been poured had become rigid and inflexible. And the major emphasis was now placed upon the form of the vessels rather than upon the wine that the vessels were designed to contain.

Contrariwise, the message of Jesus was the demand for absolute obedience to the will of a God who encountered men in such a manner that no predetermined external expression could serve as an adequate response. His was the message of a living God whose requirements for mankind could not be contained within the dried skins which comprised the institutional framework of Judaism. Therefore, implicit in the proclamation of Jesus were both the fulfilment and abrogation of Judaism. Initially, the early Christian community, as the Jewish community, did not recognize this absolute incompatibility between the old skins and the new wine, but inevitably these were severed one from the other: "No one places new wine in old skins."

3

The Ministry of Jesus

—THE FRUIT PRESSED OUT

Oral Tradition

The writing of the Gospels.—There existed a *gospel* before the Gospels; the Christian message was preached before it was written. Behind the written Gospels stands the spoken word, the early Christian tradition concerning the meaning of the Christ event. From these various strands of tradition the Gospel writers selected those materials which they felt best demonstrated the emphases they desired to make. Luke explicitly states that he pursued this methodology:

Inasmuch as many have undertaken to compile a narrative of the things which have been accomplished among us, just as they were delivered to us by those who from the beginning were eyewitnesses and ministers of the word, it seemed good to me also, having followed all things closely for some time past, to write an orderly account for you, most excellent Theophilus, that you may know the truth concerning the things of which you have been informed (1:1-4).

The author of the Fourth Gospel likewise affirms that from the many traditions available he selected those which would convey his thesis that "Jesus is the Christ, the Son of God, and that believing you may have life in his name" (John 20:30-31). Thus, one must remember as he reads the Gospels that these are *confessions of faith*, written by men who were disciples rather than historians. Their purpose was not to record objective, historical data—if, indeed, that should be possible in the writing of any records. These men wrote to interpret the events of Jesus' ministry in light of their belief in him as the Lord of heaven and earth.

The Gospels were not written immediately after the events of Jesus' life had transpired. A primary reason for this was the belief, prevalent within the early church, that their Lord would return within the lifetime of the generation who had known him in the flesh. In the earlier part of his ministry, Paul certainly felt that he would be alive at the Lord's return (1 Thess. 4:17); and this was perhaps the feeling of Mark (9:1). However, certain factors did come about that encouraged the writing of a permanent source.

(1) Eye (and ear) witnesses were passing from the scene. After the midpoint of the first century several of the eyewitnesses had died, and there was danger that more would soon be passing on. In order to preserve an accurate record, especially in a community where the Lord's return was no longer felt to be quite so immediate, certain persons began to jot down events, either as they had seen or as they had heard them.

(2) As the church responded to the universal implications of its message, men like Luke recognized the necessity to formulate the Christian message in a manner that would make it relevant for the Gentile world.

(3) The needs of Christian worship became another factor in the writing of the Gospels. The first Christians were Jews who had been accustomed to the reading of Scripture in their synagogues. Therefore, since the redemptive history had culminated in the person of Christ, it was only to be expected that the church should desire to have read before them narratives pertaining to this One.

(4) Apologetic[1] factors must be taken into consideration. Through false accusations Jesus had been crucified as an insurrectionist, an enemy of Caesar. The church must demonstrate where these charges were without foundation and affirm that the church and her Lord were not in opposition to government.

(5) Judaism had refused to acknowledge Jesus Christ as the fulfilment of its hope, and there were followers of John the Baptist who declared that John was superior to Jesus. These and other factors produced a polemical situation for the Christians wherein they were required to argue the fulfilment of Judaism in Jesus and the superiority of Jesus to the Baptist.

(6) The most weighty motif in the Gospels is the Christological, an attempt to give answer to the question, "Who is Jesus?" Somehow the church must share with the world the truth that the Lord of the church is also Lord of history and of mankind.

---

[1]An "apology," in its technical sense, is the presentation of a reasoned basis for one's faith.

The oral period.—During the period immediately antedating the composition of the Gospels, those traditions which later were incorporated into the written Gospels circulated primarily by word of mouth, hence the phrase, oral period. No doubt during the oral period some of these traditions had already received a written form. But these were without connection to their original context, with the possible exception of the passion narrative, which likely would have been remembered in more detail. Ultimately, what determined the preservation and selection of the traditions were the interests and needs of the early Christian community. Each person would remember a narrative or a saying that had meant something to him. Certain individuals might retain more than others, but none could recall all the events of Jesus' ministry in their exact chronological order.

The technical science for the study of this preliterary period is termed *form criticism,* or better, *form history. Form history* proceeds upon the presupposition that the situation of Jesus' ministry and the situation of the early church reflect somewhat different backgrounds, and, therefore, the sayings and teachings of Jesus would have been applied by the developing church to meet the needs of the later period. For example, much of Jesus' ministry was exercised against the background of Judaism as it was before the catastrophe of A.D. 70, whereas three of the four Gospels were not written until after this date, which brought significant modifications into Judaism.

Again, Jesus lived in Palestine and spoke to the Jews, while, at the time of the writing of the Gospels, the church was existing primarily on Gentile soil in an entirely different milieu. Many parables and sayings of Jesus would have become ineffective in the changed situation unless the preachers of the congregations had applied them to their own contemporary needs. So it was that when the Gospels were written, they related the traditions, not solely in the context in which the events had originally transpired, but oftentimes in the new context that these traditions had acquired in the early church's life.

Indeed, the editor of each Gospel was a preacher himself, who on occasion, would add fresh light to a narrative through including it in his Gospel in a context different both from the original context of Jesus' ministry and from the way it had come to be used since Jesus' time. Therefore, the role of the form historian is to trace, if possible, the history of a particular narrative (or saying) through the Gospels and the early church back to its original setting in Jesus' lifetime. The purpose of this highly technical, and sometimes arbitrary, skill is to understand the Word of God both in its original context and in the way it was used in the early church, so that this ever living Word might speak with clarity and significance to the present generation.

The Synoptic Gospels

The Synoptic problem.—The first three Gospels, Matthew, Mark, and Luke, are called the Synoptic Gospels, because in large measure they present the same basic viewpoint and outline of Jesus' ministry. On the other hand, there are a multiplicity of variations, sometimes significant ones, both in the viewpoint and the outline represented by these three Gospels. The problem raised through the recognition of these similarities and differences within the first three Gospels is known as the Synoptic problem. Presently two basic solutions are suggested for the Synoptic problem: one posits the priority of Matthew; the other, the priority of Mark.

Matthean priority is supported by B. C. Butler in a work entitled *The Originality of St. Matthew*. Recognizing that any solution to the problem must take into consideration the similarities and differences between the Gospels, as well as any unique material that is contained within any one Gospel, Butler offers the following hypothesis. Matthew wrote the Aramaic version of the Gospel that carries his name. This volume would have found ready acceptance by the Christian missionaries and preachers, especially those among "the twelve."

When, a few years later, the Christian movement spread to Greek-speaking quarters, each disciple would have had to translate this Aramaic volume impromptu as the occasion demanded. How much they would have welcomed "an authentic translation of the work." As soon as this translation appeared it would have received numerous copyings and from then on would have been the basis for the teaching within the early Christian community. To the details in Matthew's Gospel, each of "the twelve" could have added his own memoirs. Mark, who was not one of "the twelve," derived his Gospel from Matthew in conjunction with the memoirs of the apostle Peter.

St. Peter made use of Matthew as the sourcebook for his own "instructions," he selected passages which his own memory could confirm and enlarge upon, he omitted incidents that occurred before he met our Lord, and most of Matthew's discourse-material, as not suitable for his purpose

and not such as he could reinforce with a personal and independent re-collection . . .

St. Mark, for his part, it would seem, "made it his own care to omit nothing of what he heard" in these Petrine instructions, "and to reproduce them faithfully." But it may well be that he had Matthew in front of him when he came to write out his Gospel, and was thus in a position to check his notes of St. Peter's reminiscences.[2]

Finally, Luke is said to have been dependent upon Matthew for the material that he and Matthew have in common apart from Mark, while he was dependent upon Mark for the general outline of his Gospel.

Despite Butler's arguments for Matthean priority, the thesis represented by B. H. Streeter's *The Four Gospels* is more generally accepted. Streeter advocated Markan priority on several bases. Among those related to content are: (1) Almost the whole of Mark's Gospel is found in Matthew or Luke or both. (2) The correspondence of language is striking. Whenever Matthew or Luke diverge, Mark is generally common to one of them; very few places exist where Matthew and Luke both differ from Mark's wording. (3) The general outline of Jesus' ministry is that of Mark's Gospel. Sometimes Matthew or Luke will depart from the Markan outline, but they never do this at the same place, and they always return to Mark's arrangement.

Certain other arguments advocated by Streeter are related to literary form: (1) Mark's Gospel is the shortest. Why would Mark have omitted the Sermon on the Mount or many of Luke's parables if he had known them? (2) Mark's Gospel is a relatively simple document when contrasted with the others; he offers very little of Jesus' teaching and places his main import upon the power and deeds of Jesus. (3) There are certain problematic and difficult passages in Mark which either have been altogether omitted or else altered to read more smoothly in the Matthean and Lukan parallels. In

---

[2]B. C. Butler, *The Originality of St. Matthew* (Cambridge: University Press, 1951), pp. 168-69. Matthean priority has traditionally been supported by the Roman Catholic scholars. For a recent Protestant scholar who argues in favor of this position, cf. William R. Farmer, *The Synoptic Problem* (New York: The Macmillan Co., 1964).

13. Jacob's well at Sychar

these passages it is easy to see why they would have been altered to read in the form of Matthew or Luke, but it is impossible to understand why they would have been changed to the Markan form.[3]

In the main, contemporary New Testament scholarship accepts the priority of Mark. Mark was the first written Gospel and was utilized as a source for Matthew and Luke. Besides Mark there was a second source (or group of sources?) common to Matthew and Luke. This source is known as Q, an abbreviation for the German word *Quelle,* meaning "source." Matthew possessed another source, unique to himself, known as M; while Luke possessed a source, not available to Matthew and Mark, known as L. The diagram below illustrates this "four-document hypothesis." In the diagram the arrows point from the sources drawn on by the different Gospels:

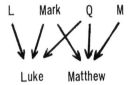

Mark.—Before an introduction to any one of the Gospels is offered, a word must be said relevant to the general approach one should take toward the Gospels. When one approaches the Gospels, he must ever be mindful that these are *Gospels* rather than biographies of Jesus. Each author intends to enshrine the "good news" (gospel) in what he writes; and the reason any particular narrative or saying is incorporated is because it in some fashion proclaims the "good news." Therefore, the Gospels are neither haphazardly arranged collections of unrelated incidents nor biographical documents, chronologically accurate in all details. The Gospels are theological works, utilizing the methodology of historical narrative to herald the "good news" from God, as it had come to man in the person of Jesus Christ.

Papias, bishop in the Phrygian city of Hierapolis during the first half of the second century, represents the earliest testimony to the authorship and source of the Second Gospel.

Mark, who was Peter's interpreter, wrote down accurately, though not

[3]B. H. Streeter, *The Four Gospels* (London: Macmillan & Co., 1956), pp. 157-69.

in order, all that he recollected of what Christ had said or done. For he was not a hearer of the Lord, nor a follower of his; he followed Peter, as I have said, at a later date, and Peter adapted his instructions to practical needs, without any attempt to give the Lord's words systematically. So that Mark was not wrong in writing down some things in this way from memory, for his own concern was neither to omit nor to falsify anything he had heard (Eusebius, *E. H.*, III, 39).[4]

It can be seen immediately that Papias attributes the Markan Gospel ultimately to the witness of Peter, for whom Mark was the interpreter (translator?). Most likely the words, "not in order," were intended to have been a contrast between the rough and ready style of Mark's Gospel as compared with the smooth flowing Matthean Gospel, which by Papias' time seems to have had more preeminence in the early church than the Markan Gospel. Papias is correct in his statement concerning a Petrine influence upon Mark's Gospel, though Mark apparently utilized other sources, both oral and written, in the composition of his Gospel. So freely has Mark combined

---

[4]Translation from James Moffatt, *Introduction to the Literature of the New Testament* (Edinburgh: T. & T. Clark, 1949), pp. 186-87.

14. Roman coin (enlarged) from Palestine: the "penny" ("farthing," KJV) mentioned by Jesus in Mark 12:42, equal to two of the so-called "widow's mites"; obverse side (left) pictures a ladle used by the Romans in augury and reads "Tiberius Caesar" (written in Greek); reverse pictures three ears of grain bound together and reads "Julia Caesar"; coins of this type were minted by Pontius Pilate during the public ministry of Jesus.

his sources that absolute agreement will never be reached with respect to the origin of all the individual parts.

The accumulation of evidence from early Christian authors suggests that the Gospel was written either immediately prior to or soon after the death of Peter in Rome about A.D. 64-65. This is harmonious with the internal data of Mark that suggests a date before the destruction of Jerusalem in A.D. 70.

Mark wrote for a Gentile audience, as is indicated by his habitual explanation of Jewish customs (7:3-4; 15:42) and his translation of Aramaic words into Greek (5:41; 7:11; 15:22). Throughout the Gospel he emphasizes the *power* of Jesus, which would have particular appeal to a Gentile reader. These and other observations have left the impression that Mark was written in a city heavily populated with Gentiles, but where the Christian message had made an impact, such as Rome, Antioch, or Alexandria.

Matthew.—Papias' testimony also supplies the earliest witness to the authorship and composition of the first Gospel: "So then Matthew composed the *Logia* in the Hebrew language, and everyone interpreted them as he was able."[5] Papias is more enigmatic than he appears on the surface. Some manuscripts substitute a word meaning "arranged" for "composed." If the latter is the true reading, then Papias may simply be contrasting the "orderly" Matthew with the "less orderly" Mark. Technically, the term *logia* means only "sayings" or "oracles," and would not have included narratives. Thus Papias could have had reference either to a collection of the "sayings" of our Lord, or else to a collection of "proof-texts" or "oracles" from the Old Testament, which were believed to have been spoken concerning the coming Lord.

However, the possibility exists that Papias did not use *logia* in its confined sense, and that he had reference to a collection of sayings *and* narratives from Jesus' ministry. But even this does not necessarily imply that Papias had reference to an Aramaic original of Matthew's Gospel. In light of the judgment that the present edition of Matthew evidently has Mark as a source and that Matthew often appears out of touch with the Palestinian situation of Jesus' day, it is safe to conclude that the author was not an eyewitness to the events, though at places he did have possession of sources from eyewitnesses, among whom may have been the disciple Matthew.

---

[5]*Ibid.*, p. 187.

It is relatively certain that Matthew wrote after the destruction of Jerusalem, since there appear to be indirect allusions in his Gospel to this as an event already past. The church of Matthew's day is developing an organizational pattern and the hope of Jesus' return has diminished considerably. These and other considerations date the Gospel of Matthew somewhere around A.D. 80.

The place of origin is no more certain than the authorship of the Gospel. Generally, students of the First Gospel believe it originated somewhere in the eastern part of the Mediterranean world— in Palestine, Antioch, Alexandria, or even in some Phoenician city.

Luke.—Early tradition assigns the authorship of the Third Gospel to Luke, the companion of Paul and author of the book of Acts. There would seem to have been no reason to have attributed the Gospel to such an obscure person as Luke, unless he actually had at least a significant hand in its writing. Beyond the external testimonies, the language, style, and theological emphases are such as one would expect to find in a volume by the type person Luke is supposed to have been.

Luke's unique utilization of sources led B. H. Streeter to a theory of composition known as Proto-Luke. Rather than interweaving his sources, so that they are separated with difficulty (as in Matthew's Gospel), Luke chose to alternate Markan material with non-Markan sources. Furthermore, Luke neither began nor concluded his Gospel with the Markan source and the Q-L section (with the Markan segments removed) is said to read like a complete book. Streeter thus concluded that Luke had composed a Gospel (Q + L) before encountering the Markan source. This Gospel, Streeter termed Proto-Luke. Later Luke combined Mark with his earlier edition, and it is this that, according to Streeter's theory, comprises Luke in its present form.[6] Needless to say, this hypothesis has not received unanimous support among New Testament scholars, but every serious student of Luke's Gospel must at least become conversant with Streeter's thesis.

Suggestions for the date of Luke vary from one extreme to another. A date after A.D. 100 is supported by those who believe Luke depended upon Josephus for some of his materials. At the opposite side of the pendulum, others feel as if Luke wrote immediately after the last events recorded in Acts, that is, about A.D. 65. A medial

---

[6] *Op. cit.*, p. 187.

date (around A.D. 80) is pursued by the majority of commentators for essentially the same reasons that Matthew is dated about that time. Whatever the specific geographical origin of Luke's Gospel, it manifestly was penned in an atmosphere where there was need for a Gospel to the Gentiles. Among other places, Antioch and Caesarea have been argued as the city of origin.

The Synoptic Tradition

The interpretation of the Synoptic tradition offered herein will follow essentially the Markan outline of events. In the compass of a brief survey one cannot discuss all the passages in the Synoptics, but an attempt will be made to include those passages that are basic for formulating a prospectus of the person and ministry of Jesus.

The Galilean Ministry

John the Baptist (Mark 1:1-8; Matt. 3:1-12; Luke 3:1-20). —Upon close examination, John the Baptist shares a significance in the New Testament that is surprising to the average reader. Mark describes the person and activity of John as "the beginning of the Gospel," which would indicate that John is an essential part of the Gospel, its "first chapter" more than an "introduction." Evidently, Luke felt this same way, for he begins his Gospel with the nativity narratives of John; and even the prologue of the Fourth Gospel permits the Baptist to peer in where he would be otherwise unexpected to appear.

The proper key for understanding the person and intention of the Baptist lies in his concept of baptism. Mark describes him "the Baptizer," while Matthew entitles him "the Baptist"; and the content of his preaching is a "baptism" characterized by the forgiveness of sins.

A number of theories exist regarding the source of John's baptism, varying from heathen or Jewish lustrations to mythological concepts concerning the purifying strength of the Jordan River. Ernst Lohmeyer[7] has offered a suggestion which seems most feasible. John may have taken over his concept of baptism as a direct counterpart to the Jewish concept of sacrifice. For him the Temple cultus had become so corrupt that John believed God desired to initiate a new

---

[7]Ernst Lohmeyer, *Johannes der Taüfer* (Göttingen: Vandenhoeck und Ruprecht, 1932), in *passim*.

and final sacrifice. John's baptism then would have been the "es-chatological sacrifice" that replaced the Temple sacrifice; and the offer of a "forgiveness of sins" would have stood in the same relation to his baptism that the same offer would have stood with reference to Jewish sacrifice in the Temple.

John thus becomes the "high priest of baptism," whom God had appointed to effect forgiveness for his people before the final era of God's judgment arrived. John's priestly heritage adds further weight to this interpretation: his father was a priest, his mother was from the tribe of Aaron, and the words of John's forthcoming birth were spoken in the Temple during the course of the Temple service. In this light must be understood the other motifs surrounding John's activity. The "desert" and no longer Jerusalem, the "Jordan" and no longer the Temple, comprise the holy places. God now creates a new people for himself in the desert as he had originally made Israel his possession in the wilderness of long ago. And these "holy people" are no longer those who can appeal to Abraham as their progenitor, but only those who receive divine forgiveness mediated through John. Even the priestly garments and food are corrupt, so John nourishes himself on locusts and honey, and wears the skins of a camel.

John's messianic preaching is not easy to decipher, but the following conclusions are possible: (1) John spoke of a Coming One who would "baptize" both with spirit and fire. The fiery baptism is parallel with "burning the chaff" and the spirit baptism is synono-mous with "storing in the barn." The work of the Coming One was to condemn those who had rejected John's baptism and to re-deem those who had accepted his work as the work of God. (2) Mark omitted reference to the fiery baptism for theological reasons. This was because he desired to emphasize the purely redemptive aspect of Christ's work apart from the judicial function at the first of Christ's ministry. (3) The work of the Coming One is called a "baptism," since it follows and fulfils what the baptism of John had initiated.

Who did John have in mind as the Coming One? Immediately, the Christian answers, "Jesus Christ!" But the answer is not that evident. The ever-present temptation in reading the Scriptures is to read them in light of what is known *at present,* rather than in light of what a person may have meant *at the time* he spoke. If one would examine the meaning of the quote from Malachi 3:1 in Mark

1:2, he would discover that Malachi's words originally referred to *God himself,* not to an earthly Messiah. Did John then expect some historical figure to follow him and complete his work, or did he expect the final inbreak of God himself into history apart from the mediation of a historical figure? Whomever John expected, the early Christians correctly interpreted the person and work of Christ as consummating what God had begun in the ministry of John.

Luke correlates the appearance of John with several other dates. Tiberias became emperor in A.D. 14, though he had aided Augustus with the government since A.D. 11. The fifteenth year of his reign would then have been A.D. 28-29, although the date of A.D. 25-26 would not altogether be excluded. As the reader recalls from the first chapter, Pilate was procurator from A.D. 26-36, while Herod Antipas and Herod Philip were tetrarchs beginning in 4 B.C. Annas was removed from the high priesthood in A.D. 15 and Caiphas, his son-in-law, was appointed high priest from A.D. 18-36. No exact data can be found concerning Lysanias of Abilene, whom Luke mentions.

The baptism and temptation of Jesus (Mark 1:9-13; Matt. 3:13 to 4:11; Luke 3:21 to 4:13).—Why was Jesus baptized? Matthew answers this question with the ambiguous, "to fulfil all righteousness," whereby the reader is left with several possible solutions, all of which are closely related. (1) Jesus intended through baptism to identify himself with the people he came to redeem. (2) Jesus wished to place approval upon and to be identified with the mission of John the Baptist. (3) This was Jesus' manner of dedicating himself to his redemptive vocation. (4) As a devout Jew, Jesus felt, as did the others who came to John, his own insufficiency before God, and accepted John's baptism as an external expression of his deep humility before and genuine commitment to God.

Several elements, conveying significant theological overtones, are mentioned in connection with the baptismal experience. The "opening of the heavens" declare the grace of a holy God who is willing to reveal himself to man on earth; and the "coming down of the Spirit" conveys further this motif. Both expressions alike declare that in Jesus Christ, God has rolled back the curtains of the heavens and has set up his dwelling with man.

The One upon whom the Spirit resides and concerning whom the heavenly Voice speaks is none other than the eschatological Redeemer and the nature of his redemption is expressed in the words from heaven. These words are a combination of two passages from the Old Testament, Psalm 2:7 and Isaiah 42:1. The first "You are my beloved Son" was used by ancient Israel in their annual coronation ceremony for the king. The second "With you I am well pleased" was the ordination formula for the Suffering Servant. Thus the baptism stands as a proleptic testimony to the final outcome of Jesus' life: He is the messianic king who achieves the salvation of his people in a manner necessitated by his relationship to God, even through suffering.

What was the true nature of these events? (1) Jesus surely was baptized by John. The fact that Jesus submitted to the baptism of John gave reason for some to believe that John was superior to Jesus; so this event would not have been recorded by the Gospels unless it had been well established in the tradition. (2) The other elements of the account are more difficult, with the result that several points of view exist. First, some indications support the events as being absolutely objective: Luke speaks of the dove in "bodily form," while Matthew records the words from heaven, *"This* is my beloved Son," with the intimation that either John or the crowd was addressed. Other words support the experience as being subjective, limited to the spiritual insight of Jesus alone: Mark and Luke state, *"You* are my Son" while Mark and Matthew state, *"He* [Jesus] saw" the heavens divided and the Spirit coming down.

Mark apparently did not possess the longer temptation account rendered by Matthew and Luke from Q. The unique orientation of his briefer account is to demonstrate the contrast between the first Adam and the second Adam (Jesus).[8] Despite all that was in his favor, the first Adam fell, while the second Adam won over evil in the most adverse circumstances. The first Adam introduced sin into the world, but the second Adam made possible for mankind the conquest over sin. Q is more elaborate and depicts Jesus faced with a series of three temptations. Each temptation is prefaced with the presupposition, "If [or since] you are the Son of God," which receives its logic from the baptismal words, "You are my Son." Satan therein sought not to make Jesus doubt his Sonship; rather he was testing to see if Jesus was willing to accept the consequences of divine Sonship. The meaning of Satan's remarks are, "Since you are the Son of God, achieve your mission without involving your-

---

[8]Joachim Jeremias, "Adam," *Theologisches Wörterbuch,* I, 141-43.

self in suffering." These temptations characterize the choices Jesus necessarily faced in deciding a proper perspective of himself and his mission; and these same choices lay before him throughout the course of his earthly life.

(1) "Turn the stones into loaves of bread." This represents the appeal to be a Redeemer who would concern himself primarily with the physical needs of mankind. Although there is nothing wrong in feeding the hungry, Jesus realized "man does not live by bread alone." Consequently, he must make his primary emphasis in another direction.

(2) "Jump off the Temple. God will preserve you and the people will acclaim you the One sent from God." At least one Jewish tradition hoped for the Messiah to appear suddenly on the Temple roof. If Jesus combined this feat with the additional one of jumping off without bodily injury to himself, many would interpret this as a

sign from God and would be willing to follow Jesus. Jesus desired that the populace accept him, but he simultaneously realized that this means of doing so would be an attempt to coerce God into intervening in a manner and a time not in accord with God's purpose.

(3) "Gather an army and free your nation from the power of Rome" was the essence of the third temptation. As a devout Jew, Jesus would have desired to see his nation free from foreign domination. Yet there was a more significant freedom—a freedom from sin—that he must offer his people, and this freedom could not be achieved through military force.

Jesus' message (Mark 1:14-15; Matt. 4:12-17; Luke 4:14-15).— The Synoptics define the time only through the observation that Jesus began his active ministry *after* the betrayal of John. As with the Baptist, so with Jesus, the Synoptics give only the essential core of his preaching. (1) "The time is fulfilled." All promise and preparation have reached their fulfilment and consummation; the "moment" is full, the presence of God fills the midst. (2) "The kingdom of God is at hand." Much controversy centers about the interpretation of this affirmation. Whether Jesus meant that the kingdom was "just around the corner," or whether he declared that the kingdom had "already arrived," is not altogether certain. Jesus may have meant that in his ministry God's sovereign power was being manifested in such a manner that the activities of Jesus were a surety of what God would absolutely accomplish at the end of all history. (3) "Repent and believe in the gospel." On the basis of God's witness to himself in the gospel, Jesus demanded absolute obedience to the will of God.

The rejection at Nazareth (Luke 4:16-30; cf. Mark 6:1-6; Matt. 13:54-58).—Luke makes a noticeable divergence from the Markan outline by including Jesus' rejection at Nazareth this early. Mark does not record the visit of Jesus to Nazareth until later in Jesus' ministry and locates the earlier work of Jesus in Capernaum. That Luke has intentionally placed this later rejection earlier is also indicated by the mention, made in Luke's account, of Jesus' *previous* work in Capernaum (v. 23). Evidently Luke placed this account at the first of his Gospel for at least two reasons. (1) He wanted to indicate, by way of anticipation, the final outcome of Jesus' ministry: rejection by his people and the subsequent mission to the Gentiles (note vv. 25-30). (2) Luke desired to introduce certain themes that were to run throughout his Gospel: emphasis on the Spirit, Jesus' concern for the poor and needy, and the fulfilment of prophecy.

Call of the first disciples (Mark 1:16-20; Matt. 4:18-22; Luke 5:1-11).—The announcement of the kingdom of God is immediately followed by the call of four Galilean fishermen as disciples. This passage forms part of Mark's theological scheme in depicting what he believes is the foundation for the Christian community: (1) The Forerunner (Mark 1:1-8), (2) the Lord (1:9-13), (3) the Christian message (1:14-15), and (4) the apostolic witness (1:16-20).[9]

Included in this brief passage are elements which constituted the meaning of discipleship within the early church.[10] (1) *The person of Jesus*. The reader wonders why four men would follow another so readily when no previous contact has been mentioned. This is as the Gospel writers intended it; this was their way of underlining the uniqueness of their Lord. (2) *Leader-follower*. When the word "follow" appears in the New Testament, it generally has a profound significance. By this term is indicated the relationship of the disciple to his Lord, whereby the "follower" accepts the same destiny for his life that his Lord shared: suffering and death which lead to life. (3) *Break with the past*. Immediately these men not only follow Christ, but, in so doing, they "forsake all." (4) *Witness*. Jesus calls these men that they may be witnesses to the grace of God. (5) *Fellowship*. Those who "follow" abide with Jesus and through fellowship with him share a common unity with one another. (6) *The "call."* Only after one is "called" may he "follow." Through this medium the Gospels emphasize the fact that God takes the initiative in the divine-human encounter; only because God comes to man is man able to "follow." Luke's account represents a somewhat different version of the experience, but he also focuses attention upon these same elements of discipleship.

Jesus in the synagogue at Capernaum (Mark 1:21-28; Matt. 7: 28-29; Luke 4:31-37).—In Capernaum, the city on the northwest shore of the Sea of Galilee, where Jesus made his "headquarters,"

---

[9]Ernst Lohmeyer, *Das Evangelium des Markus* (Göttingen: Vandenhoeck und Ruprecht, 1959), p. 31.

[10]Cf. Eduard Schweizer, *Lordship and Discipleship* (Naperville: Alec R. Allenson, 1961).

16. Street in Bethany

Mark locates an early miracle by Jesus, the healing of a demon-possessed man. To the modern reader the existence of demons raises questions; but it must be noted that the ancients attributed all illnesses, mental and physical, to the powers of demons. When a person was healed, this signified that the power of God had over-thrown the demons. Thus it was only natural to classify the healing of this man as a "casting out of demons" through the "Holy One of God."

Several observations might be made concerning the presence and exorcism of demons. (1) The people in Jesus' day believed in demons. (2) Either Jesus himself believed in demons, or else he was accommodating his words to the thought patterns of his hearers when he spoke of demons. One's own solution to this problem will ultimately depend upon how much one feels Jesus was a man of his own day. However, it would seem that Jesus did believe in demons, yet knew that by the Spirit of God they were cast out. (3) That the historical appearance of Jesus came at a moment when people believed in demons is part of the biblical concept of "the fulness of time." At no other moment in history could such a vivid revelation of the true power of God have come about except in a milieu where a belief in demons was current and men interpreted healings as an inbreak of the kingdom of God.

To this initial act of healing, Mark immediately attaches two others: the healing of Peter's mother-in-law (1:30-31) and the sick healed at evening (vv. 32-34). After praying all night (vv. 35-38; cf. 6:46 and 14:32), Jesus departed from Capernaum and began a preaching and healing crusade in Galilee (1:39). Mark intentionally places these varied experiences on the first day of Jesus' ministry in order to express the manifold grace revealed in the "appearing of our Lord and Saviour" (2 Tim. 1:10).[11]

The Sermon on the Mount (Matt. 5-7).—Matthew incorporates the Sermon on the Mount into his Gospel at this point. Later Luke includes many of these same teachings in his "Sermon on the Plain" (6:20-49). Matthew and Luke have collected sayings that were originally separate, but this does not signify that the evangelists have created these sayings, for they are essentially the teachings of Jesus. Many parallels to these teachings may be found in Jewish sources, but no parallel to the Sermon as a whole exists.

[11]*Ibid.,* p. 34.

Matthew intentionally locates the Sermon on a mountain. Judaism considered "mountains" as sacred places of divine revelation. In particular, God had confirmed Israel as his chosen people around a sacred mountain; and upon this same holy mountain Moses had received the legislation relating to the old covenant. Mention of the many people from various geographical regions who *follow* Jesus indicates that in Jesus these people have found an inner unity. These humble followers of Jesus, rather than the self-righteous professional religionists, are now the holy people of God; and this is so because they follow God's Chosen One. Thereby the key to the Sermon on the Mount is the contrast between the old and the new, between the way of Judaism and the way of Christ. In accord with this thesis the Sermon may be outlined:[12]

I. The Old and New People (5:3-20)
 1. Beatitudes
 2. Salt and Light
 3. Law and Fulfilment
II. The Old and New Law (5:21-48)
 1. Murder
 2. Adultery and Divorce
 3. Swearing
 4. Eye for an Eye
 5. Command to Love One's Enemies
III. The Old and New Righteousness (6:1-18)
 1. Almsgiving
 2. Prayer
 3. Lord's Prayer
 4. Forgiveness
 5. Fasting
IV. The Old and New Life (6:19 to 7:12)
 1. Riches
 2. Anxiety
 3. Judging
 4. Holy Things
 5. Golden Rule
V. The Old and New Promise (7:13-27)
 1. Summons
 2. False Prophets
 3. True Prophets
 4. Hearers and Doers

---

[12]This outline is adapted from Ernst Lohmeyer, *Das Evangelium des Matthäus* (Göttingen: Vandenhoeck and Ruprecht, 1958), pp. 74-152.

At the beginning (5:3) and at the end (5:20) of the initial part of the Sermon, mention is made concerning the kingdom of heaven and those persons to whom the kingdom is a reality. These citizens of the kingdom of heaven are addressed in the *indicative* rather than in the imperative, as were the people who belonged to the kingdom of Israel. Whereas, the people of the old covenant were commanded, "Keep my commandments, so shall you be my people," the people of the new covenant are assured, "You are my people, so keep my commandments." This observation harmonizes with the recognition that in Matthew's setting Christ delivered the words of the Sermon only to those who were following him; that is, those who in Christ had *already* accepted the kingdom of God as the determinative factor for their existence.

Viewed in this context the Beatitudes must be recognized as descriptive characteristics unique to the lives of those who have entered the kingdom of God. A more popular method of interpretation is to look upon the Beatitudes as "virtues" that one should imitate in order to become a "Christian." But there is an eternal gulf between those who follow Christ in the New Testament sense

17. Roman silver denar (enlarged), the type of coin mentioned by Jesus in Mark 12:15, showing the "likeness and inscription" of Tiberius Caesar; coins of this type were minted in Rome but were used throughout the empire; the denar (or denarius, KJV "penny") was a day's wages for a worker

and those who would adopt the Beatitudes (or any other part of Christ's teachings) as a pattern for conduct. No matter how excellent an attempt one makes at imitating these "virtues," an imitation remains but an imitation. The Beatitudes represent traits produced from the inner resources of a man's life because the kingdom of God reigns within.

"Blessed" is quite ambiguous to the ears of the modern reader and is better replaced by the more contemporary, "How fortunate are." The purpose of the Beatitudes as a whole is to emphasize certain basic characteristics of Christian discipleship, and to reveal to the disciple the inevitable "reward" that comes to one who is motivated by these inner traits of life. On this basis the disciple is "fortunate" because his manner of life is founded upon the values of the kingdom rather than upon the standards of the world in which he lives. A somewhat free translation will serve as a brief commentary on the Beatitudes.

> How fortunate are those disciples who are poor in spirit,
> In them does God reign supreme!
> How fortunate are those disciples who have endured
>   deprivation and suffering,
> God himself shall console them!
> How fortunate are those disciples who have given themselves
>   irrevocably to the call of God,
> God himself shall reward them!
> How fortunate are those disciples who suffer
>   that righteousness may triumph,
> They will share the victory of God!
> How fortunate are those disciples who deal mercifully
>   with others,
> God will be merciful to them!
> How fortunate are those disciples whose sole desire is to see God,
> To them shall God disclose himself!
> How fortunate are those disciples who bring about peace,
> For this is the work of God!
> How fortunate are those disciples who know the cost of discipleship—
>   persecution, insult, and ill-treatment—
> God will permit them to share the fulfilment of discipleship
>   with their spiritual forerunners, the prophets!

The parables of salt and light speak forth the very essence of the Christian faith. One thing alone do these two elements share in common: both must "die" in order to accomplish their task. Salt is dissolved; oil is consumed. Discipleship compared to salt and light is discipleship that acknowledges the declaration of Jesus, "He who would gain his life must first of all give it up!" To become the "salt of the earth" or the "light of the world" requires that one "take up his cross and follow Jesus."

Matthew 5:17-20 is extremely difficult to interpret. Perhaps the first two verses should be understood as a description of Christ's relationship to the law of God revealed in Judaism, while verse 19 should be held to describe the proper relation of the Christian disciple to the "law" of Christ. If this is the case, the entire passage indicates that Christ is the consummator of the old era and the initiator of the new era in God's dealings with man, and obedience to the law of God must now become absolute obedience to the person of Christ. Verse 20 is the conclusion to this first part of the Sermon.

Contrast between the old Law and the new Law forms the subject of 5:21-48; or, to use the words of 5:20, the "more" in contrast with the teaching of the scribes. This section is clearly marked off through the repetition of the formula, "You have heard it said . . . but I say," and is concluded by the command, "Be perfect as your Father in heaven is perfect." All sections of this second part are in reality contrasts between the radical obedience demanded by Christ and the formal obedience required by Judaism.

Hatred is not equated with murder, nor is adultery of the heart equated with the act of adultery. What is affirmed is that in each instance the deed is an expression of one's inner being. Whereas, in Judaism no guilt was incurred unless one committed the actual act of murder or adultery, Christ condemned the inner desire that leads to the act. Matthew's statement concerning divorce was likely attached to his paragraph on adultery because of the catchword, "adultery," that appears in the Matthean tradition on divorce (5:32). Mark (10:11-12) and Luke (16:18) make no stipulation for divorce and perhaps represent more exactingly the words of Jesus.

As murder and adultery are not redemptive measures in human relationships, neither does divorce resolve redemptively the injured human relationship. Murder, adultery, divorce, and retaliation (5:38-42)—along with their inner seeds—destroy human personality; and the only adequate answer to the despairing problem of distorted human relations is that of unselfish and redemptive love. The disciple becomes "perfect" (mature) only when he learns to love in the same self-giving and uncalculating fashion that his Father in heaven loves the world of men, good and evil alike.

The third part (6:1-18) deals with the new righteousness of the kingdom in opposition to the old righteousness of Judaism; to use again the words of 5:20, the "more" than the righteousness of the Pharisees. Pharisaic righteousness was hypocritical (6:2,5,16) from the standpoint that there was no vital concord between the inner impulse and the external religious performance. Their pietistic expressions had become none other than superficial deeds done for the sake of astonishing the "less righteous" men with the strict Pharisaic fervor for religious duty. When onlookers became amazed at the religious devotion of the Pharisee, he had thus been "paid in full."

In sharp contrast to this superficial righteousness, Jesus demanded an inner righteousness effected through an alliance with God rather than with men. In his religious service the disciple of the kingdom must concern himself solely with pleasing God, and the judgment of the world must be forgotten altogether.

The Lord's Prayer appears both in Matthew (6:9-13) and Luke (11:1-14). It also is contained in the *Didache,* an early Christian writing dating about A.D. 100, with the instruction, "Pray thus three times a day." Matthew offers the prayer as a portion of Jewish-Christian teaching.[13] There is also a different introductory formula to each version: Matthew connects it with the *how* to pray; Luke with the *what* to pray. In Luke the prayer is a summary of the correct life of faith; and Jesus prays, not as an individual, but as the representative of the disciples. In Matthew the prayer also is for the community rather than for the individual; it deals not with the needs of daily life but with the exigencies of discipleship in the eschatological hour that is about to dawn.[14] Allusion to several aspects of the prayer will indicate its eschatological orientation.

(1) The disciple prays that the immediate consummation of God's kingdom on earth might come; that men on earth might in this moment know the reality of the kingdom of God.

(2) To the traditional translation, "Give us this day our daily bread," the Revised Standard Version has appended a note, "our bread for the morrow." The translators of the Revised Standard Version have attempted to point out the ambiguity of a Greek word

---

[13]Joachim Jeremias, "The Lord's Prayer in Recent Research," *The Expository Times,* LXXI (February, 1960), 142.

[14]Ernst Lohmeyer, *Das Vater-Unser* (Göttingen: Vandenhoeck und Ruprecht, 1960), pp. 10-12.

which may be translated with several different meanings. It is quite possible that the translation in the footnote of the Revised Standard Version is more nearly correct in light of the remainder of the prayer. One way the early church described the consummation of the kingdom was by a banquet over which Christ would preside. Here the church is enjoined to pray that the bread of this coming kingdom feast might be theirs today; that today God might bring history to its consummation and celebrate his victory through a banquet with his people. This interpretation receives indirect support from the content of two other prayers of the church: "Our Lord, Come!" (1 Cor. 16:22) and "Amen. Come, Lord Jesus!" (Rev. 22:20).

(3) The last petition, "Lead as not into temptation, but deliver us from evil," should also be understood in this eschatological context. The "temptation" mentioned is not temptation in general, but the last period of extreme hardship that the Jews and early Christians alike felt was to befall mankind immediately prior to the end of time. "May we be faithful when the final period of extreme testing comes upon us" is the heart of this petition; and, logically, it is offered in conjunction with the prayer for the immediate realization of the kingdom.

The fourth part of the Sermon (6:19 to 7:12) is designed to depict the dangers which the disciples, as the community of the poor and persecuted, must endure because of their historical situation and eschatological destiny. Members of the Christian community are not of the world; therefore, the world does not acknowledge them as its own. But, though the disciples are not of the world, they, nevertheless, must live *in* the world; and this existence in a world dominated by the "Evil One" inevitably produces conflicts for the community of faith. The disciple cannot find ultimate security in the "treasures" of this world (6:19-21); his eye must be fastened upon God (6:22-23); he must serve only one Master (6:24). When he is tempted to become frustrated with his lot in life, the disciple must not forget that God knows how to provide what is necessary for life (6:25-34) and that God delights in giving "good gifts" to his children (7:7-11).

Amidst a world of men whose lives are profligate, the man of faith is ever confronted with the temptation to feel self-righteous and to condemn others; should he yield to this temptation, he would come into a status worse than those he condemns (7:1-5). The ethic for this new life is not easy: one must learn to encounter all

persons, within and without the community of faith, in the manner
that he would desire they treat him (7:12).

As the old Law contained its promise along with its demand,
so does the new Law. The new promise (7:13-27) constitutes the
final portion of the Sermon and is made to those whose "teaching"
surpasses that of the scribes and whose "righteousness" supersedes
that of the Pharisees, even to those who possess the new righteousness and share the new life. This is the eschatologically conditioned
promise offered to the eschatologically new people who await its
fulfilment and consummation. It is offered not to the scribes and
Pharisees but to those who are poor and persecuted for the sake
of the kingdom of God. Accepting the summons to this new life
demands that one enter through the "narrow gate" (7:13-14); and
the consequences are so monumental (7:24-27) that one dare not
be misled, either through feigned piosity (7:15-20), or through self-
deception (7:21-23).

The great healing ministry (Mark 1:40-45; 5:1-43; 7:31-37; 8:
22-26; 9:14-29; 10:46-52; Luke 7:11-17; 17:11-19; Mark 4:35-41;
6:31-42,45-52; 11:13-14,20; Luke 5:1-11).—Space will not permit
a detailed analysis of these miracles individually, therefore
they will be examined in light of their general characteristics
as *miracle stories*. The earlier discussion of *form history* pointed
out that the narratives which finally became incorporated into the
Gospels originally circulated as independent accounts, without integral attachment to one another. One of the forms in which these
stories about Jesus circulated may be designated "miracle stories."
There are two basic types of miracle stories in the Gospels: healing
(including raising the dead) and nature miracles. Whereas, healing
miracles report Jesus' compassion upon the mental and physical infirmities of people, nature miracles report Jesus' miraculous power
over the forces of nature.

All the miracle stories possess a common literary form which may
be divided into three parts: (1) the illness or danger is depicted;
(2) Jesus heals the illness or removes the danger; and (3) the effect
of the miracle upon the onlooking crowd is described. The fact that
the miracle stories in the Gospels share this form in common with
similar stories contained in secular literature does not vitiate the miracle stories in the Gospels, for this is the natural form that one would
expect any miracle story to have. One basic and significant difference between the miracle stories in the Gospels and those recorded

18. Traditional home of Mary, Martha, and Lazarus in Bethany

in secular literature is that Jesus interprets his miracles as indications of God's compassion and grace, while the miracle stories of secular literature are recorded for the sake of mystifying the reader with the magical powers of the miracle worker.[15]

Since nature miracles evoke the most difficulty for the modern reader, several observations are in order.

(1) Nature miracles cannot be immediately rejected upon rationalistic or scientific grounds. There is much mystery that will ever surround these stories because the contemporary world is removed, both in time and outlook, from the world of the first century. But the men who repeated and recorded these narratives believed they happened.

(2) The nature miracles held a Christological significance for the disciples. For example, the stilling of the tempest was to attest the

---

[15]E. Basil Redlich, *Form Criticism* (London: Duckworth, 1948), pp. 128-34.

lordship of Christ over death, symbolized in the devouring waves, while the feeding of the multitudes bore witness to Christ as the Lord of life.

(3) The *primary significance* of the miracles, healing and nature, was to herald the presence of the long-awaited salvation of God, and, in this sense, they are as inseparable from the life of Jesus as are his teachings. Each miracle was the manifestation in a given instance of what God would do for all mankind when the kingdom of heaven was finally revealed "in power." Each act of mercy was a testimony to the moment when God would make all men whole; each nature miracle was a guarantee that God would redeem his creation, and from it create a "new heaven and a new earth."

(4) In the final analysis, one's solution to the problems connected with the miracles, especially with the nature miracles, will be based upon one's own understanding of the incarnation.

Either we must reject the nature-miracles, and hold that the humanity of Jesus did not include the power to control Nature, or we must accept the stories and choose the more difficult conception of His humanity. . . . This is the very razor edge of decision. I do not think that we are guilty of intellectual vacillation if we hesitate between these alternatives, now inclining to the one, now to the other. Those of us who think that the incidents were natural events ought to keep an open mind, since we may have misread the limitations of the Incarnation; and, on the other hand, those who accept the stories should ask if they do not rob the Incarnation of its grace and infinite condescension. In these matters we face unsolved problems, and each man must follow the light which he has.[16]

Conflict stories (Mark 2:1 to 3:6; Matt. 9:1-17; 12:1-14; Luke 5:17 to 6:11).—Mark aligns a series of five "conflict stories" with the intention of indicating the nature of the opposition between Jesus and the religious authorities that led to their rejection of him. It will be noticed that the conflicts heighten until there is open rejection. "Immediately the Pharisees counseled with the Herodians against him, so that they might kill him" (3:6). That this counsel between the Pharisees and the Herodians is not mentioned again until 12:13 has led some to believe these five stories were originally prefixed to Mark's passion narrative for the sake of explicating the reason the Jews caused Jesus to be put to death.

---

[16]Vincent Taylor, *The Formation of the Gospel Tradition* (London: Macmillan & Co., 1953), p. 140. Used by permission of the Macmillan Co. and St. Martin's Press.

A significant question looms about the interpretation of the phrase "Son of man" (2:10,28). As a rule, the Son of man passages in the Gospels are classified into three categories: (1) the earthly life of Jesus, (2) his passion and death, and (3) his exaltation and return. In reading these passages where reference is made to the Son of man, one never knows whether the reference is individual (Jesus alone) or corporate (Jesus and the Christian community), since there is precedent for a corporate interpretation in Daniel 7:13, where the Son of man comprises the "saints of the Most High." Thus a passage like, "The Son of man possesses authority on earth to forgive sins" (Mark 2:10), has a variety of possibilities.

If the Son of man is Jesus (individual interpretation) this passage represents the claim that while on earth Jesus had the divine prerogative to forgive sins. On the other hand, should the corporate interpretation be pursued, the words may declare the church's feeling that they, as the "saints of the Most High," shared the prerogative of offering forgiveness in the name of their Lord. This latter interpretation is not so improbable when one considers the words of John 20:23 ("If you forgive the sins of any, they are forgiven; if you retain the sins of any, they are retained") and notices that the Matthean parallel to Mark 2:10 concludes with, "The whole crowd feared and glorified God who had given this authority to *men*" (9:8).

The call of the twelve (Mark 3:13-19; Matt. 10:1-4; Luke 6:12-16; cf. Acts 1:13).—Matthew places the call of the twelve earlier in his outline so he can incorporate thereafter some special teachings of Jesus to his disciples (10:1 to 11:1). As of old God called unto himself the twelve tribes of Israel around Mount Sinai, so now Jesus calls whom he will upon this sacred mountain that these few may form the nucleus of his new people. It is from the analogy of the twelve tribes that the number "twelve" gains its significance in this context. Within the twelve, three are marked out through the granting of new names. This gift is not based upon their connection with the twelve, but upon the special nature of their relationship with Jesus. The New Testament presents four lists of the twelve, and though the lists vary somewhat in the order of names, only the name Thaddaeus is uncertain in the manuscripts.

The Beelzebul controversy (Mark 3:19b-30; Matt. 12:22-37; Luke 11:14-23).—Sometime in the course of Jesus' ministry a group of scribes from Jerusalem raised the accusation against him, "He possesses Beelzebul and in the prince of demons he casts out demons."

There was an intended parallelism in this judgment: the scribes meant that Jesus *was* Beelzebul, the prince of demons.

To this accusation Jesus retorted: (1) A kingdom divided against itself cannot stand. It would be illogical for a prince to destroy his own domain; thereby, One stronger than Satan had spoiled the stronghold of Satan. (2) The "sons" (i.e. disciples) of the Pharisees were performing similar deeds. Why did the Pharisees not attribute *those* deeds to the power of Satan? (3) Destruction of demonic powers was an indication that the Spirit of God was active and the kingdom of God a present reality. (4) Through deliberately attributing the beneficent deeds of healing wrought by the Spirit of God to the agency of Beelzebul, the Pharisees had committed blasphemy.

The reason Jesus affirmed this blasphemy would not be forgiven was because the Pharisees had already decided that whatever Jesus did, no matter how much it evidenced the power of God, they would attribute it to the agency of Satan. Forgiveness, therefore, *could not* be found, for there was no willingness on their part to repent.

The parables of Jesus.—One of the primary obstacles to a study of the parables is the unconscious presupposition held by many that the parables of Jesus were "illustrations" used by him to clarify dark issues in his teachings.

Two observations militate against this definition of a parable. (1) This definition is not broad enough to include all that the Gospels designate as parables. For example, "Physician, heal yourself" (Luke 4:23), and, "There is nothing outside a man which by going into him can defile him; but the things which come out of a man are what defile him" (Mark 7:15), are both termed parables, but neither suits this limited definition of a parable. (2) Nor does this definition cohere with some things said concerning parables, such as, "To you has been given the secret of the kingdom of God, but for those outside everything is in parables; so that they may indeed hear but not understand" (Mark 4:11-12).[17]

The Greek word transliterated "parable" is used in the Septuagint to render the Hebrew word *mashal,* which has several diverse meanings. A *mashal* may be a parable, similar to most of those in the Gospels, or it may be simply a saying of popular wisdom, or even a "byword." Every genuine Hebrew parable is significant in several

---

[17]T. W. Manson, *The Teaching of Jesus* (Cambridge: The University Press, 1951), pp. 57-81.

ways and the Old Testament parable of the ewe lamb (2 Sam. 12: 1-14) will prove most helpful in demonstrating these unique traits of Hebrew parables.[18]   (1) As a story, the parable of the ewe lamb possesses a meaning of its own: a rich man has taken advantage of a poor man's position. (2) There exists a second meaning to the story that cannot be understood unless one knows the specific event to which Nathan has reference: the adultery and murder committed by David. (3) The effectiveness of the parable depends upon the insight and response of the hearer: David must acknowledge that he is the guilty man and confess, "I have sinned against the Lord."

With these considerations in mind, the following will serve as a definition for an Old Testament parable: A "parable" is a word addressed to a specific situation to call the hearers to a decision in their relationship with God.   And since the Hebrew parable is the pattern for the parables of Jesus, this definition will also serve for those parables contained in the Gospels.

Jesus delivered his parables as "weapons of warfare" in confrontation with his opponents, the Pharisees and Sadducees; thereby, Jesus' parables reflect moments of crisis and conflict in his ministry. After the specific situation of Jesus' ministry had passed, the early church applied his parables to their own historical situation.   So as one reads the parables in the Gospels, he must realize that they reflect this "double situation"—the ministry of Jesus and the life of the early church.

The recognition of this fact indicates the nature of our task. Jesus spoke to men of flesh and blood; he addressed himself to the situation of the moment. Each of his parables has a definite historical setting. Hence to recover this is the task before us. What did Jesus intend to say at this or that particular moment? What must have been the effect of his word upon his hearers? These are the questions we must ask in order, so far as possible, to recover the original meaning of the parables of Jesus, to hear again his authentic voice.[19]

This task is not simple, and it requires the proper utilization of the *form history* technique, along with a number of other technical tools of biblical study. Since it would require an extensive amount

---

[18]*Ibid,* pp. 65-66.
[19]Joachim Jeremias, *The Parables of Jesus,* trans. S. H. Hooke (London: SCM Press, 1955), p. 19.

of space to elucidate only a few of the many detailed involvements
of this type investigation, it is best at the moment only to mention
the problem involved and to present the reader with the results provided by Joachim Jeremias, who has produced a definitive work in
this area of New Testament study. The most importance attached
to the work of Jeremias is his understanding of the *message of Jesus*
contained within the parables and attention will now be drawn to
this aspect of the parables.[20]

(1) Jesus spoke concerning the *great assurance*. The mustard seed
(Mark 4:30-32; Matt. 13:31-32; Luke 13:18-19) and the leaven
(Matt. 13:33; Luke 13:20-21) present a striking contrast between
the small beginning made by Jesus' disciples and the final consummation of the kingdom: as it is with the mustard seed and the leaven,
so it is with the kingdom of God! One must realize that Jesus did
not intend to describe a process of growth within the kingdom, but
rather to signify the awful contrast between the present world's
evaluation of the kingdom and the evaluation which the eschatological moment will indicate that God has placed upon the kingdom.

The patient husbandman (Mark 4:26-29) is to encourage patience
in the grace of God. As the farmer marvels at the way wheat is
produced from a small seed, so will the patient disciple marvel at
the final revelation of God's kingdom. The sower (Mark 4:19; Matt.
13:1-9; Luke 8:4-8) teaches that "the one thing needful is to take
God seriously in spite of all outward circumstances." Though the
seed appears to fall upon dead soil to no avail, God's kingdom will
ultimately triumph.

(2) Both the deeds and words of Jesus herald, "Now is the day
of salvation!" The compassionate acts of Jesus (Matt. 11:2-6; Luke
7:18-23) are parables which attest the inbreak of the new day. No
need "to patch" the old age, the new age has dawned (Mark 2:
18-22; Matt. 9:14-17; Luke 5:33-39). This is the day of the wedding, the time of sorrow has passed (Mark 2:19), and the time has
come to reap rather than sow (Matt. 9:37-38; Luke 10:2).

(3) In at least three ways the parables indicate *God's mercy for
sinners.*

First of all, Jesus draws the attention of his opponents to the
outcasts who have received the good news. Not the whole, but the
sick, need the services of a physician (Mark 2:17), and these outcasts

---

[20]*Ibid.*, pp. 89-159.

realize their lack of wholeness before God. One is an obedient "son
of God" only because he responds to the will of God as these "sinners" have at last done (Matt. 21:28-32). Like this woman, only
those who have experienced forgiveness acknowledge their indebtedness to God (Luke 7:36-50).

Second, Jesus focuses the spotlight upon the critics of his actions.
These hypocrites are comparable to a son who obeys in word only
(Matt. 21:28-32), or to a guest who rejects the requirements of his
host (Matt. 22:11-14), or to a sharecropper who refuses to share
(Mark 12:1-12; Matt. 21:33-46; Luke 20:9-19).

Third, Jesus validates his actions by appeal to the "boundless love
of God." The prodigal son (Luke 15:11-32) at once appeals to the
boundless love of God and makes a frontal attack upon the self-
righteous sophistication of the Pharisees. God's "redemptive joy" is
depicted in the parables of the lost sheep and the lost coin (Luke
15:1-10). The Pharisees "murmur against God's goodness" because
God delights in bestowing his benefits upon those who possess no
claims against him (Matt. 20:1-16). Only when one voids himself
of any merit except God does he experience the mercy of God (Luke
18:9-14).

(4) Before the scribes (Matt. 24:45-51; Luke 12:42-46; Matt.
25:14-30), the members of the Sanhedrin (Mark 12:1-12; Matt. 21:
33-46; Luke 20:9-19), the Pharisees (Matt. 7:1-5), and the nation
as a whole (Luke 13:1-9), Jesus announced the *imminence of the
catastrophe,* and warned that the *challenge of the crisis* demanded
immediate readiness (Matt. 25:1-13) and resolute action (Luke 16:
1-13) because evasion of God's judgment was impossible (Luke 16:
19-31).

(5) Finally, both through words and parabolic actions, Jesus spoke
of *his own impending suffering* (Mark 10:38; 14:22-25; Matt. 26:
26-29; Luke 22:15-20), of the *paradox of discipleship* which meant
suffering and joy (Mark 8:34 to 9:1; Matt. 13:44-46), and of the
consummation when God would be worshiped as King and would
banish all evil.

The confession at Caesarea Philippi (Mark 8:27-33; Matt. 16:
13-23; Luke 9:18-22).—Doubtless Mark intends the confession at
Caesarea Philippi to have been a turning point in the ministry of
Jesus, and so indicates this as much through the change in geographical orientation as through the new emphases that are established in his Gospel pursuant to this event: the confession of Jesus'

messiahship is first made *outside* the Holy Land proper and his is a hidden messiahship which entails *suffering*.

Evidently Peter himself did not understand at that moment the implications of Jesus' messiahship, for his confession appears to have been predicated upon the assumption that Jesus would be a militant Messiah whom the masses would gladly accept, rather than a humble "Son of man" to whom they would not so readily respond (Mark 8:32). At least Mark so interprets the confession and describes Jesus as utilizing this for an opportunity to *reprimand* the disciples for their lack of spiritual perception into the nature of Jesus' person and mission (8:33).

Matthew tends to place the disciples in the best light (cf. 20:22 ff. with Mark 10:35). He sees Peter's confession as a moment of exalted revelation, which qualifies the apostle for the spiritual leadership of the community (Matt. 16:17-19). This account may reflect the fact that Peter later emerged as a leader. In any case, the confession is a turning point in Jesus' ministry. From this time on he begins to correct his disciples' false opinions concerning his mission (cf. Mark 8:31; 9:31; 10:32-34).

The transfiguration (Mark 9:2-8; Matt. 17:1-8; Luke 9:28-36).— Each of the Synoptics explicitly connects the transfiguration in chronological sequence with the confession at Caesarea Philippi (Mark 9:2; Matt. 17:1; Luke 9:28), but no such unanimity of opinion exists with respect to the method of interpretation rendered the passage. For that reason three interpretations which are representative will be presented:

(1) *Resurrection story*. It is believed that the unique elements of the story (especially the mention of six days, the mountain, Elijah and Moses, the voice from heaven, and the change in Jesus' body), as well as the purpose of the account ("to confirm Peter's confession [Mark 8:29] and to ratify Jesus' prediction of his suffering and resurrection [Mark 8:31]"), are best understood as a resurrection appearance of the risen Christ read back into his earthly ministry.[21]

(2) *Symbolic interpretation*. One example of the symbolic approach is the affirmation that the event is neither a postresurrection narrative nor an actual historical event. Rather it is felt that the story serves a double purpose: it validates the apostles, Peter, James,

---

[21]Charles Edwin Carlston, "Transfiguration and Resurrection," *Journal of Biblical Literature*, LXXX (September, 1961), 233-41.

and John, as leaders of the Jerusalem church and declares the truly divine nature of Jesus Christ.[22]

(3) *Literal view.* Those who pursue this approach accept the actual historicity of all facets of the narrative, including the appearance of Moses and Elijah. It is believed that for a moment of time the true nature of Jesus' person flashed through the limitations of his humanity and was manifested to his disciples. Through this experience these three disciples were granted the realization that in the earthly life and person of their Teacher had appeared a revelation of the heavenly Lord. With him appear Moses and Elijah, indicating that he is the fulfilment of the Law (Moses) and the Prophets (Elijah); and on this account the voice from heaven commands that his disciples hear and obey his words.

One realizes immediately that each of these viewpoints is beset with its own peculiar difficulties. Yet each sheds some light upon this extremely significant passage. In the final analysis the particular conclusion with which the reader will agree will be determined in some measure by his own understanding of the incarnation. Perhaps the words of Vincent Taylor will prove beneficial: "In sum, we may say that, while it is impossible to say exactly what happened upon the mount, we may well believe that the confession of viii 29 was deepened and confirmed in an incommunicable experience of prayer and religious insight."[23]

The journey to Jerusalem (Mark 10; Matt. 19-20; Luke 9:51 to 19:28).—Immediately the reader recognizes that the mass of Lukan material relating this "journey" of Jesus far outweighs the amount of material either in Mark or Matthew. As a matter of fact, Luke 9:5 to 18:14, known as the "Lukan Travel Narrative," constitutes approximately a third of Luke's Gospel. In this section Luke does not include any Markan material and shares approximately half the material with Q. It is generally recognized that this section of Luke's Gospel reflects something of the *theological intention* of Luke.

Some of this material has already been discussed, and it is the

---

[22]Hans-Peter Müller, "Die Verklärung Jesu," *Zeitschrift für die Neutestamentliche Wissenschaft,* Band 51 (1960), 56-64.

[23]Vincent Taylor, *The Gospel According to St. Mark* (London: Macmillan & Co., 1955), p. 388.

19. Mount Zion, Jerusalem

purpose of this paragraph only to introduce the student to certain theories that have been developed with regard to this section of the Third Gospel. All theories have in common the recognition that Luke composed his Gospel with literary and theological aims. The only question is, "What were these aims?"

(1) One suggestion is based upon the assumption that Luke's writings (Luke-Acts) describe the "continuity of the history of salvation as a course or a way," and that this section fits logically into such a framework. According to Acts 13:31, the requirements of witnesses are that they be "those who went up with him from Galilee to Jerusalem," and that is precisely the purpose that this trip serves. Thereby this section attests that those men who made this journey with Jesus, from beginning to end, are *authentic witnesses* to the redemptive act of God in Jesus Christ.[24]

(2) Hans Conzelmann believes that Luke has described this journey to Jerusalem as a "Way to Death." Hence it differs significantly from the previous wanderings in Galilee and follows the unveiling of the necessity for his death which must be accomplished in Jerusalem.[25]

(3) A third suggestion is that Luke intends to picture Jesus as the Chosen One of God, through whom God himself seeks men; but to the eyes of men this One is but a wanderer who visits with men as the "Unknown Guest" (9:52-53,58; 10:5-11,16,38 ff.).[26]

The Jerusalem Ministry

The entry into Jerusalem (Mark 11:1-10; Matt. 21:1-9; Luke 19:28-38).—Both the occasion and the nature of the Jerusalem entry lead the interpreter into a quandary. The actions and words of the crowd are as much suited to the Feast of Tabernacles as to the Passover. This observation has caused some to conclude that the entry actually took place during the Feast of Tabernacles, but was remembered as this final entry of Jesus into Jerusalem during the Passover. On the other hand, since Jesus immediately cleansed the

---

[24]William C. Robinson, Jr., "The Theological Context for Interpreting Luke's Travel Narrative," *Journal of Biblical Literature*, LXXIX (March, 1960), 20-31.

[25]*The Theology of St. Luke*, trans. Goeffrey Buswell (London: Faber & Faber, 1960), pp. 60-73.

[26]Walter Grundmann, "Fragen der Komposition des Lukanischen 'Reiseberichts'," *Zeitschrift für die Neutestamentliche Wissenschaft*, Band 50 (1959), 252-70.

Temple, Burkitt has conjectured that the entry happened on the occasion of the Feast of Dedication, when Jesus himself "rededicated" the Temple.[27]

Whatever the original occasion of the event, the Synoptics intend it to be understood as the entry of Jesus into Jerusalem during his final Passover Week.

Two major questions loom about the nature of the event: (1) Did Jesus intentionally plan this entry, or was it a spontaneous outburst of the crowd? (2) Did the entry have "messianic" significance initially, or was it later interpreted as having messianic significance, perhaps under the influence of Zechariah 9:9?

The most satisfactory solution appears to be the suggestion that Jesus intentionally planned the entry. He, as the Son of man, chose to enter Jerusalem in such a fashion that the crowd would become responsible for making their own decisions concerning his

[27]F. C. Burkitt, "W and Θ: Studies in the Western Text of St. Mark (Continued)," *Journal of Theological Studies,* XVII (1916), 139-52.

20. Valley of Gehenna, Jerusalem

person. The words of Rabbi Joshua Ben Levi (A.D. 250) are pertinent to illustrate this opinion: "See the Son of Man comes 'on the clouds of heaven,' and 'meek and riding on a donkey.' If they [Israel] are worthy of this one, he comes on the clouds of heaven; if they are not worthy, he comes meek and riding on a donkey."[28]

The cleansing of the Temple (Mark 11:15-19; Matt. 21:12-13; Luke 19:45-48; cf. John 2:13-22).—Matthew states that Jesus immediately cleansed the Temple upon his entry into Jerusalem (21:12), while Mark and Luke place the cleansing on the next day after Jesus had returned from Bethany, where he had spent the night. John, contrary to all the Synoptic writers, places this event at the first of Jesus' ministry. One feels as if it is unlikely that this is something Jesus would have had occasion to do twice, and concludes that the event more logically would have taken place during the last week of Jesus' ministry. Perhaps John placed the occurrence earlier for the sake of declaring at the outset of his Gospel the superiority of Jesus to the Jerusalem Temple.

Only approved animals and special Jewish coins could be used in the Temple, so it had become customary to provide pilgrims with the opportunity to purchase approved animals and exchange their Roman coins. No doubt this transaction, conducted in the Court of the Gentiles, had become a lucrative business for the Temple personnel. Jesus' purgation of the Temple represents the climax in his conflict with the Temple authorities for their abuse of this sacred place: the Court of the Gentiles was established that "all nations" might approach God, not that the Jews might manipulate it as a lever to pry men away from God (Mark 11:17). It was this event which finally induced the "chief priests" and the "scribes" to rid themselves of Jesus because "they feared him" (Mark 11:18; Luke 19:47-48).

Jesus and his opponents in dialogue.—The Synoptics enumerate a series of controversies that erupted between Jesus and his critics during the days of his Jerusalem ministry. Inasmuch as each dialogue is differentiated from the others both by way of the interrogators and the themes of the questions, it seems probable that these controversies are intended to be representative of those faced by Jesus throughout the course of his ministry. The purpose of these dialogues is to demonstrate the superiority of Jesus to all his opponents

---

[28]Quoted from Lohmeyer, *Markus,* pp. 232-33.

and is so indicated by the observation of Mark, "No one dared question him further" (12:34).[29]

The first question (Mark 11:27-33; Matt. 21:23-37; Luke 20: 1-8) relates specifically to the nature and use of Jesus' spiritual authority: "Are you a true prophet and does your authority come from God?" It may be that this problem had become particularly acute after the cleansing of the Temple, and one notes that the "chief priests" take the initiative in this inquiry. Jesus replies by making the "work" (baptism) of the Baptist analogous to his own "works" (mighty deeds in combination with the cleansing of the Temple), and asserts that before one can discern by what authority he performs his "works," one must acknowledge the divine origin of John's rite. To misinterpret the source and purpose of John's "work" is to misunderstand the "works" of Jesus.

Next, the Pharisees encounter Jesus with a question that echoes enormous political overtones: "Is it proper for the Jew to pay taxes to Caesar, or not?" (Mark 12:13-17; Matt. 22:15-22; Luke 20:20-26). Had Jesus replied yes, many of his followers would immediately have turned aside; had he answered no, he would have been accused of insurrection before the Roman court. Jesus' response maintains that the state is within the divine intention, so that one's obligation to the state is involved in the claim of God upon one's total life. What one's exact obligation to his state should be is not defined by Jesus, but Jesus' reference to Caesar's coin implied his feelings were that the Roman government was not contrary to peace and order.

A third inquiry arises from the Sadducees, who, as the other interrogators, seek to snare Jesus by what he says and so discredit him in the eyes of his disciples. It is altogether probable that this was a standard question that the Sadducees had prepared for the Pharisees and one to which the Pharisees had been able to give no satisfactory reply. "Which of this woman's seven legitimate husbands will be her husband in the afterlife?" is the essence of this question (Mark 12:18-27; Matt. 22:23-33; Luke 20:27-40).

Jesus' incisive retort indicates a lack of spiritual perception on the part of the Sadducees: "Evidently you Sadducees do not comprehend either the nature of the afterlife or the nature of God." Through this affirmation Jesus points out that in the final analysis

---

[29]*Ibid.*, p. 249.

human relationships are not based upon marital bonds, or even upon accident of birth, but upon one's relationship to God. This is, of course, analogous to what Jesus said elsewhere: "Whoever performs the will of God, this one is my brother and sister and mother" (Mark 3:35).

"What is the greatest commandment?" asks a scribe (Mark 12: 28-34; Matt. 22:34-40; Luke 10:25-28). This question had been discussed rather freely among the Jewish teachers, and Rabbi Hillel (*ca.* 70 B.C.-A.D. 10) actually had stated the "Golden Rule" in its negative form as a summary of the Law. Jesus' answer combined the Shema (Deut. 6:4-5) with love for one's neighbor as the summary of God's demands upon man's life: were devotion to God and redemptive love the essence of one's life, no external regulations would be necessary.

According to the Synoptic arrangement (except for Matt. 22:41), Jesus initiates the next question concerning the Davidic descent of the Messiah (Mark 12:15-37a; Matt. 22:41-46a; Luke 20:41-44), and follows this with some extremely rasping "woes" upon the hypocrisy of Pharisaic Judaism (Mark 12:37b-40; Matt. 23:1-36; Luke 20:45-47). The purpose in raising the question concerning the Messiah's origin is to exhibit the emptiness of hope in a forthcoming earthly Messiah, and, at the same instant, to portray the inability of the Jews to recognize the true origin of the One who stands in their midst. Especially in Matthew's Gospel the "woes" constitute a critique of the blind Judaism that rejected its fulfilment in Jesus Christ.

The apocalyptic discourse (Mark 13; Matt. 24; Luke 21).—More often than not this so-called "little apocalypse" is viewed as revealing an outline of world events from Jesus' day until the end of time, and as providing signs whereby one may ascertain when the end of the world is at hand. However, it seems more in harmony with the details of this passage to interpret it otherwise.[30]

(1) *The questions of the disciples* (Mark 13:1-4; Matt. 24:1-3; Luke 21:5-7). As Jesus and his disciples were leaving the Temple in Jerusalem, one of them observes: "What magnificent stones and what a marvelous structure!" To this Jesus responds, "Notice this majestic building? There will not be left one stone of it touching

---

[30]Cf. Hans Conzelmann, "Geschichte und Eschaton nach Mc 13," *Zeitschrift für die Neutestamentliche Wissenschaft,* Band 50 (1959), 210-21.

another!" When they had separated themselves from the crowd around the Temple, several of the disciples inquired with reference to this remark, "When will these things come to pass? And what sign will there be for the consummation of all things?"

The disciples considered these to be companion questions, for in Jewish and early Christian thought the end of the world was to be preceded by the oppression of the believers and by the destruction of those things sacred to them, Jerusalem and the Temple included. Therefore, they ask when the destruction of the Temple would take place and, beyond that, what would be the specific sign indicating the end of this affliction and the consummation of all things. Jesus' reply to their questions is unexpected and altogether astonishing to the disciples.

(2) *A warning* (Mark 13:5-8; Matt. 24:4-8; Luke 21:8-11). The disciples are warned against being *deceived* by false messianic pretenders who would appear and attempt to lead the people after them. In A.D. 70 and again in A.D. 132 this very thing happened. Each time the Jews were led by one (or several) who claimed to be the Messiah and who announced that God would intervene to help them throw off the Roman yoke, if they would rise in arms against Rome. On both occasions the Jews were deceived and their city destroyed. Jesus warns his followers not to be led astray by such revolutionaries.

Furthermore, the disciples are warned against being *disturbed* by any historical events such as wars and earthquakes, as though these in any fashion could determine the end of the world. Such occurrences are a normal part of the flow of history and cannot indicate the time of the end. "The end is not yet." Therefore, the believer should not experience the present through speculation but by the following manner.

(3) *The task of the disciple at present* (Mark 13:9-13; Matt. 24:9-14; Luke 21:12-19). The believer must experience the present in a twofold relationship. In his relationship to the world he must *endure persecution* (Mark 13:9,11-13). As the world treated the Lord, so it treats the disciple. Another relationship, this time imposed upon the believer from within, is that in which he stands with regard to the Christian message. His obligation is *to proclaim the gospel* to all peoples. After prefacing his remarks with these warnings, Jesus now approaches the specific questions themselves. He answers them, not as one question, but as separate questions which cannot be dealt with in the same terms.

(4) *Answer to the first question* (Mark 13:14-23; Matt. 24:15-25; Luke 21:20-24). Jesus treats the first question as one that relates strictly to *historical* events: "When will the destruction of Jerusalem occur?" This is a historical event which one may predict with reasonable certainty by other events. Jesus' reference to the "abomination of desolation" (a phrase first used in Daniel 9:27 and 12:11 to refer to the desecration of the Temple by Antiochus Ephipanes in 167 B.C.) is now used as a reference to the Roman army in its approach to the city. This is explicitly stated by Luke, who replaces this phrase with, "When you see Jerusalem surrounded by armies, then you know that its desolation is near" (21:20).

The verses immediately following lose all their meaning unless they refer to strictly historical events. Yet if these verses relate to the destruction of Jerusalem they abound with meaning: "When you see the army approaching, do not turn back to save your possessions, run to save your skin! Woe to the pregnant woman, and to those with small children, for they cannot flee so speedily! Pray that this invasion will not take place during the rainy winter season lest you cannot cross the swollen Jordan to escape in the desert! Let me emphasize again that you watch out for the false Messiahs. When they appear, remember that I have warned you beforehand!"

(5) *Answer to the second question* (Mark 13:24-27; Matt. 24:29-31; Luke 21:25-28). The disciples' question regarding the time of the end pertains to suprahistorical events that cannot be determined by historical occurrences. The signs for the end and the time of the end appear at the same instant. The phrase "and then" (Mark 13:26-27) must be interpreted as simultaneous with the events mentioned in Mark 13:24-25, and both should be understood together as one momentary act. *When the signs appear one can no longer prepare himself;* before he would be able the Son of man would be there.

(6) *Two illustrations* (Mark 13:28-32; Matt. 24:32-36; Luke 21:29-31). The parable of the fig tree is used to point out that one can reason the outcome of historical events by the "signs of the times." Such fervor against Rome could possibly lead to nothing else other than destruction. As one can predict the time of figs by the foliage on the tree, so one can predict the arrival of Rome by the events in Jerusalem. Recognizing the degree that this hatred of Rome had already reached, Jesus states, "This generation will not pass away until all these things come to pass." On the other hand,

"that hour"—the consummation of all things—is not a historical event of cause and effect; it is suprahistorical, and, therefore, within the will and knowledge of God alone!

(7) *The conclusion* (Mark 13:33-37; Matt. 24:34-36; Luke 21: 32-33). Even the Son himself does not know the hour of the end. Yet there is a quite definite task assigned for the interval: the disciple must be alert and maintain his faithfulness, for he does not know when his Lord may appear. Now the reader can understand why the Synoptics connected these sayings in the manner they did. Their purpose was to exhort the believers to avoid empty and vain speculations concerning the signs of the end and to encourage them to be faithful in the task to which they were called—the proclamation of the gospel to all nations.

The anointing at Bethany (Mark 14:3-9; Matt. 20:6-13. Cf. Luke 7:36-50 and John 12:1-8).—Mark, followed by Matthew, includes the mention of an anointing of Jesus at Bethany immediately prior to the celebration of the Passover. In lieu of this account, Luke records an earlier anointing by a "sinful woman" in the house of Simon the Pharisee. The Gospel of John mentions an anointing at Bethany six days before the Passover and names Mary as the one who anoints Jesus. Possibly the knowledge of an anointing was circulated in various forms and each of the Gospel writers utilized the tradition that had come to him.

At least two alternate possibilities exist with regard to the interpretation of Jesus' words, "Wherever the gospel is preached in all the world, what she has done will be remembered." (1) These words are intended to imply a mission to the Gentiles, during the course of which time her deed will be recounted. (2) Otherwise, Jesus' words may be completely eschatological, especially if the word rendered "wherever" really means "when." Thereby Jesus would have said, "When on the last day all creation hears the Good News, her deed will be proclaimed."[31]

The betrayal (Mark 14:10-11; Matt. 26:14-16; Luke 22:3-6). All four Gospels indicate that Judas Iscariot betrayed to the enemies of Jesus where and when they might arrest him apart from the crowd. Suggestions will never end with regard to the reason that Judas "betrayed" Jesus, but the most likely possibility seems to be that Jesus

---

[31]Joachim Jeremias, *Jesus' Promise to the Nations,* trans. S. H. Hooke (Naperville: Alec R. Allenson, 1958), pp. 22-23.

had disappointed the hopes of Judas when he refused to become a political Messiah.

Institution of the Lord's Supper (Mark 14:22-25; Matt. 26:26-29; Luke 22:15-30). It is not certain whether the last meal Jesus ate with his disciples was a Passover meal. In only two passages (Mark 14:1-2; Matt. 26:1-5; Luke 22:1-2; and Mark 14:12-16; Matt. 26:17-19; Luke 22:7-13) is the meal specifically referred to as the Passover, while two other passages may imply that Jesus did not get to eat the Passover with his disciples (Mark 14:2; Matt. 26:5; and Luke 22:15-16). As often interpreted, the Fourth Gospel states that Jesus did *not* eat the Passover meal but that he was put to death at the time the Passover lamb was being slain in preparation for the meal (John 19:14; 18:28). However, the problem appears not to be insurmountable when one recalls that both John and the Synoptics wrote to emphasize certain theological aspects. A suggested reconstruction of events is offered as follows.

Jesus customarily ate fellowship meals with his disciples, as other teachers often ate with their disciples; and it was remembered that he had eaten one such meal with them during the events of the Passover Week. Before the Gospels were written, two traditions were circulating with respect to this last meal that Jesus had eaten: one suggested a Passover meal (represented by the Synoptics) and the other a fellowship meal prior to the Passover (represented by the Fourth Gospel). Because the Synoptics understood the death of Christ as a "new exodus," they perpetuated the tradition that the last meal was a Passover, so as to have Christ, the "new Moses," inaugurate a meal in anticipation of his redemption as Moses had done in ancient days with respect to the redemption from Egypt. On the other hand, the author of the Fourth Gospel was more concerned to depict Christ as the "Lamb of God who bears the sin of the world," and so selected the tradition whereby Christ was put to death at the time the Jewish Passover lamb was being slain.

The theological significance of the Last Supper reflects the leader-follower motif that permeates the New Testament. Jesus' action with the bread was a type of prophetic symbolism whereby he signified that what had happened to the bread was about to happen to him. By "taking" the bread, the disciples accepted his destiny for themselves. The cup was a "covenant" between Jesus and his disciples by which they were consecrated to identify themselves with him in his passion. And, if Luke 22:28-30 originally followed the words concerning the cup,[32] consecration to the destiny of their Lord further indicated victory achieved through suffering.

Gethsemane, arrest, trial and crucifixion.—Jesus' demeanor in the Gethsemane experience (Mark 14:32-42; Matt. 26:36-46; Luke 22:40-46) demonstrates as much as any other one event the reality of his incarnation and genuine manhood. As with other men, Jesus must decide upon the intention of God for himself and he must enter into this intention with absolute faith. Very vividly the Synoptics portray the loneliness with which a man must stand before God and make the decision that is absolutely binding upon himself.

After Judas had identified Jesus for the Temple police (Mark 14:43-52; Matt. 26:47-56; Luke 22:47-53), Jesus was arraigned before a nocturnal gathering of the Sanhedrin (Mark 14:53-72; Matt.

---

[32]Rudolf Otto, *The Kingdom of God and the Son of Man,* trans. Floyd V. Filson and Betram Lee-Woolf (London: Lutterworth Press, 1951), pp. 265-330.

26:57-75; Luke 22:54-71). According to the Synoptic tradition, the Jewish charge against Jesus was twofold: (1) Jesus had affirmed that he would destroy their handmade Temple; and (2) in three days he would erect another temple, not made with hands, to succeed their Temple (Mark 14:58; Matt. 26:61). Whether or not Jesus had actually ever uttered these assertions, both were implied in his work and words. The first affirmation meant the eschatological liberation from the Jewish cultic system of blood and sacrifice; the second meant that in a miraculously brief span of time God would create a better mode of worship than the Jerusalem Temple. Thus Jesus' words meant: I am at once the consummator of the Jewish religious system and the initiator of the eschatological community of God.[33]

The exact content of the questions asked Jesus and the precise answers given by Jesus are not clearly evident. Mark relates that to the question of the high priest, "Are you the Messiah, the Son of the Blessed?" Jesus answered, "I am." Matthew's account somewhat alters the question to read, "Are you the Messiah, the Son of God?" and makes the answer less positive, "You are saying this." Luke divides the question into two parts, the first of which is, "Are you the Messiah?" Jesus responds, "If I told you, you would not believe." The second question transmitted by Luke is, "Are you the Son of God?" To this Jesus answers, "You are saying this."

Whatever the exact dialogue between the court and Jesus, they decided he was guilty of blasphemy and worthy of death. Evidence from the Mishnah and other sources makes it highly probably that the Jews had the authority to exact the death penalty from men of their own race on religious charges, especially on the charge of blasphemy.[34] Why did they not then stone Jesus? The answer is not difficult. There was another way, a better way, whereby they might have Jesus put to death and have themselves exonerated from guilt in the eyes of the masses: they would accuse him of insurrection before the Roman governor.

Early the next morning Jesus was delivered to Pilate (Mark 15:1; Matt. 27:1-2; Luke 23:1) with several related accusations against him (Mark 15:2-5; Matt. 27:11-14; Luke 23:2-5). First, Jesus was accused of attempting to instate himself as the Jewish messianic king. Second, he was charged with speaking against Roman taxation. Third,

[33]Lohmeyer, *Markus*, p. 327.
[34]Paul Winter, "Marginal Notes on the Trial of Jesus," *Zeitschrift für die Neutestamentliche Wissenschaft*, Band 50 (1959), 14-33.

the charge was that Jesus was misdirecting the Jewish nation through his false teachings. Pilate obviously conjectured that these were trumped-up charges and sought to place the responsibility of the decision on another. Luke states that upon learning that Jesus was from Galilee, Pilate sent him to Herod Antipas, who was in Jerusalem for the Passover (Luke 23:6-16). When this did not effect a betterment of his own situation, Pilate sought to barter with the Jews, but to no avail. Finally, Jesus was sentenced by Pilate to be crucified (Mark 15:6-15; Matt. 27:15-26; Luke 23:17-25).

After receiving the customary maltreatment designated for condemned criminals (Mark 15:16-20; Matt. 27:27-31), Jesus was led out to be crucified (Mark 15:21; Matt. 27:32; Luke 23:26-32). With some detail the Gospels elaborate the mocking Jesus received while on the cross (Mark 15:22-32; Matt. 27:33-44 and Luke 23:33-43). The underlying significance to the entire passion narrative is contained in words too often neglected: "The curtain of the temple was torn in two from top to bottom" (Mark 15:38; Matt. 27:51). This is the fulfilment of the charges made against Jesus in the Jewish trial: Now is the Jewish Temple destroyed! Now has God laid the foundation for the new temple! And the mention that the veil was split from top to bottom is not accidental: in the death of Jesus Christ it is *God himself* who has destroyed the old and initiated the new!

The resurrected Lord.—Even the most limited survey of the traditions concerning the resurrected Lord should incorporate some mention of the accounts contained in the remainder of the New Testament outside the Synoptic Gospels. For that reason this present discussion will include not only the Synoptic traditions but those of the Fourth Gospel and 1 Corinthians as well.

The Markan tradition is complicated by the textual difficulty relating to 16:9-20. Though manuscript evidence is overwhelmingly in favor of deleting these verses, this is only a negative conclusion and does not suggest what might have been the original ending of Mark. Was the original ending lost, or did the Gospel end with the statement that they told no one because they were frightened? It is possible that the last part of the Second Gospel was accidentally torn away. But it is also possible that Mark intended to end his Gospel upon the note of fear, thereby emphasizing the magnitude of impact that the resurrection initially had upon the first witnesses. When the two Marys enter the tomb they are commanded by the angel, "Tell his disciples and Peter that he goes before you into Galilee: there *shall you see* him, as he told you" (16:7; 7 cf. 14:28). Customarily these words are read to mean that "the disciples and Peter" were to journey to Galilee where a resurrection appearance of the risen Lord would take place. Doubtless this is the interpretation given the command by Matthew, who emphasizes it through a further statement to the women (28:10); but it is questionable whether Mark intended the injunction to be understood in this fashion. In light of two other considerations, Mark's words *may* imply something more than another resurrection appearance.

First, certain New Testament passages use the future expression, "You shall see," with reference to the final appearance of the Lord. "You shall see the Son of man sitting at the right hand of the power, and coming with the clouds of heaven" (Mark 14:62) and "Behold, he is coming with the clouds, and every eye will see him" (Rev. 1:7) are two examples. The reader might also refer to Mark 13:26, Matthew 16:28, and John 16:16.

Second, a Jewish hope existed that God would make his final appearance in Jerusalem and there gather unto himself all his people from the four corners of the earth. It is possible that Mark has reoriented this Jewish expectation in light of his confession of the lordship of Jesus Christ: the final manifestation of God must be accomplished through the person of Jesus Christ and it must take place in Galilee. If this is the case, what Mark expects is the *final* appearance of Jesus rather than another resurrection appearance; and it is to be accomplished in Galilee, the new Holy Land, where God will fulfil his promises to his new people who follow him there.[35]

Matthew's resurrection narrative may be divided into two parts, 28:1-10 and 28:16-20. Verses 11-15 do not deal with the resurrection appearances proper, but point out the lying and fraudulent attempt of the high priest to pervert this truth. The first narrative (28:1-10) seems to have as its purpose that of verifying the fact that the Lord lives and so achieves this goal through the witness of

---

[35]Ernst Lohmeyer, *Galiläa und Jerusalem* (Göttingen: Vandenhoeck und Ruprecht, 1936), pp. 10-14.

the empty tomb (v. 6), the words of the angel (vv. 5-7), and the appearance of the Lord himself (vv. 9-10). Matthew 28:16-20 serves to announce the *lordship* of Christ; other factors, such as seeing Christ or verification of the resurrection, are subservient to this theme of Christ's lordship. Thereby this second appearance in Matthew's source emphasizes Galilee as the midpoint from which the redemptive message of the lordship of Christ is to be carried to all the world.[36]

Luke's narrative concerning the appearance of Jesus to the disciples on the road to Emmaus (24:13-35) declares that, indeed, Jesus is the "Redeemer of Israel" (v. 21), even though the eyes of the disciples cannot recognize this reality until Jesus himself breaks through to reveal it to them (vv. 16, 30-35). The appearance of the risen Lord to the disciples gathered in Jerusalem (vv. 36-51) involves several motifs that subsequently dominated the life of the early church: the necessity of witnessing (vv. 47-48), the presence of the Spirit in the life of the church (v. 49), and the fulfilment of God's purpose in Jesus Christ, indicated through the phrase, "according to the Scriptures" (v. 44; cf. vv. 26-27).

John 20 is filled with major themes of that Gospel. For the sake of discussion, it is best to divide the chapter into three divisions. In the first (vv. 1-18), the discovery of the empty tomb by Peter and "the other disciple" is climaxed by the appearance of the risen Lord to Mary Magdalene. For these disciples belief in the resurrection is established through the testimony of the empty tomb (v. 8), apart from the appeal to Scripture (v. 9), which must have developed later as a proof in the thinking of the early church. Jesus' words to Mary may be rendered, "Stop trying to hold on to me; I have not yet ascended to the Father" (v. 17). If this rendering is correct, then these words of Jesus indicate that in light of the resurrection "the old physical contacts are no longer appropriate."[37] Further elements in this account are those of Jesus' ascent to the Father and the necessity of witnessing to this event (vv. 17-18).

The second appearance (vv. 19-23) takes place as all the disciples, except Thomas, are gathered together behind closed doors. Again the purpose of this appearance, like all the other Jerusalem appearances, is to verify the reality of the resurrection. However, a unique feature about this passage is the explicit assurance that

---

[36] *Ibid.*, pp. 15-17.
[37] C. K. Barrett, *The Gospel According to St. John* (London: S.P.C.K., 1955), p. 470.

the resurrected Christ is the same One who was crucified (v. 20). In common with Luke, this narrative emphasizes the presence of the Spirit as the constitution of the church's fellowship (vv. 21-22) and indicates that because the church possesses the Spirit it may mediate forgiveness of sins in the name of Christ (v. 23).

Eight days later Jesus appears again to the gathered disciples, this time with Thomas present (vv. 24-29). Previously, Thomas had rejected the apostolic witness to the resurrection, but at the sight of the risen Lord he believes. The purpose for recording this event is at once to confirm the faith of those later disciples, "who had believed though they had not seen," and to affirm the validity of the apostolic witness to the resurrection.

The author of the Fourth Gospel originally concluded his work with the statement of his purpose in 20:31. Appended to these closing remarks is the report of a resurrection appearance on the Sea of Galilee (21:1-23). Three themes dominate this chapter. Foremost is the confession, "It is the Lord," which was made in conjunction with the miraculous draft of fish (vv. 1-7). Second, the theme of fellowship is suggested through the disciples' participation in the common meal shared with their Lord (vv. 12-14). A third theme arises in connection with the dialogue between Jesus and Peter (vv. 15-17), which is the Johannine version of founding the church and installing its leader (cf. Luke 5:1-11 and Matt. 16:16-20).

Evidently the passage that Paul includes in 1 Corinthians 15:5-8 goes back to an early tradition. Several facets are outstanding: (1) No place is mentioned where the appearances happened; (2) Paul's tradition is careful to enumerate a sufficient amount of witnesses so as to leave no doubt concerning the actuality of the event: Cephas (Peter), the twelve, five hundred brothers, James, the apostles, and Paul himself are included; and (3) the Old Testament Scriptures are enjoined as a further evidence for the resurrection.

The Nativity Narratives

Only Matthew and Luke, among all the New Testament writers, reflect any knowledge of or interest in the events surrounding Jesus' miraculous conception and birth. This is not to suggest that these accounts are of little or no importance. But it is to say that even though the birth narratives are chronologically first, they were evidently not the primary concern of the earliest disciples. The primary confession of the first Christians was, "Jesus Christ is Lord," which they validated by an appeal to his resurrection. Other events in Jesus ministry were important too, but at first the disciples did not raise the question concerning the nature of his coming into the world.

On the basis of the account of Jesus' baptism in Mark's Gospel, one can possibly see one of the primary reasons that some Christians may have concerned themselves about the *how* of Jesus' entry into the world. Mark states that the Spirit came upon Jesus *at the time of his baptism.* Mark meant by this that the entirety of Jesus' ministry was under the guidance of the Spirit, and all of Jesus' actions were done in the power of the Spirit. But some people concluded from Mark's account that Jesus *became* the Son of God at his baptism.

Because of this and other reasons, Matthew and Luke incorporated the nativity narratives into their Gospels. They intended to point out that *the very conception of Jesus was by the Holy Spirit* (Matt. 1:18 ff.; Luke 1:35 ff.). In the Gospel of John this truth is unfolded even further, for he affirms that the Son of God (whom he calls the "Word") has eternally existed with the Father; therefore,

23. Traditional site of the Last Supper

the event of Jesus' coming was in reality the medium through which God himself entered the human arena.

It should be recognized from the outset that the nativity narratives of Matthew and Luke are independent of each other.

The account in Matthew.—Matthew's account falls into two major divisions: genealogy and birth-childhood.

The genealogy (1:1-17) is divided by Matthew into three parts. The first is from Abraham to David, the second from David to the Exile, and the third is from the Exile to Jesus (v. 17). By drawing attention to these divisions, Matthew seems to be pointing out to his readers that the revered Davidic kingship led only to the Exile, whereas the true King leads his people into the light of God's salvation. Significant also is the mention of the women in the genealogical account. That Tamar, Ruth, Rahab, and the wife of Uriah are included, along with Mary, intimates that the ways of God are beyond the comprehension of men. Who would have suspected that the mother of the Lord, and the Lord himself, would have descended from a lineage such as this!

The birth-childhood (1:18 to 2:23) subdivides naturally into five divisions, each of which is understood as the fulfilment of God's promise made to his people in times past.

(1) The birth account (1:18-25) carries through three themes. The first is the creation of the child by the Holy Spirit; the second is the conception and birth by the virgin Mary; and the third is the giving of the name, Jesus. That the child is created by the Holy Spirit verifies his *deity;* that he is conceived by a woman validates his *humanity;* and because he is both God and man, he is able to bear the name Jesus and deliver his people from their sins.

(2) The second scene is that of adoration in which three men from the East (perhaps intended as Persian astrologers) have come to offer homage to the newborn King (2:1-12). The connection of their coming with the quote from Micah 5:2 signifies two things: The arrival of these men from a distant land hints at the universal nature of his salvation, and the quotation from Micah indicates that the true King comes from the insignificant village of Bethlehem instead of the noted city of Jerusalem, where lived the noted kings of Israel's past.

(3) The flight to Egypt (Matt. 2:13-15) looks forward to the time when this child will deliver his people from the bondage of sin as Moses led Israel out of Egypt in their ancient past.

(4) The murder of the infants at Bethlehem (vv. 16-18) further demonstrates the parallel between the "first" and "second" Moses. As Moses of old was divinely protected from Pharaoh, so God now delivers his Son from the hands of Herod. Although there is no record of this event other than the account of Matthew, it is not at all out of keeping with what is known of Herod's character.

(5) Matthew understands the return of Jesus to Nazareth (vv. 19-23) as the fulfilment of prophecy (v. 23), in the same way that he understands all the other happenings thus far mentioned. But the difficulty in this instance is that there is to be found no passage in the Old Testament to which Matthew had reference. Various solutions have been offered to this problem, but none of them is entirely satisfactory.

The account in Luke.—Luke includes in his account the birth narratives both of Jesus and of John the Baptist. The form and style of the stories strongly suggest that they were originally told in Aramaic, which would indicate that they represent a very early source. And it is possible, as many have suggested, that this record goes back to Mary herself. The narrative consists of seven individual sections.

(1) The annunciation of John's birth (1:5-25) has woven into it at least three major themes. First, Luke calls attention to John's priestly heritage, since the annunciation to Zechariah, who is a priest and whose wife is from a priestly tribe, takes place in the Temple. Second, of significance is the recognition that he, like the Lord, is to be "filled with the Holy Spirit" (v. 15). Perhaps this is in some way understood as the fulfilment of Joel's words, that in the last days God would pour out his Spirit (Joel 2:28-29). A third evident theme is that this child is to be the one who prepares the way for the Lord (Luke 1:17).

(2) The annunciation of Jesus' birth (vv. 26-38) follows immediately. Here also several motifs dominate the story. The name of the child is to be Jesus, meaning "Deliverer." This was not an uncommon name among Jewish children, for each mother hoped that her child would be the Chosen One of God. However, in this instance it is not the mother who names the child; the name is given by the messenger of God. When Mary is told that she would have a child, she evidently expected the conception of the child to come about through the normal means of human procreation (v. 34); but she is informed by the angel that the Spirit of God would create

in her this child (v. 35). For this reason he would be called the "Son of God." Luke also emphasizes the virginity of Mary. This, of course, indicates that the child could not possibly have had a human father. But, even more than that, the fact that Mary was a *human mother* verifies the *genuine humanity* of her Son! It should not be forgotten, as was mentioned above, that the *creation by the Holy Spirit* is the *evidence of Jesus' divine origin,* whereas the *conception by a virgin woman* is the *validation of his human origin.*

(3) After Mary is told of the forthcoming birth of her child, she goes for a visit of three months with Elizabeth, the wife of Zechariah (vv. 39-56). The Magnificat (vv. 46-55) reads like an Old Testament psalm and has many parallels to the song of Hannah in 1 Samuel 2:1-10. The general content of the Magnificat is the praise for the salvation which God gives to those who are faithful to him.

(4) Following the account of Mary's visit with Elizabeth is the story of John's birth (Luke 1:57-80). Zechariah gives him his name and breaks forth in a song of praise (known as the Benedictus) which highly exalts the person and role of John the Baptist. In fact what is said of John more nearly describes the person and work of Jesus; and this recognition has led some to believe that this hymn of praise was originally circulated by certain of John's disciples who looked upon him as the Messiah.

(5) The birth of Jesus is told in an almost poetic fashion (2:1-20). In conjunction with his birth the Gloria in Excelsis (v. 14) is sung by the angels to the shepherds in the fields.

(6) The account of Jesus' presentation in the Temple unites several elements (vv. 21-40). According to Jewish law the mother had to go through the ceremony of purification forty days after the birth of the child, at which time an offering was made in the Temple (Lev. 12:1-8). That she offered a pair of doves, rather than a lamb, signifies that the family was not well-to-do. The significance of Jesus' coming is sung by Simeon in words that have become known as the Nunc Dimittis (Luke 2:29-32). This song is highly flavored by Old Testament reflections, and it expresses the belief that this child will become not only the Redeemer of Israel but also a "light to the Gentiles." And the words of Simeon are confirmed by Anna, a prophetess, who herself had longed for the salvation of God.

(7) The brief account of Jesus' boyhood (vv. 41-52) is perhaps told by Luke for the sake of emphasizing the genuine humanity of Jesus, as well as his profound understanding of the things of God.

The Fourth Gospel

The Fourth Gospel and the Synoptics

In several significant aspects the Fourth Gospel differs from the Synoptics. The *content,* both by way of inclusions and omissions, is different. John includes a series of "seven signs" that are not in the Synoptics: the changing of water to wine (2:1-11), healing the nobleman's son (4:46-54), feeding the multitude (6:1-14), walking on the water (6:16-21), giving sight to the man born blind (9:1-39), and raising Lazarus (11:1-44). Some of these signs may have their analogies in the Synoptics, but the Fourth Gospel treats them in an entirely different manner. Lengthy dialogues are mentioned that have no counterpart in the Synoptic framework: Nicodemus (3:1-36) and the Samaritan woman (4:1-42). Jesus exercises a ministry in and near Jerusalem (2:13; 5:1; 7:10; 10:22; 11:7-8) and is in Jerusalem for three Passovers (2:13; 6:4; 12:1). On the other hand, John omits mention of such crucial events as the baptism and temptation, the confession at Caesarea Philippi, and the transfiguration, as well as the Gethsemane experience and the Synoptic accounts of healing.

There are basic variations in the *outline of events.* According to the Fourth Gospel, Jesus and John the Baptist exercised simultaneous ministries (3:22-24; 4:1), while the Synoptic tradition explicitly states that Jesus did not begin his ministry until after the incarceration of the Baptist. As previously noted, the cleansing of the Temple occurs at the first of Jesus' ministry, whereas the Synoptics interpret this event as the climactic event which made the Jews decide to rid themselves of Jesus, a decision which John attributes to the raising of Lazarus (11:47 ff.). Nor, as the reader will recall, is the Last Supper a Passover meal in the outline of the Fourth Gospel.

Perhaps the primary difference between the Fourth Gospel and the Synoptics is the difference in *methodology.* From the very first of his ministry, as presented by the Fourth Gospel, Jesus is acknowledged to be the Messiah (1:45,49; 4:29; 6:68-69) and he himself openly declares both his Messiahship (4:26; 9:37) and his unique relationship to the Father (7:25-36; 8:12-30). John the Baptist serves only as a "witness" (1:15) to point men to the "Lamb of God" (1:29); no longer is he a herald of repentance. Finally, the kingdom of God, which is the essence of Jesus' proclamation in the Synoptic tradition, receives only sparce allusion (3:3,5); and Jesus becomes the major topic of his own message.

Why did John write as he did? Did he write with a knowledge of the Synoptics or did he write independently of them. To say that John wrote to correct the Synoptics is to misunderstand both the Synoptics and the Fourth Gospel. Whether or not John wrote with a knowledge of the Synoptics, he certainly wrote with a familiarity of at least *some* of the traditions contained within the present texts of the Synoptic Gospels. It may be that the best opinion is to suggest that both John and the Synoptics wrote from the vast storehouse of early Christian traditions, and that each source serves as an independent witness to the rich variety of interpretation given the person of Christ within the early church. The difference between the Fourth Gospel and the Synoptics, rightly understood, ought to be looked upon, not as a problem, but as a *contribution,* for their diversity in approach means that each tradition has supplemented the other and has given the contemporary Christian community a more complete portrayal of her Lord.

Origin of the Fourth Gospel

Authorship.—In at least one respect the Fourth Gospel is similar to the Synoptics: the authorship is anonymous. The words of 21:24, composed after the analogy of 19:35, were perhaps written by a later disciple to authenticate the apostolic authority of the Gospel in a period when much emphasis was placed upon apostolic authority. But, if the reader will read carefully, 19:35 actually seems to differentiate between the author of the Gospel and the witness "who saw it."

The external evidence, which centers in large measure about the evidence of Papias and Irenaeus (a church leader in Gaul *ca.* A.D. 185), is in line with the internal evidence of the Gospel itself. Papias refers to two Johns who resided in the city of Ephesus, the "apostle" and the "elder"; and Papias seems to indicate that it was not the "apostle" who planned the Gospel. Irenaeus only states that John "set forth" the Gospel. Even if Irenaeus meant thereby that the "apostle" wrote the Gospel, this is not evident; and Irenaeus' judgment may not be exact, because elsewhere he reveals certain inaccuracies in historical details.

While we thus cannot definitely name the author of the Gospel, we can share the faith of Christians from the earliest centuries to the present—the Gospel was written by one who had a deep and true knowledge of who Jesus is and what he does for men. Whether or not he had seen Jesus in the flesh, we cannot say. Clearly, however, he belonged to the community of those who had. If not with his physical eyes, with the eyes of faith he stood among those who "beheld his glory (1:14; cf. 20:29).

Date and place of origin.—A papyrus fragment of the Fourth Gospel has been found which dates somewhere around A.D. 135-50, while certain indications from the content of the Gospel intimate that the Gospel could not have been written prior to the last decade of the first century A.D. Therefore, a date between A.D. 90-100 is suggested. The learned and often enigmatic combination of Jewish and Hellenistic motifs within the Fourth Gospel causes one to seek as a place of origin a metropolitan area where Jewish and Hellenistic thought patterns had previously intermingled. For this reason Alexandria, Ephesus, and Antioch in Syria are presented as possible locales of publication.

Interpretation of the Fourth Gospel

Before the interpretation is entered into, several observations should be made concerning the complexity of interpreting this Gospel. Often the devout churchgoer expresses his appreciation for the Fourth Gospel because it is "so simple." This is a perfect example of the paradoxical nature of the Fourth Gospel which at once is both "simple" and difficult. Every believer, regardless of his degree of learning, can receive devotional values from its pages. Yet its author has purposely planned each word and phrase so that the concerned reader must ponder before deciding upon the emphasis that was originally intended.

In the author's day there was a massive theological and philosophical vocabulary, which included a number of words and phrases that could be understood differently, depending on whether one read them from a Jewish or Greek background. This very factor, which facilitated the writing of the Gospel, has intensified the problem of its interpretation. The contemporary reader must first familiarize himself with the theological thought patterns of the first-century world, and then he must decide with what tint of Jewish or Greek emphasis the author wrote a given passage.[38]

A second, even more difficult problem of interpretation, is that

---

[38]For an excellent study of the background of the Fourth Gospel, the reader is referred to C. H. Dodd, *The Interpretation of the Fourth Gospel*, pp. 3-130.

24. Gethsemane

of gaining a proper insight into the author's perspective of the relationship between faith and history. In a degree that far outstretches the grasp of most, the author of the Fourth Gospel has perceived the impossibility and vanity of separating event and interpretation. It is impossible for the believer to behold any event in the life of Jesus except through the eyes of faith; no event has meaning unless faith establishes that event in its proper light.

When, for example, the man of faith relates Jesus' healing of the lame man, he must recognize that therein is a witness to the unity between the Father and Son. The Son is thus able to make alive whom he will in the same fashion that the Father raises the dead (John 5:21). Every other event in the history of Jesus' ministry likewise emerges from this union with the redemptive grace of God —and the Fourth evangelist must so testify—or else the words and deeds of Jesus are but the echo of empty human dreams, rather than "signs" of the presence of God. Hoskyns expresses this idea classically:

> In other words, the theme of the Fourth Gospel is the non-historical
> that makes sense of history, the infinite that makes sense of time, God
> who makes sense of men and is therefore their Saviour. . . . Moreover,
> the non-historical cannot be dismissed aṣ Johannine interpretation. It is
> rather the veritable meaning of the history that has been set forth.[39]

The prologue (1:1-18).—The prologue comprises more than an introduction to the Fourth Gospel; it summarizes the entire contents of the Gospel and conditions the reader's mind for all that comes ıfter. For purposes of comment, the prologue may be divided into four parts: 1-5, 6-8, 9-13, and 14-18. Two basic themes of the Gospel are included in the first five verses: (1) An essential unity exists between the Father and the preexistent Son, spoken of as the Word of God: "The Word eternally has abided in a unique relationship with God [the Father] and, indeed, is himself Deity [Godness]" (1:1-2). (2) The Word of God is both creative and life-giving; the power of darkness (evil) neither can comprehend nor conquer this Word which is Light (vv. 3-5).

Immediately the second division of the prologue (vv. 6-8) serves to differentiate John the Baptist from the Light and to validate John as a witness to the Light. Evidently these verses, along with verse 15, were intended to refute the claims of a "Baptist sect," which exalted John the Baptist over the Lord of the church. A subsidiary purpose of these verses is to introduce the theme of "witness" which is a vital part of the Gospel.

The third section (vv. 9-13) affirms the significance of the coming of the Light into the world, the consequences of which are elaborated in more detail throughout the remaining chapters of the Gospel. Several aspects of this coming are evident. (1) The true Light shows up every man for what he really is (v. 9). (2) Though all the world owes its life to this Light, mankind in general, and the Jews in particular, rejected the Light when he came to them (vv. 10-11). (3) Whoever responds in faith to the Light of God in Jesus Christ receives this grace from God and becomes a child of God (vv. 12-13).

Finally, the last division of the prologue (vv. 14-18) also declares

---

[39]Edwyn Hoskyns and Francis Davey, *The Fourth Gospel* (London: Faber & Faber, 1961), pp. 129-30.

concepts that are of the very core of the Fourth Gospel. (1) The Word of God became *truly man* and lived his life among men (v. 14). (2) The church confesses that this man, Jesus Christ, was also *truly God,* who mediated to the church the grace of God, and who alone can bear a valid witness to the Father, for he alone has known the Father absolutely (vv. 14,16,18). (3) Thus the claim of God which comes in Jesus Christ is superior even to the claim of the Law, which was given through Moses (v. 17).

The witness of the Baptist (1:19-34).—The author of the Fourth Gospel has a twofold purpose in these paragraphs. (1) Verses 19-28 relate the words of the Baptist himself in answer to the questions presented him by the deputies from Jerusalem: I am *not* any of the persons anticipated by the Jewish messianic expectations; I am only a voice of *witness* to the Coming One. (2) In verses 29-34 is contained the content of John's witness: "Jesus of Nazareth, upon whom the Spirit abides permanently, is at once the Lamb of God and the Son of God."

What is indicated by the phrase "Lamb of God" is not easily decided upon. It is quite possible that the concept of the Passover lamb (which in itself possessed no sin-bearing functions) has been interwoven with connotations of a sacrifice for sins, in light of Christ's death, which transpired during the Passover season and effected a forgiveness of sins. According to the Synoptic tradition, the open confession of Jesus as the Son of God does not come this early in Jesus' ministry; but this is in keeping with the intention of John, who desires for his readers to recognize from the very first who Jesus truly is.

The witness of the disciples (1:35-51).—Upon the basis of John's confession two of his disciples separate from him so as *to follow* and *to abide* with Jesus, which means that they have become permanent disciples of Jesus. These disciples themselves now become witnesses through whom others make the decision to follow Jesus. Among these newer disciples is Nathanael, who is intended to personify the ideal Jew through his confession that Jesus is the "King of Israel," a theme reverberated elsewhere in the Gospel (6:15; 18: 33,36).

The first sign (2:1-12).—At Cana in Galilee the first of Jesus' seven "signs" takes place. In the Fourth Gospel a "sign" is an event that attests to a deeper reality than the actual event itself. That this "sign" is called the *first* "sign" further signifies that it is basic in understanding the essential significance of Jesus' coming. Taken as a whole, the story is to affirm the consummation of Judaism in Jesus and, consequently, the superiority of the Christian faith to Judaism. Both of these ideas are signified by the actions of Jesus: the first in the filling of the water jars, and the second in the changing of water into wine. After the six jars, symbolic of Judaism, were filled, Jesus sent the servant to draw fresh water,[40] and it was this water that was transformed into wine. In characteristic Johannine fashion the truth of it all is declared in veiled language, "You have kept the good wine until now." For the Christian reader there is no doubt that the steward has unwittingly confessed the new wine of the Christian church is superior to the old wine of Judaism. Another facet of the Johannine "signs" is seen in the response of those persons who had witnessed the event: the blindness of the world is typified by the amazement of the steward who saw only the externals of the miracle, while the spiritual perception of the church is typified in the disciples who believed in Jesus through the medium of this "sign."

Cleansing the Temple (2:13-25).—The particular emphases made through the Johannine episode are two. (1) Mediating the presence of God to man, the intended function of the Jerusalem Temple, is realized in Jesus Christ, the true temple. Hence the implied destruction of the Jewish cult. (2) As the function of the Temple is fulfilled in Jesus Christ, so the role of the people of God is fulfilled in the church, the body of Christ.

Conversation with Nicodemus (3:1-21).—Much symbolism is involved in Nicodemus' encounter with Jesus: although Nicodemus is a leader of the Jews and a Pharisee he dwells in spiritual darkness and cannot see (enter) the kingdom of God. Nicodemus represents the Jewish people, as is indicated through the use of the plural form of *you* in verses 7 and 12, *"You* must be begotten from above . . . I spoke to *you* earthly things and *you* did not believe." On the other hand, Jesus speaks as the representative of the Christian community in dialogue with the Jewish community: *"We* know that which *we* are speaking and *we* have seen that concerning which *we* are

---

[40]In support of this interpretation, see B. F. Westcott, *The Gospel According to St. John* (Grand Rapids: Wm. B. Eerdmans Publishing Co., 1950), pp. 37-38, who bases this judgment in part upon the meaning of the Greek verb, which most naturally means to draw water from a well. For an opposing viewpoint, C. K. Barrett, *op. cit.,* pp. 160-61.

bearing witness, but *you* [plural] did not receive *our* witness" (v. 11). The purpose of incorporating this dialogue is to declare that neither Nicodemus as an individual, nor the Jewish people as a nation, can possibly enter the kingdom of God unless they experience a transformation of life as radical as the change wrought through the physical birth. And this transformation is possible only through the power of the Spirit, mediated via the church's witness to the exalted Son of man.

A further witness by the Baptist (3:22-36).—In these few verses the Gospel reiterates John's witness to Jesus and mentions several themes that are dealt with in more detail elsewhere: the divine initiative, eternal life, judgment, and the unity between Father and Son.

Conversation with a Samaritan woman (4:1-42).—In typical Johannine fashion several major emphases of this passage are introduced either through misunderstandings or questions on the part of the one in conversation with Jesus. (1) "Are you greater than Jacob who was the father both of the Jews and the Samaritans?" The appropriate answer is to recognize that Jesus *is* superior to Jacob. Jesus grants life-giving water to all who ask, whereas Jacob's well satisfies only the temporary needs of those few persons who happen by. (2) "Where is the proper place of worship—in the Samaritan or Jewish temple?" Jesus' response indicates that historically the Jewish religious tradition, rather than the Samaritan faith, has pointed toward God; however, the Jewish faith is now consummated and true worship may be offered wherever the Spirit bears witness to the reality of God in Jesus Christ. (3) To the woman's question, "Can this be the Christ?" the Samaritans themselves give answer, "We have heard for ourselves, and we know that this is indeed the Saviour of the world."

The second sign (4:43-54).—The healing of the Gentile's son, which takes place in Galilee rather than Jerusalem, intends to convey to the reader the truth that the farther away from Jerusalem Jesus works, the better he is received, for even the Gentiles confess, in agreement with the Samaritans, that Jesus is the Saviour of the world.

The third sign (5:1-47).—A third sign, the healing of the lame man on the sabbath, affords Jesus opportunity to confirm the absolute identity of his activity with the activity of the Father. Because of this deed and the claim of Jesus in conjunction with it, the Jews seek to kill Jesus (vv. 17-18). From this Jesus draws several conclusions.

(1) Since the work of the Son is in essence the work of the Father, rejection of the Son on the basis of his work is rejection of the Father, whereby the Jews bring judgment upon themselves (vv. 19-20,22-23). (2) The healing of the paralytic is a "sign" pointing to the Son's authority to raise the dead and to judge them either unto life eternal or unto destruction (vv. 21,27-30). (3) It is not the witness of Jesus alone that the Jews reject, but the witness of God (vv. 32,37-38), of John the Baptist (vv. 33-35), of Jesus' works (v. 36), and of the Scriptures (vv. 39-47).

The fourth and fifth signs (6:1-71).—Jesus' feeding of the multitude and its effects comprise the fourth "sign" (vv. 1-15,22-71), while the fifth "sign," walking on the Sea of Galilee, is woven into the context in accordance with the Synoptic order of events (vv. 16-21). That the feeding occurs during a Passover season (v. 4) indicates Jesus is the fulfilment of the Jewish Passover and no longer will it be necessary for the Jews to continue that feast. As customary, the Jews miss the true significance of the "sign" and interpret it as confirmation of their suspicions that Jesus desires to become an earthly king, a move they are willing to support (vv. 14-15).

In order to avoid this temptation, Jesus withdraws to a lonely place and his miraculous walking on the sea serves as the medium to reunite Jesus and his disciples in Capernaum, where the deeper implications of the feeding are given: Jesus is the Bread of life, apart from whom man cannot live; and his body and blood accomplish in reality for man what the Passover could effect only by way of symbol (vv. 22-59). As an outcome of this "sign" and its interpretation, a firm line is drawn between the disciples who perceive 'ts meaning and the Jews who stumble at its severity (vv. 60-71).

Controversy during the Feast of Tabernacles (7:1 to 8:59).[41] —Jesus' decision to go to Jerusalem during the Feast of Tabernacles (7:1-13), as his decision to perform the sign at Cana (2:3-5), indicates his complete independence of human authority in all actions. Two themes are interwoven into this narrative of Jesus' visit to Jerusalem.

(1) As Jesus is the fulfilment of the Passover, so also he is the fulfilment of the Feast of Tabernacles. This Feast commemorated God's provision of Israel during their sojourn in the wilderness and

---

[41]"For Jesus as the fulfilment of the Jewish feasts, see T. C. Smith, *Jesus in the Gospel of John* (Nashville: Broadman Press, 1959), pp. 145-83.

testified to the continuing provision of Israel by their God. The Fourth Gospel states that what the Jews professed as part of their sacred past and anticipated as part of their future through the Feast of Tabernacles had been accomplished in Jesus Christ. In Jesus' day the symbols of light and water had been incorporated into the celebration of the Feast, and it is against this background that the claims of Jesus to be the Light of the world and the Water of life must be understood: the material blessings of light and water, memorialized in this feast, discover their spiritual counterpart in Jesus.

(2) The Jews, who do not possess the Light of the world, are blind both to their own origin (8:31-47) and to the origin and destiny of Jesus (7:25-44; 8:1-30,48-59).

The sixth sign (9:1-41).—Jesus' act of healing the man born blind at once demonstrates that he is the Light of the world and that the Jews are walking in spiritual darkness because they *will not* acknowledge him as the true Light from God. Through this brief narrative one is presented the Johannine concept of judgment. Judgment is the inevitable consequence of one's wilful rejection of Jesus as the One sent from God; and this judgment is a present reality in the lives of those who choose to reject Jesus. Granting of sight to a man born blind should have been sufficient indication that the power of God was operative in the person of Jesus, and the sin of the Jews consisted in their deliberate misinterpretation of this obvious act of God. On this account, the answer to the Pharisee's question, "Are we also blind?" is a categorical, "Yes, you are spiritually blind because you have wilfully closed your eyes to the Light of God which has just flashed in your midst!"

Controversy during the Feast of Dedication (10:1-42).—Chapter 1 of this book mentioned the Feast of Dedication, which was inaugurated by Judas Maccabee in 164 B.C., when the Jews gained repossession of the Temple from the Syrians. It is extremely probable that Jesus' allegory of the Good Shepherd should be interpreted against the background of this Feast, especially since the Gospel alludes to the Feast of Dedication immediately following Jesus' discourse on the Good Shepherd (v. 22).

If this is the case, the allegory becomes a contrast between the type king the Jews would follow and the type king that Jesus was. The Jews would follow a man of military might, such as Judas Maccabee, who would lead them to certain destruction in an insurrection against Rome, but they would not follow the king by whose death they would be delivered from the suzerainty of sin. Accordingly, the Jews could not recognize Jesus as the Christ (Messiah) because they were proceeding on false premises concerning Jesus' messiahship (vv. 23-42).

The seventh sign (11:1-57).—In similar fashion to the first "sign," the seventh "sign" affirms the basic meaning of Jesus' historical appearance. As always, the Jesus of the Fourth Gospel knows the final outcome of all events and so his every movement is made with deliberation. There is no need to hasten to Lazarus' side, for his illness is not ultimately to end in death but in a manifestation of the true power of God (vv. 2-4).

Insight into the Johannine concepts of eschatology and life eternal may be gained from an examination of Jesus' words to Martha. The only death that is to be feared does not affect the Christian believer; for him eternal life is a present reality (v. 26). Even though he should die, he will be restored to life again (v. 25). When Jesus raised Lazarus from the dead, this act became the realization and seal of these words to Martha. Unable to deny the presence of God in what Jesus had done—but, nevertheless, unwilling to con-

25. Olive trees, Gethsemane

fess Jesus as the Son of God—the Jews decided they must destroy him. And the record of Caiaphas' words reflect the bold irony of the Fourth Gospel: through rejection of this one Man, the Jews had unwittingly destroyed their nation.

The arrival of the Greeks (12:20-36).—The anointing at Bethany (12:1-11) and the entry into Jerusalem (12:12-19) have already been discussed in connection with the Synoptic tradition and will not receive further mention. And verses 37-45 deal again with the theme of Jesus' abiding unity with the Father. That the Greeks should approach Jesus immediately prior to the crucifixion is a proleptic hint at the universal appeal of the One who, when lifted up, will draw all men unto himself.

The Last Supper (13:1-38).—In light of the earlier discussion of the Last Supper it is necessary to discuss only the unique Johannine inclusion, Jesus' washing of the disciples' feet (vv. 1-20). One feels it extremely unlikely that this last act of Jesus with his disciples could express anything less than the very heart of the Christian message. No doubt Jesus was demonstrating the true meaning of the incarnation by this act of condescension. To use Pauline terminology, this is the picture of the One who emptied himself and became obedient unto death, even the death of the cross (Phil. 2:5-11). Furthermore, the teaching of Jesus following the washing of the disciples' feet signifies that the destiny of the disciple must be like unto that of his Lord: the disciple must also endure the ignominy of the cross in his service to the unredeemed world.

Fellow-travelers along the way (14:1 to 17:26).—These four chapters may be surveyed together since the latter three chapters reiterate and elaborate themes begun in chapter 14.

(1) Jesus' death will effect the possibility of a more vital union between himself and his disciples than was possible during his earthly sojourn. Before his resurrection-exaltation the presence of Jesus was limited by the confines of his earthly body; but after the resurrection-exaltation his presence can abide permanently with all disciples, no matter how far apart the disciples are from one another. From this recognition develops the further truth that the spiritual presence of Jesus, present wherever disciples exist, can effect "greater works" than the earthly Jesus who was spatially limited by his body of flesh. However, as the analogy between the vine and the branches interjects, the life of discipleship is possible only so long as the disciple remains in union with his Master.

(2) Effectual love is the evidence of true discipleship and of union with Christ. It is important to note that the Fourth Gospel, when speaking of union between the disciple and his Lord, does not concern itself with false notions of a mystical absorption of the one into the other. Rather, union with Christ is evidenced by the disciple's willingness to "lay down his life for his friends," as "Christ loved the church and gave himself up for her," to use again Pauline terminology.

(3) Victory is the final outcome for the life of faith. Although the eyes of the unbelieving world can at present see nothing but defeat for the life of discipleship, the disciple has already seen the victory of God achieved in the work of the Son. And it is the power of God, effective in the spiritual presence of Christ, that enables the disciple to achieve the life of faith amidst the unbelieving world.

Death and resurrection (18:1 to 21:25).—For interpretation of these events, the reader is referred to the previous discussion in conjunction with the Synoptic tradition.

26. Gordon's Calvary, regarded by some as the place of Jesus' crucifixion

4

Jesus Christ and the Kingdom of God

—THE WINE IN FERMENT

So far, we have seen various aspects of the nature of Christ and his message as these are related to the structure of the Gospels. The present chapter will view the same truths from a different perspective. Teachings from the Gospels will be pulled together around certain key ideas, of which the kingdom of God is central. By this approach the unity and coherence of the Gospels' teachings can be brought into clearer focus.

The Person of Jesus Christ

Son of God

Son of God in the Old Testament.—In the Old Testament Israel is often spoken of as the son of God. This is so because there was a peculiar bond existing between God and the nation Israel. The Greeks among others thought of themselves as the offspring of their respective deities, but there was no such idea in Israel. Israel was not the offspring of God; they belonged to God because he had chosen them from among the nations of the earth. From this choice of God grew a reciprocal responsibility between God and Israel; and it was to this mutual relationship that Israel referred when they spoke of themselves as the son of God. When had Israel become the son of God in this sense? Generally the Exodus from Egypt was thought of as the moment when they became the son of God. Hosea (11:1) echoes the voice of God: "When Israel was a child, I loved him; and out of Egypt I called my son."

The more limited concept of the Son of God as Israel's king developed from the larger concept of the nation of Israel as the son of God. Israel's king was the representative of God among the people of the nation. His function was not only to lead the nation in military victories but he was also to keep the attention of the people upon God, their true King. So it was, that at the annual coronation ceremony of the king, God could address the king through the congregation of Israel: "You are my son, today I have begotten you" (Psalm 2:7).

Wherever the notion of sonship to God appeared, whether national or personal, two basic recognitions were present: (1) To be the son of God depended upon the free and sovereign choice of God. (2) Sonship required that the nation (or person) accept the sovereignty of God in obedient trust.

Jesus, the Son of God.—By a voice from heaven at his baptism, Jesus was affirmed to be the Son of God (Matt. 3:17; Mark 1:11; Luke 3:22). The specific words which the Gospels record reflect two Old Testament passages, and so offer a clue to the meaning of Jesus' sonship. Psalm 2:7 ("This is my beloved Son") identifies the one who is baptized as the "King of Israel"; while Isaiah 42:1 ("With whom I am well pleased") describes him as the Servant of God, who suffered without cause for the sake of Israel. When these two ideas are combined, the baptism declares that Jesus, the Son of God, must fulfil his task as the King of Israel through the route of undeserved suffering on his part.

Matthew and Luke, realizing that some readers of Mark's Gospel might conclude that Jesus *became* the Son of God at his baptism, include their nativity narratives to void this faulty judgment. Actually Mark's gospel does not intend to state that Jesus was adopted as the Son of God at his baptism. Rather, Mark is saying that Jesus' entire earthly ministry must be understood as under the direction of the Spirit of God. The First and Third Gospels go a step beyond and remind the readers that the conception of Jesus was by the Holy Spirit as well (Matt. 1:18 f.; Luke 2:25 f.). In the Fourth Gospel the mystery of Jesus' person is unfolded a step further. The Son of God, entitled the Word of God, is shown to have existed eternally in a unique relationship with God the Father. Furthermore, he is himself of the very essence of God and is both creative and life-giving (John 1:1-5).

From the foregoing the reader can immediately see a new dimension in the phrase "Son of God" when referred to Jesus. Whereas, in the Old Testament a uniqueness of relationship to God was implied wherever the term was used, the one referred to was never thought to be of the same essence as God. Viewed from this perspective, Jesus is *the only* Son of God, since he alone bears the divine nature.

What did Jesus' sonship mean for him during the course of his earthly ministry? Perhaps this may best be answered from a glance at the temptation narrative, since it seems to be the purpose of this narrative to answer that question. Each of the three temptations represents a route that Jesus as the Son of God could have chosen for his ministry. Would he concern himself primarily for the physical needs of the people (Matt. 4:1-4; Luke 4:1-4)? Would he attempt to coerce God into proving to the people who he [Jesus] was (Matt. 4:5-7; Luke 4:9-12)? Would he submit to the methods of Satan in order to be victorious over the world (Matt. 4:8-10; Luke 4:5-8)?

That Jesus rejected these more popular concepts and surrendered himself to God in a way that ultimately led to rejection and death intimates what divine sonship involved for Jesus. It meant identity with God to such a degree that the world's attitude toward God would be expressed toward Jesus himself. This truth is explicated most dynamically in the Gospel of John, where Jesus is constantly rejected because of his absolute union with God the Father.

For Jesus then, sonship meant all that it did in the Old Testament, and more. (1) He acted and spoke as he did because it was the will of the Father. (2) Jesus' relationship with God was based upon absolute obedience and trust. (3) Finally, and most significantly, the absolute nature of Jesus' union with the Father necessitated his absolute rejection at the hands of the world in a way that no other person has been rejected. All other men, even those who are "sons of God," are in some measure "of this world," and so are not absolutely rejected by the world. On the other hand, Jesus, who was not "of this world," is necessarily rejected by the men "of this world."

Son of Man

Methods of interpretation.—Without hesitation one can say that the title, "Son of man," is the most enigmatic phrase in the entire New Testament. This is the phrase used most often in the Gospels to refer to Jesus, and so holds an important clue to the understanding of Jesus' person. How can one best discover its meaning?

The son of man in Daniel 7:13 is generally assumed to refer to the "saints of the Most High" (v. 18), by which is meant the nation Israel as opposed to the "animal-like" nations pictured elsewhere in Daniel. That is, the son of man in Daniel is not an individual, but a corporate representative of the entire nation conceived of as the people of God. If Jesus used the term in this corporate sense, it could imply that he thought of himself as the representative of the new people of God, the church.[1]

In the Jewish book of 1 Enoch, a popular treatise written in the first century, the son of man is a preexistent heavenly being who comes at the end of time to vindicate the cause of the righteous and judge the wicked.[2] It may be that this is the best background for understanding the title as it applies to Jesus. But Jesus went far beyond all that is implied in 1 Enoch, for the son of man in 1 Enoch does not have to suffer and he does not forgive sins.

Another viewpoint is to interpret the son of man in the light of the Aramaic (Jesus' language) *bar nasha*. *Bar nasha* literally translated means "son of man," but had a much wider meaning. It was equivalent to the contemporary use of "one" or "we" when used by a speaker to refer to himself. Thus it is suggested that Jesus used a term which could be filled with different implications, depending upon the attitude of the hearer. Were one to know the mystery of Jesus' person, he must have faith to penetrate the meaning of this term; otherwise, like the Pharisees, he would altogether fail to recognize who the Son of man truly was.

Others think the best commentary on the term is the book of Ezekiel, where it appears a number of times, always with reference to the frailty of man as opposed to the eternalness of God. Thereby the term in application to Jesus would be a medium of identifying him with the humanity he came to redeem.[3]

One more recent theory is the attempt to render the phrase in light of Judaism's presentation of the righteous man who suffers unjustly because of his faith in God amidst a perverse society.[4] In God's time the circumstances are reversed. God vindicates the cause of the righteous man and punishes the world of sinners; and through this action the righteous man is "exalted" to a unique relationship with God. One must certainly agree that this "humiliation-exaltation" theme is at the heart of the New Testament doctrine of Christ; and it may be that this is the basic key to understanding what is indicated by the description of Jesus as the Son of man.

[1] T. W. Manson, *op. cit.*, pp. 211-36.
[2] Rudolf Otto, *op. cit.*, pp. 176-261.
[3] George S. Duncan, *Jesus, Son of Man* (London: Nesbet & Co., 1948), pp. 135-205.
[4] Edward Schweizer, *op. cit.*, pp. 22-76.

The Son of man in the Gospels.—Whatever the best route toward understanding the title Son of man, and all those suggested above add some light, it is valuable to note the three categories in which the Son of man references appear in the Gospels. A first group of sayings relate to the humble life of the Son of man on earth. In two of these passages the Son of man is the mediator between God (represented in his Law) and men: he has authority to forgive sins and to abrogate the law of the sabbath (Mark 2:10,28 and parallels). From another aspect the earthly Son of man is mediator, for he stands like Jonah as a sign to call the nation to repentance (Luke 11:30). Although he lives among men, he finds no absolute security in this world, and so "has no place to lay his head" (Matt. 8:20). Thus the Son of man is a being of mystery, for he possesses divine authority, yet appears to the eyes of men as one who is like them.

A second category of sayings declares that the Son of man must suffer and be rejected by men (Mark 8:31; 9:31; 10:32-34 and parallels). The Son of man, obedient to God in all respects, is rejected by men who refuse obedience to God and by men whose lives his presence disturbs.

A final group of sayings deal with the victory and exaltation of the Son of man, who will be elevated to the right hand of God and come with the full authority of heaven (Mark 8:38; 14:62 and parallels). Rejected by men, the Son of man is marked out by God as his "Chosen One."

From these sayings can be perceived a definite pattern for the way of the Son of man: "humiliation-exaltation." The Son of man, rejected among men, is none other than the possessor of God's Spirit and authority. He stands in the midst of men as the authentic witness to God; and so is spurned and put to death. Yet by his resurrection God reveals the secret of the Son of man to his disciples; a truth which the unbelieving world will be called upon to confess.

Christ (Messiah)

Messiah in Jewish thought.[5]—First, it should be pointed out that the terms "Messiah" and "Christ" are synonyms. "Messiah" is the Hebrew word meaning "an anointed one"; while "Christ" is its Greek counterpart. Anointing was the means in ancient Israel whereby one

---

[5]For a more detailed explanation of the Messiah in Jewish thought, see the previous discussion, "Messiah and messianic age," in chapter 2.

was set aside for some special service to God. Therefore, prophets, priests, and kings were all spoken of at various times as the "anointed of God." However, the phrase, "anointed one of God," when used absolutely, finally came to indicate none other than the king of Israel. Thereby the Messiah was immediately identified with the nationalistic hopes and aspirations of Israel, especially as they had been realized in David the ideal king.

Jesus the Messiah.—A close reading of the Gospels will immediately reveal Jesus' reticence to make openly any messianic claims for himself. From all indications he also apparently attempted to suppress any aspirations of this sort on the part of his followers. Near Caesarea Philippi Jesus asked his disciples who they believed him to be, whereupon Peter responded, "You are the Christ [Messiah]" (Mark 8:29).

According to Mark's account, Jesus sternly prohibited Peter to repeat this to anyone, and followed this warning with the surprising statement, "It is necessary for the *Son of man* to suffer many things" (Mark 8:31). One must conclude from this narrative either that Jesus did not understand himself to be the Messiah, or else he reinterpreted his messiahship in a way others would not understand. As the reader will recall from the preceding discussion, the Jews did not understand the Messiah as a spiritual leader; and no doubt Jesus' hesitation to accept this title was due to the popular conception of the Messiah in the minds of the people. Jesus was, indeed, the "anointed one of God," but his anointing was other than to be a political sovereign of the Jewish nation.

Matthew's account of Peter's confession adds a new perspective, but first it is important to recall that Matthew's Gospel was written with a different emphasis than the Gospel of Mark. In Matthew's Gospel, Peter not only declares that Jesus is the Christ but further characterizes him as the Son of God (16:16). This indicates that Matthew's usage of the title is conditioned, not by the narrow messianic viewpoint of Judaism, but by the broader Christian concept of Christ as a universal Saviour and the very Son of God. Thereby, Matthew does not hesitate to have Jesus praise the confession of Peter as a deep spiritual insight effected by God himself (16:17-18).

Of course Mark also believes that Jesus is the Son of God, but he does suggest that this was not what Peter meant when he *originally* confessed at Caesarea Philippi that Jesus was the Christ. Mark likely intends his readers to recognize that Peter himself was earlier conditioned by the nationalistic hopes of Judaism, and saw the possibility of their fulfilment in Jesus. But this earlier misconception had to be corrected, so that Peter would come to recognize what it really meant for Jesus to be the "anointed one of God." Matthew writes more from the perspective of what Peter subsequently came to discover concerning the significance of Jesus' messiahship: he was the anointed Son of God who achieved his purpose for mankind through suffering and death.

Later, Mark does record Jesus' affirmation that he *is* the Christ (14:62). Strangely enough this is the *only* passage in the Synoptic Gospels where Jesus himself explicitly states that he is the Christ, and it is made in answer to the question of the high priest at Jesus' trial. But serious questions are raised regarding exactly what Jesus did say, inasmuch as all three of the Synoptics differ at this juncture (Matt. 26:64; Mark 14:62; Luke 22:67-70). Mark, in fact, is the only one of the three Synoptics to say that Jesus answered affirmatively. What can be concluded from this passage? Negatively, it is impossible to draw from this passage a conclusion regarding Jesus' "messianic consciousness"; the passage is too ambiguous for any dogmatic conclusion in this direction. Positively, one must conclude that Mark felt compelled at some point in his Gospel to state forthright his conviction, in the full Christian sense, that Jesus was the Christ. Thus, at a very climactic moment in his Gospel, Mark openly presents Jesus as the Christ. The Christian reader realizes what this implies; but the Jewish high priest in his spiritual blindness condemns to death the "anointed of God."

Servant of God

The servant in the book of Isaiah.—In the last half of Isaiah are at least four so-called "servant songs" (42:1-4; 49:1-6; 50:4-9; 52: 13 to 53:12). Opinions differ widely with regard to the interpretation of the servant figure. Some see in the servant either the nation Israel or a righteous group within the nation; others believe the servant to have been an individual figure such as Moses, Jeremiah, or Isaiah. For purposes of this study the identity of the servant is not as important as the recognition of certain traits that characterize him.

Basic in the servant songs is the recognition that God has chosen the servant and given him his Spirit. God addresses him as "my chosen [one], in whom my soul delights" and declares, "I have put my spirit upon him" (Isa. 42:1). And the servant acknowledges,

"The Lord called me from the womb, from the body of my mother he named my name" (49:1). This chosen servant does all according to the divine will; and even of his suffering it may be said, "It was the will of the Lord to bruise him" (53:10).

The servant was chosen that he might effect the redemption of God's people by bearing their iniquities and becoming "an offering for sin" (53:10-11). Because the servant was not believed by the people to whom he ministered, he was "wounded," "bruised," and "oppressed." Yet it was by the stripes laid upon him that the people were healed (53:3-5).

However, the servant's destiny remains unfulfilled until God elevates him to a status beyond the imagination of his adversaries:

> Behold, my servant shall prosper,
>   he shall be exalted and lifted up,
>   and shall be very high. . . .
> so shall he startle many nations (Isa. 52:13-15)

Jesus as the Servant of God.—Only a few passages in the Gospels characterize Jesus by specific reference to the servant songs, but New Testament scholars tend to maintain that Jesus was significantly influenced by the life of the Suffering Servant. In general support of this supposition is the undeniable argument that Jesus was thoroughly familiar with the Old Testament and seemed especially attached to Deuteronomy and Isaiah. Also the Gospels themselves appeal to Isaiah in relation to aspects of Jesus' ministry other than in the matter of his suffering and death. For example, Matthew 8:16-17 quotes Isaiah 53:4 as having its fulfilment in Jesus' healing ministry, "He took our infirmities and bore our diseases." Matthew 12:18-21 quotes Isaiah 42:1-4 in a similar fashion. When Jesus reads from the Old Testament in the synagogue at Nazareth (Luke 4:16-19), he selects a passage from Isaiah, "The Spirit of the Lord is upon me" (Isa. 61:1-2).

More specifically, reflections on the servant passages glimmer through the passion narratives of the Gospels. Luke's account contains a saying from Jesus which incorporates a direct quote from Isaiah, "For I tell you that this scripture must be fulfilled in me, 'And he was reckoned with transgressors'" (22:37). "For the Son of man also came not to be served but to serve, and to give his life as a *ransom* for many" (Mark 10:45) may be a direct allusion to Isaiah 53:5. Furthermore, the words of Jesus at the Last Supper

27. Gaza (see Acts 8:26-40)

intimate in this direction: Jesus' body is to be broken and his blood shed *for many* (Isa. 53:11). Finally, as previously indicated, the voice at Jesus' baptism identifies him with the Suffering Servant.

From the foregoing, it can be seen that each of the names applied to Jesus in the Synoptic Gospels contains essentially the same content and pattern. (1) Jesus, the Chosen One of God, possesses God's Spirit and authority, and so is an authentic witness to God. (2) At all times and under all circumstances Jesus is absolutely submissive to the will of God. (3) He meets rejection at the hands of men, because men are unwilling to receive his person and message. (4) God, in his own time, will vindicate Jesus and grant him to share the final victory.

It is in no wise unexpected that all these names of Jesus should converge on these primary traits of Jesus' person. The Gospels utilize various names to describe Jesus, but they all refer to the *one*

Lord. Nor is it surprising to discover the apparent analogies between Jesus and certain figures at the heart of the Jewish faith and hope. In the same manner that men of God in the past had walked by faith and obedience, so did Jesus. Thus the nature of his life and the attitude of the world toward him would be expected to be analogous to what the men of God had experienced in times past. However, as the Gospels bear abundant testimony, Jesus achieved what others could not, for he alone stood in an absolute relationship with the Father.

Jesus in the Gospel of John

Jesus in the Gospel of John is the same Jesus one finds in the Synoptic Gospels, only John carries further the implications of Jesus' person. John and the Synoptics differ not so much in their understanding of Jesus as in their presentation of him. In the Synoptic Gospels the disciples gradually come to realize who Jesus is; but from the very first of John's Gospel the messiahship and divine sonship of Jesus are openly acknowledged (1:45,49; 4:29; 6:68-69). Thereby John makes *explicit* from the beginning of his Gospel what was *implicit* throughout the Synoptics: Jesus is at once the Christ and the Son of God. Since a relatively full discussion has been given each of these names of Jesus as they appear in the Synoptic Gospels, the discussions in this section will be limited to the peculiar emphases rendered these same names in the Gospel of John.

Son of God.—After Jesus had healed a lame man on the sabbath, the Jews became further angry with him because he made himself equal to God (5:18). These words express not only the judgment of Jesus' opponents, but much more the basic theology of the Gospel: an essential *unity* exists between the Father and the Son. Accordingly, the Son acts solely upon the authority of the Father (5:19). Growing out of this oneness is the fact that the Son possesses both the power to give life and the authority to exercise judgment for the Father (5:21-23). The most climactic revelation of the identity between the Father and the Son is the realization that God's love for mankind is seen in the self-giving of the Son (3:16).

Son of man.—The Son of man has his origin in heaven, "No one has ascended into heaven but he who descended from heaven, the Son of man" (John 3:13; see 6:62). While on earth the Son of man is the ladder between God and man: "You will see heaven opened, and the angels of God ascending and descending upon the

Son of Man" (1:51). Because the Son of man has come from heaven, he can offer to men "food which endures to eternal life" (6:27).

Central to the doctrine of the Son of man is the declaration that he must be "lifted up" (3:14; 8:28; 12:32,34). In the Gospel of John this statement is made only of the Son of man, and it always has a twofold meaning. To be "lifted up" refers immediately to the Son of man's exaltation and to the route by which it is accomplished, that is, to the cross. The highest glory of the Son of man is paradoxically revealed in his moment of deepest humiliation.

Messiah.—Jesus' disciples immediately acknowledge him to be the Messiah, but in typical Johannine fashion "the eyes of sinful man his glory cannot see." Herein lies the double aspect of Jesus' messiahship in the Gospel of John: it is both revealed and hidden. Although the Jews are initially prepared to accept him as the messianic King (6:15), they miss the real significance of Jesus' messiahship and so finally reject him (6:66). Only the faithful perceive who he truly is and what he has to offer (6:67-69).

In the allegory of the sheep this "revealed-hidden" motif is further elaborated (10:1 ff.). The Jews willingly accept the false messianic pretenders with their selfish nationalistic hopes and lack of concern for the "sheep." On the other hand, the majority of the Jews reject Jesus, the true "Shepherd Messiah"; only a few "hear his voice." Before Pilate this theme is again introduced (18:33 ff.). Jesus is, indeed, "King of the Jews," but Pilate cannot penetrate the depth of Jesus' person or conceive the nature of his kingdom. None other than a "true Israelite" like Nathanael can recognize: "You are the Son of God! You are the King of Israel!" (1:49).

Word of God.—It is necessary to discuss in more detail the phrase "Word of God," which is applied to Jesus only in John's Gospel. Both in its Greek and Jewish heritage the term "Word" connoted much more than is apparent in English translation.

The Stoics, a pre-Christian philosophical school, had utilized the term "word" to great advantage in the formulation of their theology and world view. For the Stoics the "word" was the rationale, an impersonal sort of "deity," which gave meaning and unity to the world order. Within each man was a "word spark," which guided him in his destiny and gave purpose to his life. In Stoicism, then, the "word" was at once their "god" and the medium through which the divine will was disclosed to each man.

In the Old Testament the "word of God" plays a significant role.

All Judaism would agree with the psalmist's declaration, "By the *word* of the Lord the heavens were made" (33:6. See also the account in Genesis 1, where God *speaks* and all creation comes into being). Furthermore, God not only creates but reveals through his word, as is recognized by the Old Testament prophets who constantly affirm, "The *word* of the Lord came to me." By way of summary, one can say that the "word of God" in Old Testament thought had functions relating both to *creation* and *revelation*. And the fact that this word is always the word *of God,* suggests an intimate relationship between God and his word, so that one can *almost* conclude that the word is God himself, described in his creative-redemptive activity.

The prologue to John's Gospel (1:1-18), especially verses 1-5 and 14, unfold his understanding of the "Word of God." The *Word* not only has existed eternally with God the Father, but is himself of the same essence with the Father (vv. 1-2). Furthermore, it was through the *Word* that all creation was brought into existence; and all creatures have their source of life in him (vv. 3-5).

Thus far John has not gone basically beyond what could have

28. Joppa (see Acts 9:36-43)

been said in Judaism or in certain segments of the Greco-Roman world concerning the "Word." Verse 14, however, expresses the dis tinctively Christian confession, "The Word became flesh and dwelt among us." By this statement the *eternal Word* is identified with the *historical Jesus.* It is imperative to realize that John indicates by this statement a genuine incarnation, for the term "flesh" includes more than merely a physical body. John is declaring that Jesus of Nazareth was at once "truly God" and "truly man" (flesh). In an event unique among all historical happenings, the eternal *Word* of God entered human history as a man among men; and it is because of this act of divine grace that mankind has hopes of redemption.

Embodied then in the Johannine doctrine of the *Word* of God are all the concepts contained in the other names of Jesus in the Gospels. Presupposed are the divine initiative and the perfect human response. And John knows that his readers will understand that the coming of the *Word* resulted in the cross, for "his own people received him not" (1:10-11). John also believes in the ultimate triumph of the *Word,* because the Son of man (the *Word* become man) must be "lifted up." An early Christian hymn very appropriately summarizes the Johannine presentation of the *Word* who,

> Because he appeared in human form,
>   He emptied himself,
>   becoming obedient unto death.
> Therefore God highly exalted him,
>   and gave to him
>   the Name above every other name (Phil. 2:7-10).

The Message of Jesus

The Nature of the Kingdom

Before entering into a discussion relevant to the meaning of the kingdom of God in the preaching of Jesus, a few preliminary remarks are necessary. It should be pointed out that the terms "kingdom of God" and "kingdom of heaven" are synonymous in meaning. The latter of these, confined entirely to the Gospel of Matthew, seems to have been chosen by him for the sake of circumventing mention of the sacred name of God. Matthew's reason for this preference may have been determined in part by his intended readers, who appear to have been Jewish Christians.

A second detail is equally as important and somewhat more dif-

ficult to formulate.   Perhaps it is best projected by way of a question:
What would the average Jew of the first century have had in mind
upon hearing the phrase "kingdom of God"?   The answer to this
inquiry is not at all easy, although there are a few generalizations
that may be made without risk of dangerous error.   First, the word
rendered "kingdom" would have had a significantly different connotation for him than it does for the man of the present day.   To
modern ears the word "kingdom" relates primarily to the *territory*
over which a sovereign rules, whereas for the Jew of Jesus' day it
would have been understood more as the *authority* or *rule* exercised
by the sovereign.   The kingdom of God must then be understood
primarily as the *authority of God* exercised among his people.

Second, since the authority of God was not executed in a vacuum,
the kingdom of God could also be interpreted as the people or territory over which God's rule was in force.   However, one should
never forget that this second definition was derived from the former,
and not vice versa.   Thus Israel could be spoken of both as the
people of God and the kingdom of God (Ex. 19:5-6), for it was in
Israel that God's rule received a unique recognition.

Third, when Jesus preached concerning the kingdom of God, he
was speaking in the primary sense of the word in that he was calling
upon men to accept the will of God in their lives.   For Jesus, the
kingdom was not limited to the nation Israel; nor was it confined
to their so-called "sacred land."   The kingdom of God was present
wherever men acknowledged the authority of God—indeed, the kingdom was present whether or not men acknowledged the will of God,
for it was there to judge those who refused his will.

With this brief definition as a background, the remainder of this
chapter will elaborate the meaning of the kingdom of God in the
proclamation of Jesus.

The Presence of the Kingdom

Mark summarized the initial preaching of Jesus with these words,
"The time is fulfilled, and the kingdom of God is at hand; repent,
and believe in the gospel" (Mark 1:15; see Matt. 4:17).   But the
meaning of the affirmation, "The kingdom of God is at hand," is
not altogether evident.   Did Jesus mean thereby that the kingdom
was *close at hand* and would soon appear, or did he mean that the
kingdom was *already present* in his ministry?   That this word was
spoken in conjunction with the statement concerning the "fulfilment

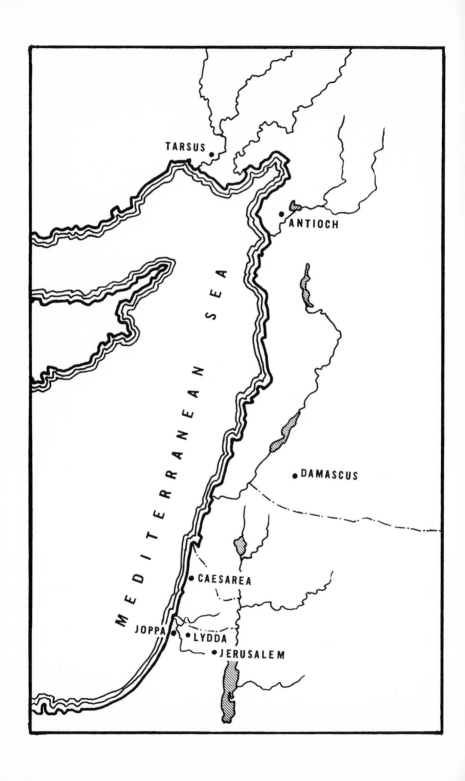

of time" suggests the latter emphasis was uppermost in the mind of Jesus. This is not to say that Jesus did not expect a future moment when the kingdom would be manifest before the entire world; it is to say that there is much evidence to support the contention that Jesus *did* believe the kingdom was present in his ministry.

Both by *word* and *deed* Jesus attested to the presence of the kingdom. At the outset of his ministry Jesus commented upon the verse of Scripture he had read in the Nazareth synagogue, "Today this scripture has been fulfilled in your hearing" (Luke 4:21). He had reference to the passages from Isaiah (61:1-2; 58:6):

> The Spirit of the Lord is upon me,
>   because he has anointed me *to preach* good news to the poor.
> He has sent me *to proclaim* release to the captives and recovering
>   of sight to the blind,
> to set at liberty those who are oppressed,
> *to proclaim* the acceptable year of the Lord (Luke 4:18-19).

Evidently Jesus interpreted his *preaching* of the "good news" as an integral part of the kingdom's presence in the midst of the people.

A similar saying, uttered under different circumstances, validates this interpretation. When John the Baptist sent messengers to ask Jesus if he was the "Coming One," Jesus' response was twofold. First, he healed several sick people and then answered, "Go and tell John what you have seen and *heard:* the blind receive their sight, the lame walk, lepers are cleansed, and the deaf hear, the dead are raised up, *the poor have good news preached to them"* (Luke 7:22). Once more the *message* of Jesus is put forth as a vital part of those events which constitute the presence of the kingdom.

After the disciples of the Pharisees and the disciples of John the Baptist questioned Jesus why his disciples were not in the habit of fasting, Jesus replied, "Can the wedding guests fast while the bridegroom is with them?" (Mark 2:19). Fasting takes place only by way of preparation for the great event; when the *wedding day is present,* one rejoices as the disciples of Jesus. The long awaited day of divine intervention had arrived; the kingdom of God was present in the person of Jesus, the "bridegroom."

Attached directly to the parable of the wedding are the parables

29. Map: Some places mentioned in the early chapters of Acts

concerning the wine skins and the new garments (Mark 2:21-22). Each of these affirms in its own way the presence of the new era. It is not possible to contain the living word of God in the dead skins of Judaism; *the new wine had come* and must form its own wine skins. Like an old dried-out garment, Judaism could not at all adapt itself to the *new cloth; the presence of the new garment* demanded the putting away of the old.

Jesus, accused of being in league with Satan, related a parable about a strong man who was able to defend his household until one stronger than he broke into the house (Mark 3:27). That Satan is the "strong man" and Jesus the "stronger one" is surely the interpretation intended. Jesus had stormed the stronghold of Satan, and the outcome was Satan's fall from heaven like a bolt of lightning (Luke 10:18). Nothing less than the inbreak of the kingdom of God could possibly have caused the downfall of Satan, an indication that the kingdom had come in power.

Several sayings declare the end of the law and the prophets, an affirmation that could not have been made without the authority of the kingdom of God. More than once Jesus remarked, "You have heard it said, but I say to you." By abrogating the ancient laws of Israel and establishing his own words in their stead, Jesus indicated that the kingdom of God had come to annihilate the "commandments of men." In the same Sermon on the Mount a "new righteousness" and a "new law" had come forth to replace the old, a further intimation of the kingdom's presence. Through no other means could the law and the prophets be fulfilled (Matt. 5:17), except in the name of the kingdom of God.

At least two other words of Jesus substantiate the thesis that the kingdom was present in his person and ministry. As the disciples were rejoicing over the outcome of their preaching-healing ministry, Jesus exclaimed, "Blessed are the eyes which see what you see! For I tell you that many prophets and kings desired to see what you see, and did not see it, and to hear what you hear, and did not hear it!" (Luke 10:23). What else had been the mutual anticipation of Israel's kings and prophets, if not the kingdom of God?

Complementary to this passage is the rebuke Jesus gave the Pharisees who were seeking celestial signs for the sake of predicting the arrival of the kingdom. Jesus adjured them, "The kingdom of God is not coming with signs to be observed; nor will they say, 'Lo, here it is!' or 'There!' for behold, *the kingdom of God is in the midst of you"* (Luke 17:20-21). There is a problem of translation involved with the Greek phrase here rendered, "in your midst." Some have translated it "within you." Two factors speak in behalf of the present translation. (1) The Greek form of "you" is plural, not singular, and so "among you" or "in your midst" is a more satisfactory reading than "within you." (2) Would Jesus have told the Pharisees that the kingdom of God was within *them?* Then one is bound to conclude that in both instances Jesus openly affirmed the presence of the kingdom.

No less than three deeds performed by Jesus during the last week of his earthly ministry reveal the presence of the kingdom. The first of these is his entry into Jerusalem. Although there are significant problems of interpretation connected with this passage, it is not illogical to suggest that Jesus' intention was expressed in the words of the populace, "Blessed be the kingdom of our father David that is coming" (Mark 11:10)! With Jesus' arrival had come the kingdom! To be sure, the people deeply misunderstood the nature of the kingdom, despite the fact that Jesus entered upon a donkey rather than upon the white charger of a warrior-king. Nevertheless, the kingdom of God *had arrived* in their midst, and Jesus had consciously attempted to disclose the mystery of its presence through this means.

A second act, the cleansing of the Temple, illustrates even more dramatically the arrival of the kingdom. It is not insignificant that the Synoptics have placed this event in immediate juxtaposition to the story of Jesus' arrival. The kingdom had come, but what did this imply with respect to the institutionalized religion of Judaism? By Jesus' actions in the Temple precincts, the answer was made evident: the Jerusalem Temple stood under the judgment of God because of its failure to adequately prepare men for the arrival of the kingdom.

During the course of the Last Supper with his disciples, Jesus spoke of a "covenant" which he was making with them (Mark 14: 22-25). The hope of a "new covenant" was spoken of earlier by Jeremiah (31:31-34) as one aspect of the day in which God would make himself immediately available to his people. Expressed otherwise, a "new covenant" could be made only as God's kingdom arrived in power.

Jesus, by his actions in conjunction with this meal, left no doubt that this hour had finally appeared.

The Crisis of the Kingdom

Hearing the message of the kingdom is in itself a most crucial event, more crucial even than the urgent demands of war. As a king must calculate the awesome risks of war, so must the hearer of the gospel evaluate seriously the binding decision which lies before him (Luke 14:28-32). Should he "go to war"? Should he "begin to build"? These questions are indicative of the tremendous decisions evoked by the kingdom's presence; and the consequences are so enormous that one dare not risk a wrong judgment. To misjudge the weight of the message or the monument of the moment would be to build one's future upon a foundation of sand (Matt. 7:24-27).

Other of Jesus' words emphasize the crucial nature of the hour ushered in by the kingdom's presence. For Israel the ultimate crisis had arrived. The entire nation, especially their religious leaders, were comparable to an unfruitful fig tree in a garden. The owner had cultivated the tree with meticulous concern, yet no figs had been produced. At last the final opportunity had drawn nigh; the long overdue harvest must come now or never! (Luke 13:6-9). As it had happened with Sodom and Gomorrah, so would it happen to this generation who had heard the message of the kingdom and refused its demands (Luke 17:28-30). Not at all unlike the sinners of Noah's day were these "self-righteous" persons who denied the appeal and the warning of the kingdom (Luke 26:25-27). This generation of "blind leaders" and "blind followers" would be struck with a sword and with fire (Matt. 15:14; 10:34; Luke 12:49).

Although many felt secure because of a "righteousness" which they presumed to possess, there was no escaping the judgment unless they too repented (Luke 13:4-5). And the murder of a band of Galileans by Pilate testified, not to a superior "goodness" possessed by the unscathed Judeans, but rather to their own need of repentance (Luke 13:1-3). Even on the day of judgment many witnesses would rise against those people who had willingly closed their ears to the words of the kingdom (Matt. 12:41-42.) Their only hope was to right themselves with God immediately, like a man on the way to be sued in court attempts to settle with his adversary (Luke 12:57-59).

However, the people as a whole failed to perceive the critical aspect of their historical situation, and so could be likened to senseless children playing in the marketplace. Children, indeed, they were, children unaffected either by the dirge of repentance or by the joyous melody of salvation (Matt. 11:16-17). Had they only recognized the moment of divine visitation, how refreshing the day would have become (Luke 13:34-35)! If they looked for a sign (Luke 11:29), a sign was there—the Son of man himself (Luke 11:30).

A few of Jesus' more familiar parables emphasize both the blindness of the people and the severity of the crisis that had befallen them. A man's crops had yielded an unusually abundant harvest, so much that it was imperative to construct new and larger barns. Because of the prosperity afforded him by this rich harvest, he could live luxuriously for many years to come. He could eat, drink, and be merry (Luke 12:13-21). How blind he was to the reality of his circumstances—this very day his soul would be required of him!

Although this parable teaches a lesson concerning the futility of an absolute dependence upon material goods, its primary purpose is to emphasize the extreme necessity of reckoning with the immediate demands of the kingdom. Jesus had heralded the claims of the kingdom, and the Jewish nation had sat idly by, charmed with their false sense of religious security. The issue was more crucial than they dared realize, for the judgment of God was imminent and they were unprepared.

The parable of Lazarus and the rich man is not far different in its emphasis. Lazarus, whose name means "God helps," represents the outcasts of society who have received the message of the kingdom. These are the "sick" who have need of a "physician," the sinners who have need of repentance. When death comes, Lazarus is taken to the "bosom of Abraham," a typical Jewish description of heaven as a banquet with Abraham at the head of the table. On the other hand, the rich man also received God's final judgment on his life. Here the main point of the parable comes to light. The rich man pleads that someone be permitted to return from the dead for the sake of warning his brothers about the severity of God's judgment. He is reminded that they have "Moses and the prophets" (i.e., the Old Testament) as a witness to them. If they will not hearken to this witness, they would not listen, even if one did rise from the dead.

Amid their constant "seeking for a sign," the Jews had missed the testimony of God both in their Scriptures and in the proclamation of the One who spoke to them of the kingdom's presence. One who does not obey the word of God will not be converted even by a "sign" from heaven.

Again the Jewish nation could be depicted as a group of "share-croppers" who refused their responsibilities to the owner of their land (Mark 12:1-9). They had rejected every past plea made to them by the owner. Now they would rid themselves of the One who offered them this final moment of repentance. Surely this parable underlines the crisis of the hour in which Jesus preached to the Jewish people. By ridding themselves of this prophet, they felt they would relinquish themselves of any demands made by his message. They were wrong. God would punish severely these ungrateful tenants (Mark 12:9).

How should they react? What was expected of them in this crisis? Jesus made reference to something that had recently happened. A man had been cheating his employer over a long period of time and was found out. Knowing that he soon would lose his employ, the man acted swiftly. He permitted all his employer's debtors to cancel out their bills at great discounts, thereby guaranteeing himself a number of friends who could help him after he was fired (Luke 16:1-8). Jesus did not commend the employee's practice, though he did point to the man's *wisdom in evaluating his situation*. Were the Jewish people half so wise, they would perceive their desperate circumstances and seek to become "friends" of God by the acceptance of his will. The kingdom of God was at hand! Would they be wise enough to *repent* and *believe* the gospel?

The Cross and the Kingdom

Thus far it has been shown that the kingdom of God, present in the person and message of Jesus, effected a crisis both for the individual and for the nation as a whole. Furthermore, this crisis was so solemnly serious that the necessity of an immediate response was laid upon the hearer. The particular goal of this section is to indicate what was involved in one's obedience to the demands of the kingdom. First, attention will be directed to what was involved for the herald of the kingdom.

At the outset of his preaching mission the masses appear to have been favorably impressed with Jesus, but this popularity was not long lasting. The religious leaders were not slow to discover that his message implied the end of their well-oiled institutional machinery, and soon the people realized that he did not intend to become a political-military leader. When these two factors were combined, hostility was the inevitable result. Must one infer thereby that Jesus had no control over his own destiny; that he was put to death solely by the power of the people? Another conclusion is more in accord with the evidence of the Gospels.

Jesus' rejection and death were of his own choosing. This is not at all to imply that Jesus died either as a hero-martyr or as a disillusioned visionary. Jesus died as he lived, a *faithful servant of God* in a rebellious and sinful society. It is in this sense that Jesus' death can be considered an act of his own will. Always he was faced with the choice of absolute commitment to God or something less. Had he chosen other than the will of God, he could no doubt have escaped the agony and ignominy of the cross. Yet he chose obedience to God, and in so doing to accept the inevitable consequences.

Nor can it be said that Jesus was oblivious to his fate. From reading the Old Testament and from observing the destiny of John the Baptist, he knew "a prophet was not honored in his own country" (see also Mark 6:4; 9:9-13). Was it strange that Jerusalem should stone those who came to her in the name of God (Matt. 23:37)? One would have to have been blind to miss the overt antagonism of his opponents. The Gospels offer typical examples of hostility from the Herodians (Mark 12:13-17), the Sadducees (Mark 12:18-27), and the scribes of the Pharisees (Mark 12:28-34). Even Herod, who mistakenly looked upon Jesus as a possible revolutionary, had indicated his desire to apprehend Jesus (Luke 9:7-9; 23:8).

So intense was the enmity encountered that Jesus even expressed his wish that it would all soon be accomplished: "I have a baptism to be baptized with; and how I am constrained until it is accomplished!" (Luke 12:50). Moreover, it is quite probable that the Gospel writers intended the transfiguration to be understood as an occasion on which Jesus was strengthened for the fate that awaited him in Jerusalem (especially Luke 9:31). Finally, how else can the words in Gethsemane be interpreted? "Father, all things are possible to thee; remove this cup from me; yet not what I will, but what thou wilt" (Mark 14:36).

From the foregoing one can see the fate that awaited the herald of the kingdom. But what was indicated by his demand of *repentance* and *faith* from those who heard the message? Jesus' demand for repentance and faith was not unrelated to his other words, "Take up your cross and follow me" (Matt. 10:38; 16:24). The obedience which Jesus himself practiced must be experienced by those who would enter the kingdom of God. Repentance and faith necessitated the absolute rejection of oneself in surrender to God. And what this submission cost Jesus, it would cost *all* others who would *willingly* go this route. If one counted self, loved ones, or posessions above the call of God, he was not able to enter the kingdom (Luke 14:25-28). Were one unwilling to place his hand on the plow and not turn back, he could not follow (Luke 9:62). As with the herald, so with the "hearer"—faithful *commitment* and the inevitable *cross!*

Why is one willing to respond to the call of the kingdom, if he knows that he must experience the cross? In part, this question is answered by the author of Hebrews in his description of Jesus as the one "who for the joy that was set before him endured the cross" (12:2). Jesus is said to have accepted the absolute call of God, not only because he felt the necessity to perform God's will, but because he was confident that the final victory belonged to God.

This judgment in no way demeans the vitality of Jesus' commitment; rather it suggests that his faith was sufficient to perceive the real dimension of life behind the veneer of this world. Despite all that the call of God cost him, he believed that the kingdom of God superseded all other values. Jesus was willing to "bet his life" that this insight was true, and he attempted to communicate this truth to his followers.

In at least two parables Jesus emphasized both the *value* of the kingdom and the genuine *joy* that comes with its discovery.

> The kingdom of heaven is like *treasure* hidden in a field, which a man found and covered up; then *in his joy* he goes and sells all that he has and buys that field. Again, the kingdom of heaven is like a merchant in search of fine pearls, who, on finding *one pearl of great value,* went and sold all that he had and bought it (Matt. 13:44-46).

No doubt these two parables were transmitted together because they convey the same truth; and it is not accidental that the phrase "in his joy" stands in the center, because this is a primary emphasis of *both* parables. The kingdom brings *joy* to its discoverer, whether the discovery comes unexpectedly or at the end of a long search. And the *value* of the kingdom—it is so great that one will relinquish all else for the sake of its possession! After one has discovered the value of the kingdom of God, he will joyfully undergo persecution, famine, peril, nakedness, or the sword, because he is confident that nothing now can separate him from the love of God (Rom. 8:35-39).

But when one accepts the challenge of the kingdom, he does so not only because of its intrinsic worth but because he knows God's kingdom will be *victorious*. Jesus knew that God would not fail and promised his disciples that they would "sit on twelve thrones, judging the twelve tribes of Israel" (Matt. 19:28). If any disciple has forsaken houses or land, friends or loved ones, he will gain all this and more in the coming age (Mark 10:28-30). As a microscopic seed produces a large garden plant, the small band of Jesus' followers will see the kingdom of God triumph (Matt. 13:31-32). No more can the kingdom be defeated than can leaven be suppressed after having been placed in a lump of dough (Matt. 13:33). Not even the "gates of Hades" can overrule God (Matt. 16:18).

To be sure, the call to the kingdom is a call to accept the cross, but in receiving the cross one discovers real joy and is confident of the final outcome. What this outcome will be is enlarged upon in the next division of this chapter.

The Consummation of the Kingdom

Nowhere does Jesus indicate *when* the consummation of the kingdom will come about. Mark 13 (and parallels, Matt. 24; Luke 21) offers the best commentary on Jesus' ideas relevant to the end of time and the consummation of the kingdom. In this passage Jesus deals with *two* questions presented him by his disciples (v. 4): (1) When will these things (i.e. the destruction of Jerusalem) happen? (2) What will be the sign for the consummation of all things? Perhaps the disciples intended these to have been two aspects of one question, but Jesus answered them separately. To their surprise he did not go immediately to the answer. Rather, he gave them a warning not to be deceived by false "messiahs" or by external events, as though these could in anywise tell one when the end was to come (vv. 5-8). Then he reminded the disciples that they were under obligation to preach the gospel and to suffer the hardships incurred thereby (vv. 9-13). Next, he gave them instructions regarding what their actions should be when the destruction of Jerusalem was felt to be nigh (vv. 14-23). When they see the "desolating sacrilege set up where it ought not to be," they are to flee as swiftly as possible. Luke, writing *after* these events had come about, specifically interprets this "desolating sacrilege" to be the Roman armies surrounding Jerusalem (21:20).

30. Mountains of Lebanon, west of Damascus

At last Jesus turns to the question concerning the end of time and the consummation of all things (Mark 13:24-32). The words in verse 26 rendered "and then" really mean "simultaneously"; thus all the cosmic events described in verses 24-26 take place *at the same time.* By this Jesus indicates that the "signs of the end" and the end itself happen concurrently. What he intimates is not difficult to decipher: there is no need to speculate about the "signs of the end"; when one sees these, it will be too late to prepare himself for the coming of the kingdom.

Jesus uses two illustrations to clarify these words he has just spoken. The former of these, that of the fig tree (vv. 28-30), suggests that the destruction of Jerusalem is a historical event of cause and effect, the time of which may be determined with relative certainty. It should be no more difficult to determine when the Jewish opposition against Rome would erupt into war than it is to predict the season of figs by the leaves on the tree. And Jesus believed this war would come about during the lifetime of those around him (v. 30).

Jesus elaborated his answer to the second question, "of that day or that hour no one knows," with the illustration of the doorkeeper (vv. 32-36). Like a doorkeeper, it is the disciple's responsibility, not to speculate concerning the time of the end, but to *watch!*

The time of the consummation no one knows, one is certain only that it comes *swiftly* and *without warning.* Already this has been demonstrated in the interpretation of Mark 13 (vv. 24-26,32-36). Jesus' parable of the two houses, one built on sand and the other on rock, also emphasizes this same truth (Matt. 7:25-27). With the suddenness and severity of a torrential flood comes the kingdom of God. Matthew relates another parable that makes this further evident (25:1-13). The kingdom of God may be compared to a group of maidens on their way to a nocturnal wedding feast. While waiting for the gates to be opened, some became careless with excitement and failed to secure enough oil to last throughout the evening. Suddenly the cry, "Enter! The feast has begun!" Those who had their lamps in order were allowed to enter, the others were turned away. "Watch therefore, for you know neither the day nor the hour" (v. 13).

Fortunately enough the disciple does not need to know the time of the kingdom's consummation. He needs only to recognize and to perform his Master's will. He must be "like men who are waiting for their master to come home from the marriage feast, so that they may open to him at once when he comes and knocks" (Luke 12:36). The disciple cannot afford to behave like the unwise steward who mistreated persons in his care (Luke 12:44-45), since he may be called to give an account at any moment (Luke 12:46).

During the interval the kingdom will become "infiltrated" with false disciples. The interpretation given to the parable of the sower makes this truth quite evident (Mark 4:15-19). Many will leave their calling to pursue the "pleasures of life" or the "vanity of wealth." Others will forsake the way of discipleship when persecution or hardship arises. From all external appearances the kingdom will be like a field producing both wheat and weeds (Matt. 13:24-30) or like a net that hauls in all kinds of fish (vv. 47-49). Such circumstances may tend to discourage genuine discipleship or to make faithfulness seem senseless. Yet the real disciple knows that it was the "enemy" who sowed the "bad seed," and God will surely deal with the "weeds" in his own time.

The consummation will be a moment of *revelation,* which will expose the innermost secrets of men. "Not every one who says to me, 'Lord, Lord,' shall enter the kingdom of heaven, but he who does the will of my Father who is in heaven. On that day many will say to me, 'Lord, Lord, did we not prophesy in your name, and cast out demons in your name, and do many mighty works in your name?' And then will I declare to them, 'I never knew you; depart from me, you evildoers' " (Matt. 7:21-23).

To do the "will of the Father" is more than the achievement of a successful ministry by the world's standards. God's will is exercised in the inner man; hence the confession, "Lord, Lord," must arise from one's heart. And this inner commitment will express itself through unselfish service, so selfless, indeed, that one is not even conscious that he is serving: " 'Lord, when did we see thee hungry and feed thee, or thirsty and give thee drink? And when did we see thee a stranger and welcome thee, or naked and clothe thee? And when did we see thee sick or in prison and visit thee?' And the

31. Damascus: arch on "the street called Straight"

King will answer them, 'Truly, I say to you, as you did it to one of the least of these my brethren, you did it to me' " (Matt. 25:37-40).

When God brings his kingdom to its final fulfilment, a *reversal* of all *earthly* values will result. The "least" in this world's judgment are pronounced the "greatest" in the kingdom; and the "last" become "first." Many who have pridefully seated themselves at the "head table" will be required to go to the lowest positions when the King alters the seating arrangements (Luke 14:7-11). The lowest man in society and the women of the street will enter the kingdom before the self-righteous, because they repented when confronted with the demand of God (Matt. 21:31-32).

He who has sought to gain his life will lose it, while he who has lost his life for the sake of the kingdom will find life (Matt. 10:39). "Many will come from east and west and sit at table with Abraham, Isaac, and Jacob in the kingdom of heaven, while the sons of the kingdom will be thrown into the outer darkness" (Matt. 8:11-12). The weeping will rejoice; the meek will inherit the earth; the hungry will be fed; and all who have been persecuted for righteousness sake will possess the kingdom (Matt. 5:4 to 6:10).

After the kingdom has been established in its fulness, God and his redeemed will *rejoice* together. A series of three parables in Luke's Gospel portrays this reality. Just as a shepherd rejoices when he recovers his one lost sheep, the heavenly hosts will rejoice over one repentant sinner (15:3-7). Again the final scene in heaven is much like that which takes place when a woman uncovers her misplaced heirloom. The woman, unable to contain her feelings, invites neighbors and friends to celebrate with her. Accordingly, the angels in heaven will join with God in exalted happiness when he has finally reclaimed his people from darkness (15:8-10).

The joy experienced by God over the return of an erring "son" is akin to the joy a father knows when his wayward son has come home. So profoundly happy is the father that he prepares a great banquet and provides his son with the choicest gifts available (15:11-24). In comparable fashion the redeemed of God share with him in the banquet prepared so abundantly for his people (22:30).

Finally, the hour of consummation is a time of *retribution* for the faithless and unrepentant. "Goats" are separated from the sheep (Matt. 25:32-33); "weeds" are removed and burned (13:30); and the "bad fish" are cast away (vv. 47-48). The servant who knew well his master's will and refused to perform it is beaten with many stripes

(Luke 12:47). Those who have failed to use wisely their trusts are deposed of their positions and lose all (Matt. 25:14-30). The steward who has taken selfish advantage of his opportunity is severely punished (Matt. 24:48-51). Salt which has lost its savor is cast out (Matt. 5:13). Those who have refused the invitation are turned away from the banquet hall (Luke 14:15-24). God's "enemies," who did not want him to rule over them, are "slaughtered" before him (Luke 19:27). Men who have not acknowledged the Son of man on earth are disowned before the angels of heaven (Luke 12: 8-9).

The Message of Jesus in the Gospel of John

With the exception of two passages (3:3,5), the Gospel of John does not mention the kingdom of God. In order to understand John's reason for this omission one must bear in mind the readers for whom the gospel was penned. John's readers, whether Jews or Gentiles, were already familiar with the basic content of the Christian message represented in the Synoptic tradition. What they needed was a more thoroughgoing theological treatise which would make explicit some of the implications contained in the Synoptic tradition.

Such a treatise is provided in the Gospel of John. This Gospel *begins* where the Synoptics leave off—with the recognition of Jesus' divine origin and destiny. Because John begins at this point, he can carry further the real significance of Jesus' message, which is *Jesus himself*. Already the Synoptic writers are conscious of this truth, but they mention it only infrequently and with reservation. That is to say, the Synoptics are more concerned to record the *actual words* of Jesus (kingdom of God), while the Gospel of John is more committed to present the *full meaning* of these words (Jesus himself).

Summarily the message of Jesus in the Fourth Gospel may be stated: I am the Redeemer of the world. Because the belief in eternal life is inseparable from the confession that Jesus is man's Redeemer, a discussion of the Johannine concept of eternal life should prove quite valuable.

Eternal life is a much less comprehensive term to the modern mind than it evidently was to the author of the Fourth Gospel, who had a rich heritage in the religious thought of his people. The

32. Old city gate, "street called Straight"

Jewish people in the first century customarily thought of two ages, the present evil age and the coming glorious age. Satan ruled in the present age; whereas, the coming age would inaugurate the reign of God. Literally the phrase "eternal life" means "life in the age," that is, life in the age of God's rule. Therefore, "eternal life" indicated primarily the *quality* of life one experienced in the kingdom of God; the quantitative notion of an unending life was secondary.

The reason the Christian can speak of "eternal life" as a never-ending life is because he concludes that his life shared with God must surely be forever, This is a valid conclusion; only one must never let the former idea slip his mind.

Furthermore, eternal life is more than a future state of the believer. As Jesus is present with the believer, so is the life he brings. John 3:16, perchance the most frequently quoted verse in the Bible, uses the present tense throughout—that he who *believes* (present) might *have* (present) eternal life. When Martha ran to Jesus with the feeling that Lazarus would not have died if Jesus had been present, she discovered an amazing truth: Jesus *is* the resurrection and the life, and whoever lives and believes in him will never die (11:25 f.). Lazarus was not "dead," he was merely "asleep," and Jesus called him forth.

By this deed Jesus evidenced that eternal life was, indeed, a present experience of the believer. Nevertheless, the "presentness" of eternal life does not exhaust its content. Like the kingdom of God, eternal life will have its consummation on the "last day" (6:39).

Through appeal to his divine origin Jesus verified himself to be the Redeemer of mankind. One route by which this identity is affirmed is by his use of the designation "I am." In the Old Testament it is said that God revealed himself to Moses as "I am" (Ex. 3:14). By this expression God declares himself to be the only being with the power of self-existence and with the strength to bring about his own will. Jesus' self-application of this name immediately identifies him with the God of Israel.

Accordingly, Jesus can confess, in agreement with the prologue of the Fourth Gospel (1:1), "Before Abraham was, *I am*" (8:58). Of himself he declares, "I am the way, and the truth, and the life" (14:6); "I am the good shepherd" (10:11); "I am the true vine" (15:1); "I am the bread of life" (6:35,48); "I am the light of the world" (8:12); "I am the resurrection and the life" (11:25). Each of these declarations, in its own fashion, testifies that Jesus mediates life and redemption to all men because he is one with God, the source of life (10:30).

Jesus of John's Gospel is the Saviour of all men, not only because he is from God, but because he is *truly man*. For John the reality of Jesus' humanity is no less significant than the truth of his deity. Unless Jesus is *fully man* as well as *fully God*, the human situation remains in darkness and death. From the very outset of the Gospel the humanity of Jesus is acknowledged, "The Word became flesh" (1:14). All that follows in the Gospel must be understood in light of this thesis statement. Therefore, Jesus hungers and thirsts (4:7-8); he can weep (11:35). So strongly does the pressure of the crowd weigh upon him that he must withdraw alone (6:15). But most of all he can *suffer and die;* and in his death he sheds genuine blood like other men (19:34).

Jesus, very God and very man, brings both salvation and judgment. In the same manner that the kingdom of God effects both the grace and judgment of God, so does the person of Jesus according to the Gospel of John. Condemnation was not at all the ultimate purpose of Jesus' coming, although it became a necessary correlative, since some refused to come to the light (3:19-21). As men were faced with an imminent crisis by the presence of the kingdom, men are presently under the judgment of God, should they reject Jesus. And the blindness of the Pharisees is a typical example of the judgment of God which abides presently upon the world of unbelief (9:39-41). Yet, with salvation, so with judgment, its final fulfilment is not realized until the time of consummation (12:48).

From this brief summary the reader should now be able to discern more completely what was indicated by the earlier statement, that the person of Jesus in the Gospel of John is equivalent to the preaching of the kingdom of God in the Synoptic Gospels. The message of Jesus has now become, as, indeed, it should have become, *Jesus himself*. This is not a perversion of the Synoptic tradition, nor is it a "contradiction" to the Synoptic account—it is, to use a Johannine word, the Spirit of God leading his people to all truth!

5

The Acts of the Apostles

—THE OLD SKINS BURST

Introduction to the Book of Acts

Title and purpose.—The earliest title to the book seems simply to have been "Acts" or "Deeds" with "of the apostles" added by a later scribe, who perhaps felt this addition would explain more accurately what the author originally intended. In light of the relatively insignificant role that the apostles play in Acts, many have doubted whether the judgment of the scribe was correct. Therefore, some have suggested that the title should have been "Acts of the Holy Spirit," since the author is manifestly concerned with the activity of the Holy Spirit. Yet the author's allusions to the Spirit are largely confined to the earlier part of the book and some eleven chapters do not even mention the Spirit.

If the original title was "Acts," it may well be that the author intended thereby for the readers to interpret the events he recorded as the continuing acts of God in the history of the church, in the same manner that the Third Gospel understands the history of Jesus to have been the act of God (Acts 1:1).

What was the author's purpose in recording the continuing activity of God in the history of the church? Did he intend to record either the geographical spread of Christianity from Jerusalem to Rome or the spiritual development of Christianity from the narrow confines of Judaism to a universal religion? Likely he intended to include both themes, since these motifs appear not to have been unrelated in the author's mind. Hence, one might say that the purpose of Acts is to describe the continuity of the salvation-history begun with Adam (Luke 3:38) and continued in the mighty redemptive acts of God in the person of Christ and in the history of the church, whereby God's salvation is made available to all men.

Authorship and historical value.—There is sufficient reason to believe that the author of the Third Gospel was also the author of Acts, but beyond this generalization one encounters much difference of opinion. Tradition has supported Luke, the companion of Paul (Col. 4:14; Phil. 24; 2 Tim. 4:11), as the author. But this opinion has been made less certain than it once was through the recognition of certain historical differences between Acts and the Pauline epistles, especially Galatians.

Though this is so, the differences are no more than one would expect had Luke collected his sources and compiled his record approximately two decades after the majority of Paul's correspondence had been written. Luke would certainly have known that Paul had written letters to various churches during his career, but this does not necessarily imply that Luke would have been familiar enough with all the specific historical allusions in Paul's letters to have avoided any inconsistencies. Nor, if Luke's utilization of Mark is any criterion for judgment, would Luke have felt obligated to remain in absolute agreement with the details of Paul's writings, even if he had possessed an exact knowledge of all Paul's correspondence.

Luke evidently used a number of sources for his composition. Some of these sources were heavily colored by the interpretative insights of their bearers, while other sources were more objective and less interspersed with interpretation. Opinion is divided whether these sources were originally attached more closely to the persons whose activities they describe (e.g., Paul, Peter, Barnabas, and others) or to the geographical centers where these activities took place (e.g., Antioch, Caesarea, and Jerusalem). Possibly the author himself was an eyewitness to some of what he records, as can be deducted from the "we" sections, wherein the author apparently includes himself among those whose experiences he narrates (16:10; 20:6; 21:2).

The overall accuracy of Luke's geographical and cultural details is currently maintained, due in large measure to the results of a series of investigations initiated by Sir William Ramsay.[1] Yet the final value of Acts is more than its accuracy as a historical record.

The historical value of the book as a whole lies, not in the accuracy of the words or actions of the persons in the drama, or the exhaustiveness of its contents, but in the general picture which the author gives of the Christianity of the time, with its endowment of spiritual enthusiasm, the

---

[1] *Saint Paul the Traveller and Roman Citizen* (London: Hodder & Stoughton, 1896).

conditions under which it struggled, and its rapid advance from Jerusalem through a large part of the empire to Rome.[2]

Outline and development.—The most natural outline for Acts is built into the structure of the book itself, wherein are six divisions, each concluded by a summary statement (6:7; 9:31; 12:24; 16:5; 19:20; 28:31).[3] Each phase in the development of Acts is initiated and determined by some individual or group within the Christian community. The first phase, in which the Gospel remains within the confines of Jerusalem, revolves primarily about the "twelve," whose narrow nationalistic outlook is reflected in the question, "Lord, will you at this time restore the kingdom to Israel?" (1:6).

In the second stage of development, Stephen is the decisive personality whose death inaugurates the spread of the faith beyond Jerusalem and Judea (6:8 to 9:31). Peter, Barnabas, and a few others, governed by presuppositions similar to those of Stephen's sermon, are responsible for the spread of the Christian message to a non-Jewish audience (9:32 to 12:24).

The three final phases of development are oriented mainly about the acts of God in the ministry of Paul (12:25 to 28:31).

Survey of the Book of Acts

The Old Wine Skins Swell (1:1 to 6:7)

According to the tradition represented by the book of Acts, the resurrected Jesus spent forty days with his disciples, during which period he taught them "things concerning the kingdom of God." One can only speculate as to the details of what Jesus taught, but whatever he taught would surely have been at one with his teachings concerning the kingdom as perpetuated in the Synoptic Gospels and opposed to the implications suggested by the disciples' question, "Lord, are you now going to restore the kingdom to Israel?" Jesus' answer, which sets the tone for the entire book, affirms that the task of the believing community is to bear witness to the universal nature of the kingdom rather than to speculate concerning matters beyond the scope of their grasp.

The Spirit is promised.—No valid witness to the reality of the

---

[2]A. H. McNeile, *An Introduction to the Study of the New Testament* (Oxford: Clarendon Press, 1953), p. 123.
[3]Moffatt, *Introduction*, pp. 284-85.

kingdom in the person of Jesus could be given by the disciples until they were "clothed" with the Holy Spirit. Luke 24:49, which should be translated, "until you *clothe yourselves* with power from on high," acknowledges the disciples' responsibility in this task, while Acts 1:5,8 recognizes that ultimately the gift of the Spirit comes only through the divine will. Further observations concerning the coming of the Spirit will be made in conjunction with the discussion of the Pentecost experience.

Not only do the disciples maintain their previous Jewish nationalistic hopes for the kingdom of God, but they desire also to hold on to the physical presence of the historical Jesus rather than to work at developing an awareness of the spiritual presence of their Lord. But now they are commanded to depart from the mountain and to return to Jerusalem where they are to prepare themselves for the reception of the Spirit. Constituting this group who gather in Jerusalem are the "three" (Peter, James, and John), along with the remainder of the "twelve", "the women," including the mother of Jesus, and James, the brother of the Lord.

An incident which all but breaks the sequence of events is recorded next: Judas' suicide and the consequent election of Matthias (1:15-26). The Matthean tradition states that Judas hanged himself (27:3-10), while Acts intimates that his death may have come about by a plunge down from a mountain (1:18). Peter's statement, that Judas' death was "to fulfil the Scriptures," represents the early Christian belief that Judas' death was used by God to accomplish his purpose and is perhaps the outcome of a reflection upon Psalm 41:10.

After the death of Judas, Matthias is elected to become one of the "twelve." This election was brought about, not to perpetuate the sacred number (when James is put to death no one is elected to take his place), but because in the thinking of the early church the number had never been complete, since Judas could not truly be considered one of the "twelve."[4] Requirements for a member of the twelve were several. (1) He must have been with the group of Jesus' disciples from the time of John's baptism on. (2) He must have been a witness to the resurrection. (3) His election must come, like that of the other apostles, by the will of the Lord (1:24-25).

Chapter two resumes the chain of thought interrupted by the

'G. B. Caird, *The Apostolic Age* (London: Gerald Duckworth & Co., 1955), p. 147.

paragraph concerning the death of Judas and the election of Matthias. Important in this chapter are mention of three elements which constitute the church in Lukan theology.

The presence of the Spirit (2:1-13).—Luke records four occasions in which the Spirit was manifest in connection with some unusual phenomena: Pentecost (2:1-13), the conversion of the Samaritans (8:17), Cornelius at Caesarea (10:44-48), and the disciples of John at Ephesus (19:1-7). On each occasion the external phenomena are so interwoven into the description of the events that one feels it difficult to separate event from interpretation.

This problem is especially acute in connection with this first description of the Spirit's coming. At least two possibilities present themselves: (1) These unusual phenomena happened as described and were the external seal of God's validation upon the internal experiences of the disciples, who had now come to perceive the spiritual presence of God. After the church had reached a certain stage of maturity in their understanding of God's leadership through his Spirit, these external witnesses were no longer necessary and ceased to be. (2) Luke incorporated a mention of these external phenomena so as to underline the significance of the moment when the early church began to develop an awareness of the spiritual presence of their Lord in their midst.

A few observations should be made concerning "speaking in tongues." (1) It may be that this was Luke's way of describing symbolically a spiritual reality recognized by the church, that is, that the gospel is for all peoples. This theory receives support from several sides. First, this ability was not a permanent gift of the church. Second, when Peter spoke, everyone understood what he said. Third, the mention of people from so many areas, though not at all impossible, may have been Luke's way of emphasizing the universal nature of the Christian message. (2) The "speaking in tongues" in 1 Corinthians appears to have been a different phenomenon from this mentioned in Acts. In 1 Corinthians the experience is definitely an ecstatic one in which the person makes no intelligible sounds. (3) Whatever the exact nature of the experience, Luke sought to emphasize through it the universal character of the Christian message rather than to draw attention to the external phenomenon itself.

The apostolic witness (2:14-41).—Peter appears as a representative of the apostles and his message is representative of their preaching.   As was customary in the early church, the Christ event is interpreted in light of the Old Testament.   Peter appeals to the prophecy of Joel and declares that the apocalyptic expectations of Joel were fulfilled in Jesus Christ (vv. 17-21).   One notices immediately that Peter's interpretation of Joel's words is symbolic and in accord with what was suggested earlier as the proper means for the interpretation of apocalyptic literature.   Upon the basis of Joel's words three emphases are made: the Christ event is eschatological (vv. 17-18) in that through it a new era is inaugurated; it is cosmic (vv. 19-20) in that it concerns the transformation of the entire universe; and it transcends racial barriers (v. 21), for "whoever calls on the name of the Lord shall be saved."

Through an examination of Peter's sermons contained in Acts 2-4, C. H. Dodd has thus reconstructed the content of the earliest Christian preaching.[5]   (1) The age of fulfilment has arrived.   (2) This new era was initiated through the ministry, death, and resurrection of Jesus Christ, who descended from David.   (3) By his resurrection Jesus has been exalted to the right hand of God and is the messianic leader of the new Israel.   (4) The presence of the Holy Spirit in the church is the witness to Christ's present glory and power.   (5) The messianic era will soon be consummated through the return of Christ.   (6) Repentance is called for, and the offer of forgiveness and of the Holy Spirit, along with the promise of eternal life, are given to those who respond to the proclamation.

The common life (2:42-47).—A final characteristic of the church is its common life shared by all the redeemed community.   Luke delineates this common life both from the viewpoint of its worship and its daily walk.   Acts 2:42 summarizes the worship shared by the church.   (1) The "teaching of the apostles" was the norm of life for the community, since they were the primary witnesses to Jesus Christ.   As yet there seems to have been no written authority. (2) Fellowship, established through their common possession of the Spirit, unified them as a worshiping community.   (3) As a seal and witness of the inner unity of the Spirit, the community shared a solemn meal, perhaps in anticipation of the forthcoming "messianic banquet."   (4) A final aspect of their common worship was the offering of prayer to their Lord.

----

[5] *The Apostolic Preaching and Its Development* (New York: Harper & Bros., 1937), pp. 20-24.

This common life experienced in worship was translated into effectual daily living. (1) Whenever an occasion of need arose in the community, each believer considered it his sacred duty to fulfil that need through sharing his own goods (vv. 44-45). Each believer continued to own his possessions as before, but the need of a fellow believer was the demand of the Lord for one to share what he owned. (2) Evidently the early community still considered themselves to be faithful Jews, because they continued to frequent the Jerusalem Temple (v. 46a). (3) Finally, there seems to have been a sharing of hospitality through a mutual giving and receiving of bread from house to house (v. 46b).

Meeting problems (3:1 to 6:7).—Peter's healing of the lame man at the entrance of the Temple (3:1-9) sets the stage for the first major problem faced by the church. The man who was healed immediately responded by leaping joyfully about on his restored limbs, whereupon a crowd gathered about Peter and John. Peter took this as an occasion to announce that the healing had been wrought through the power of Jesus, whom God had raised from the dead.

Such a proclamation was unsatisfactory to the Sadducees, the official authorities for the affairs conducted in the Temple, because of two reasons: (1) They had been the leaders of the people who had crucified Jesus, and (2) they did not hold on to the doctrine of the resurrection (4:1-2). As a result they had Peter and John taken into custody. However, the Sadducees had no grounds on which to initiate any official charges against the apostles, who appear to have been in good stead with the masses, and so dismissed them with only a threat (4:3-22). Quite obviously this was not the only time that the early church was faced with a threat from the political-religious authority and Luke has included this experience because it was typical of many others.[6] As a sequel to the arrest, the apostles offer a prayer expressing their joy for the opportunity to suffer for their Lord (4:23 ff.).

A second major problem faced by the church is typified in the Ananias-Sapphira incident, through which Luke indicates to his readers that the early church had to face problems from within their fellowship as well as problems from without the church (4:32 to 5:

---

[6]Note, for example, 5:17-42, which is essentially one with this account and which is understood by some to be a doublet of the earlier account.

11). Barnabas, and others like him, had been especially benevolent with their possessions and had received the commendation of the community for their generosity. Ananias and Sapphira plot to receive the praise without making the sacrifice. That they were found out by God and subsequently punished by the hand of God suggests the enormity of the sin, which Peter describes as "lying to the Holy Spirit."

What is meant by Peter's accusation is that Ananias and Sapphira had denied the reality of a spiritual religion, since they had failed to believe that God, through his Spirit, could effectively reveal his will to someone and hold that one responsible for the accomplishment of his will. Furthermore, these two had denied that the Spirit of God could grant to the believing community the ability to discern between genuine piety and hypocrisy.

Evidently the early Christian community, as the Jewish community

before them, felt the obligation to provide the necessities of life
for those of their membership who were not able to provide for
themselves. Among this group widows would have been more numerous than any other persons because there were very few honorable
ways that a woman could make a living on her own.

In the course of this ministry, the "Hellenists" began murmuring
against the "Hebrews" because they believed their widows were being
slighted (6:1-2). Normally the word "Hellenist" would refer to one
who lives according to the culture of the Greeks, but that does not
solve the problem in the present context. It is unlikely that Hellenist
in this context has reference to Gentiles because, as yet, no Gentiles
appear to have been a part of the Christian community.[7] Neither
does it seem likely that the term is used to contrast non-Palestinian
Jews with Palestinian Jews, called Hebrews, since these persons
under discussion appear well established in Jerusalem. Probably the
Hellenists represent the more liberal Jewish element within the church,
while the Hebrews describe those who were the champions of the
traditional Jewish culture.[8]

From the group who initiated the complaint seven men were
appointed to oversee this ministry (6:3-6). Whatever term one might
use to designate the office held by these men, it appears that the office
is surely not to be identified with the office of deacon,[9] which is a
somewhat later development within the church. Two of this group,
Stephen and Philip, play a prominent role in the expansion of the
faith beyond the borders of Palestine.

The New Wine Reaches Throughout Palestine (6:8 to 9:31)

The witness of Stephen (6:8 to 7:60).—No one man was more
responsible for the bursting of the old skins than Stephen, the first
person to declare openly the absolute incompatibility between the
new wine and the old skins. From the synagogue of the "Freedmen,"
men who had previously been slaves,[10] arose men who made serious
accusations against Stephen: "We have heard him speak blasphemous

[7]Henry J. Cadbury deems this not to have been impossible. F. J. Foakes–
Jackson and Kirsopp Lake (eds.), *The Beginnings of Christianity* (London:
Macmillan & Co., 1920-1933), V, 59-74—especially 69.

[8]*Ibid.,* IV, 64.

[9]Richard Belward Rackham, *The Acts of the Apostles* (London: Methuen &
Co., 1953), p. 86.

[10]Emil G. Kraeling, *Rand McNally Bible Atlas* (New York: Rand McNally
& Co., 1956), pp. 415-16.

words against Moses and against God." The order, Moses-God, indicates that for these men any breach of the Mosaic traditions constituted blasphemy against God. Incipient, in the words of Stephen, is the theology of a universal gospel, and it will be worthwhile to examine his sermon in some detail. Stephen's thesis is stated in the words of his accusers, "Jesus of Nazareth will destroy this place, and will change the customs which Moses delivered to us" (6:14). Thereby is affirmed the consummation of the Temple in the person of Jesus Christ, through whom all people might approach God apart from the regulations of the Mosaic cult.

The entire seventh chapter of Acts is an elaboration of this theme from various angles. God is not confined to the Holy Land; before Abraham settled in Haran, God appreared to him in Mesopotamia (vv. 1-3). God's promise to Abraham was the promise of a people, not of a territory, and this promise was made to Abraham before he was circumcised (vv. 4-8).

Joseph and Moses, typical of those whom God chose to lead his people, were rejected by those who should have followed them; and, had God not intervened, God's chosen leaders would have been put

34. Street at Ephesus

to death by the rebellious actions of these "chosen people" (vv. 9-29). Moses, initially rejected by the Israelites, became their re-deemer from Egypt and promised that God would later raise another like himself, to whom the people should hearken (vv. 30-37). In the wilderness the Israelites rejected the living oracles of God and turned to idols, for which rebellion God caused them to die, without entering the Land of Promise (vv. 38-43).

The tabernacle, Stephen went on to point out, was not confined to a given locale. It thus was a better witness to the omnipresence of God than is the stationary Temple, which restricts the presence of God (vv. 44-50).

Finally, through rejecting Jesus, the Jews have placed themselves in a position comparable to their rebellious forefathers, who rejected both the prophets and the appointed leaders of God's people (vv. 51-53).

Found guilty of blasphemy, Stephen was stoned by the Jewish court. The only mention of the term "Son of man" outside the Gospels is given in this context (v. 56). By *standing,* rather than the customary sitting, at the right hand of God, the Lord signifies his coming to help and to accept the one who has just been stoned "in his name." Incidental mention is made of Saul, a witness to the execution, who later becomes a witness to the gospel.

An immediate result of Stephen's death is the attempt to drive from Jerusalem any others who hold similar views. By this per-secution the gospel is spread to regions beyond the immediate vi-cinity of Jerusalem. Of interest is the observation that the apostles, still failing to perceive the universal nature of the gospel, do not have to flee Jerusalem.

The witness of Phillip (8:1-40).—Acts 8 records two steps forward in the emancipation of the gospel from the limitations of Judaism. First, Philip, one of the seven, takes the gospel to the Samaritans who are not full-blooded Jews (vv. 1-25). When the Jerusalem church hears of this venture they send Peter and John as a com-mittee to investigate the propriety of such a movement. The in-dication that the Spirit of God could come upon the Samaritans, as it had come upon the Jews, caused Peter and John to feel favorable toward this initial step of the gospel away from Judaism proper.

35. Athens, Acropolis

Among those interested in the Christian movement was Simon Magus, a sorcerer, who had been taken by the miraculous power manifest by the Spirit through the hands of Philip. This man, whom the early church fathers characterize as the father of all heresy, was immediately rebuked by Peter because of his attempt to purchase the power of the Spirit for his selfish advantage, a sin not unlike that committed by Ananias and Sapphira.

Second, Philip's next appearance is on the road leading from Jerusalem to the city of Gaza, where he enters into conversation with an Ethiopian eunuch, the official in charge of the treasury of Candace,* the Ethiopian queen (vv. 26-40). Strange, indeed, is the picture of Philip's running beside the chariot of this man, inquiring if he understands what he reads! But this oddity is minimized by the importance of what the event has to say. (1) Given indirectly is an insight into the manner of the early church in reinterpreting their Old Testament in light of what Jesus Christ had been, and how they saw him revealed in its pages (vv. 30-35). (2) A further stride is taken away from Judaism when Philip preaches to this Ethiopian who has no Jewish blood in his veins. Because of his physical imperfection as a eunuch, it was impossible for him to become a full proselyte (convert) to Judaism, but he had accepted the God of Judaism and the moral regulations of Judaism. Although this man could never have become a fully accepted member of the Jewish faith, upon his confession of the lordship of Christ he was accepted into the fellowship of the Christian community and baptized as a seal of his confession.

Saul's conversion (9:1-31).—Introduced next in the sequence of events is the conversion of Saul, known better by his Christian name, Paul. Paul was a native of Tarsus, located in the Cilician region of Asia Minor on the Cydnus River, about ten miles inland from the northeastern shore of the Mediterranean Sea. He was born a Roman citizen somewhere about A.D. 1-5, took his rabbinical training with Gamaliel, a noted Jewish rabbi, and learned the trade of tent-making. Other than the fact of his zeal for the religious traditions of his nation and his quest for personal righteousness beside God, all else that is known about him before the time of his conversion is that he witnessed Stephen's death, and took an active part in perse-

---

*Actually, Candace was the official title for the Ethiopian queen, rather than her name.

cuting the "apostate Jews" who were going over to Christianity.

Precision in the details connected with Paul's conversion experience cannot be gained, inasmuch as the details are different in the three accounts in Acts (9:1-29; 22:3-21; 26:9-23).[11] Nevertheless several basic observations are possible. (1) No doubt the influence of Stephen's sermon, as well as the testimony of the other Christians whom Paul had arrested, had left its impact upon Paul's thinking and he began to feel that persecution of these persons was in reality persecution of the Lord (9:4). (2) As evidenced by his own writings, Paul had been struggling with the problem of his personal sin, which problem was resolved in the discovery of the resurrected Lord who imparted forgiveness to men apart from human merit. (3) Paul's vision of the resurrected Christ would also have answered his questions regarding the sufferings of Christ. (4) Paul's outlook becomes universal through the recognition that God had set him apart as a herald to the Gentiles.

Immediately following his conversion Paul began a preaching mission in Damascus, but was feared by the Christians and despised by the Judaizers, who finally decided to rid themselves of him. However, Paul escaped during the night and fled from Damascus (vv. 19b-25). Deleted from Acts is the journey that Paul took in the regions of Arabia, perhaps not far from Damascus, where for three years he tarried in consideration of the theological implications of his experience on the road to Damascus (Gal. 1:17). Finally, when Paul did come to Jerusalem, he was still under suspicion by the majority of disciples, but Barnabas took him under his watchcare. Paul then preached in Jerusalem until the disciples feared for his life, at which time they sent him to Caesarea and then to Tarsus.

The New Wine Reaches Antioch (9:32 to 12:24)

Another decisive stage in the liberation of the gospel comes in connection with the conversion of Cornelius, the God-fearing Gentile (10:1-48). For a man to become a full proselyte into Judaism required that he accept circumcision, be baptized, and offer certain designated sacrifices. But there were a number of Gentiles who were not willing to undergo these rituals and thereby become a Jew, but who, nevertheless, were strongly attracted by the strict

---

[11]Compare Acts 9:1-9 with 22:3-11.

monotheism and morality of Judaism. These persons seem to have been known as "God-fearers,"[12] and Cornelius would have been of this group. Even though the summons from Cornelius came in conjunction with an unusual dream-vision, the apostle Peter was not altogether certain that he should go to the home of one who was a Gentile. When Peter does go, he is careful to take along with him two fellow Jews as witnesses to what he haltingly feels may be the will of God. As Peter proclaimed the message of Christ, Cornelius believed, along with some other Gentiles, and the Holy Spirit's presence was so genuine that Cornelius was received into the community of faith.

Acts 11:1-18 relates the outcome of Peter's preaching to Cornelius. The remainder of the Jerusalem brethren were not at all satisfied with his actions and so called upon the apostle to explain. Thereupon Peter narrated his experiences, beginning with the dream-vision and culminating with the coming of the Spirit, and simultaneously declared his conviction that he had done the right thing in light of the evident manifestation of God's Spirit, witnessed in the conversion of these Gentiles. Luke summarizes the judgment of the Jerusalem church, "When they heard this they were silenced. And they glorified God, saying, 'Then to the Gentiles also God has granted repentance unto life'" (11:18). On the surface the issue seemed settled, but there was yet much prejudice to overcome.

A final step in the emancipation of the gospel from the bonds of Judaism takes place as certain disciples preach to the Greeks ıt Antioch in Syria (11:19-26). At this moment the Christian faith begins to come into its own. As soon as the news of this venture reached the church in Jerusalem they sent Barnabas to investigate, with the result that he was thrilled at the sight of Jew and Gentile alike rejoicing in the grace of God. Barnabas then took it upon himself to attend the needs of the congregation and called upon Paul, who also had perceived the universal implications of the gospel, to assist him in the ministry at Antioch. The overall significance of this Antiochian mission is suggested in the annotation that "in Antioch the disciples were for the first time called Christians" (11:26). Initially the name "Christian" appears to have been employed as a title of derogation by which the pagan world derode the believers

[12]Frederick M. Derwacter, *Preparing the Way for Paul* (New York: The Macmillan Co., 1930), pp. 24-40.

for their confession, "Christ is Lord," as opposed to the commonly accepted confession, "Caesar is lord." However, Luke relates with pride this name by which the faith had now come to be known.

Specific notations of time are conspicuously lacking throughout Acts, but at this juncture two relatively pointed dates are supplied. (1) Agabus' appearance is dated immediately prior to the famine which struck Rome with severity during the reign of the Emperor Claudius in the year A.D. 46/47 (11:27-30). (2) Herod Agrippa I, grandson of Herod the Great, died in A.D. 44, after previously having been responsible for the death of James, the brother of John. These dates indicate that the struggles of the church thus far depicted were taking place during the first decade and a half of the church's life.

Since the death of James pleased a number of Jews, Herod Agrippa subsequently arrested Peter, with the intention of treating him in the same fashion. After Peter's miraculous escape from prison, it is simply stated that "he departed and went to another place" (12:17). Only one other time does Peter appear in the Acts account and this is at the Jerusalem council of Acts 15. Evidence is strongly in favor of the tradition that Peter afterwards left Jerusalem and journeyed to Rome, where he was put to death about A.D. 64 in the Neronian persecution.[13]

The New Wine Reaches Asia Minor (12:25 to 16:5)

A further token of the universal climate of the Antiochian church is indicated through their desire to spread the gospel beyond their own region. Therefore, they send forth Barnabas and Paul, accompanied by John Mark. This band of missionaries traveled by land to the seaport of Seleucia, whence they sailed to the island of Cyprus, landing at the eastern port of Salamis and journeying the full breadth of the island to Paphos, the administrative city on the western coast. Here they were encountered with a favorable response on the part of Sergius Paulus, the Roman proconsul in charge of the small territory.

Sir William Ramsay concluded there was sufficient evidence from several inscriptions to indicate that Sergius Paulus must have become

---

[13]Oscar Cullmann, *Peter, Disciple, Apostle, Martyr,* trans. Floyd V. Filson (Philadelphia: Westminster Press, 1953), pp. 70-152; Jack Finegan, *Light from the Ancient Past* (Princeton: Princeton University Press, 1954), pp. 297-304.

a Christian and that his daughter and grandson later made open confession of their faith.[14] Until this point in the narrative, Luke has consistently used the name Saul to refer to the apostle, but from 13:13 on he refers to him as Paul. Emil G. Kraeling believes that Paul intentionally changed his name to that of the proconsul as a means of honoring the one whom he was seeking to win to the faith,[15] but this seems not to be a necessary conclusion.

Paul and his company sailed from Cyprus and landed on the shore of Asia Minor, where they walked inland to the city of Perga in the province of Pamphylia. Here John Mark left them and departed to Jerusalem (13:13). No reason for Mark's departure is given, but it is logical to conclude that he had not yet been able to open his eyes to the universal call of the gospel, and so returned to the security of Jerusalem where there were others of the same persuasion. Trudging northward through a hundred miles of mountainous terrain, Paul and Barnabas reached "Antioch of Pisidia," in the Roman province of Galatia. At this point in the record is a summary of Paul's preaching.

Paul's gospel.—From a comparative study of the Pauline epistles and the sermons of Paul recorded in Acts, C. H. Dodd has constructed the following compendium of the Pauline gospel[16]: (1) By the appearance of Christ the Scriptures are fulfilled and the new age inaugurated. (2) Christ was born of the seed of David, (3) died "according to the Scriptures" to deliver us from the present evil age, (4) was buried, and (5) arose on the third day "according to the Scriptures." (6) At present he is exalted as Son of God and at the right hand of God, (7) whence he will come as Judge and Redeemer of men.

Although Paul is considered the "apostle to the Gentiles," one notices that in Antioch, as elsewhere, he begins his ministry in the Jewish synagogue. No doubt there were good reasons for this procedure. Paul himself was a Jew who loved his people and could not overcome the desire to witness to them whenever the occasion permitted. Also, the synagogue granted Paul an entrée for his preaching such as would not have been gained elsewhere. First of all, the Jews had the expectation of a Saviour ingrained in their think-

---

[14]*The Bearing of Recent Discovery on the Trustworthiness of the New Testament* (London: Hodder & Stoughton, 1915), pp. 150-72.

[15]*Op. cit.,* p. 431.

[16]*Apostolic Preaching,* pp. 7-20. For a comparative study of the Petrine and Pairline preaching, cf. *ibid.,* pp. 25-35.

ing and would have known what Paul meant when he stated that all this was "according to the Scriptures." Second, there would have been Gentiles in most any synagogue gathering of reasonable size, and through them Paul would have had access to the ears of other Gentiles.

Provoked to jealousy by the eager response of the Gentiles to the Christian message, "the Jews incited the devout women of high standing and the leading men of the city, and stirred up persecution against Paul and Barnabas, and drove them out of their district" (13:50). After this had happened Paul and Barnabas traveled eighty miles east and south to the city of Iconium, where a similar fate was incurred. Learning of a plan to stone them, Paul and Barnabas fled to Lystra, a city due south of Iconium. Because of Paul's power to heal a lame man, the Lystrians understood him and Barnabas as gods come down to bestow their favors upon the city. This caused no small degree of excitement, and the people began speaking in their native tongue, rather than in Greek, so that Paul was unable to communicate with them in their frenzied state. When envoys of ill will arrived from Iconium, the Lystrians were as easily incited to hatred as they had been to benevolence, and so stoned Paul, leaving him for dead. On the next day, however, Paul was able to travel to Derbe, where he established a church. From Derbe the two traveling companions retraced their footsteps back through Lystra, Iconium, Antioch, Perga, and finally to the port city of Attalia, where they set sail for Antioch in Syria.

The Jerusalem Conference.—Some Jewish Christians from Jerusalem were strongly opposed to the judgment of Paul and Barnabas that God had "opened a door of faith to the Gentiles" (14:27). Consequently, these men came to Antioch with the demand that the Gentile converts become circumcised, which would have meant that they were virtually Jewish proselytes. A debate arose over the issue, with the result that "Paul and Barnabas and some of the others were appointed to go up to Jerusalem to the apostles and the elders about this question" (15:2).

When the conference convened, opposition arose from those who were believers among the Pharisees (15:5). They demanded that the new converts be circumcised and keep the law of Moses. To this Peter replied that God had evidently made no distinction between Jews and non-Jews; all alike were saved by faith. Furthermore, Peter pointed out, even the Jews themselves had been unable to fulfil all the legalistic requirements of the Mosaic law.   Why then should they expect the Gentile Christians to be bound by these same regulations (15:6-11)?   At the words of Peter the entire congregation was silenced; then Paul and Barnabas related from their own experiences the many ways in which God had worked among the Gentiles (15:12).

Climaxing these testimonies was the address of James, who seems to have been of the greatest influence among the Jewish believers. He concluded that since God had given salvation to the Gentiles, they could not be required to be circumcised or keep the Law.   But James did recognize the problems that would inevitably arise when Jews and Gentiles should come together, so he suggested that the Gentiles be directed not to do those things by which they would knowingly antagonize the Jewish believers (15:13-21).   All present favored the opinion of James, and their judgment in the matter was conveyed to the church at Antioch by a letter in the hands of Paul and Barnabas (15:22-30).

Two major problems loom about the Jerusalem conference of A.D. 49, discussed in Acts 15:1-30.   (1) Does the decision of the council relate primarily to "religious" or "moral" issues?   (2) What is the relationship between the events of Acts 15:1-30 and the events of Paul's ministry alluded to in Galatians 1:18 to 2:10?   The answer to this second question is not immediately integral to an interpretation of the present passage and more nearly falls into the scope of a discussion of Galatians. Hence a decision on the second question will be withheld until a consideration of Galatians is undertaken.

The first question arises because the manuscripts of Acts offer significantly different renderings of 15:20,29. The customary rendering exhorts the Gentiles "to abstain from the pollutions of idols and from unchastity and from what is strangled and from blood," and makes the decree of the council relate strictly to religious issues whereby the Gentiles are encouraged to cease those activities by which they openly affront Jewish scruples.   On the other hand, the alternate reading deals with the question of Gentile morality and encourages the Gentiles "to abstain from the pollutions of idols, and from murder, and from immorality, and do not do unto others what you would not want them to do unto you."

Most probably the first reading is correct and the second represents an expansion of the original text, since it is not uncustomary for this latter manuscript (known as D or Beza) to expand the text of Acts for one reason or another. If this opinion is valid, then the Jerusalem conference is significant for its open statement that Gentiles could be received into the fellowship of the church through faith, but they were simultaneously encouraged to avoid those mannerisms by which they knowingly would contradict Jewish scruples.

Paul and Barnabas returned to Antioch and presented to the church the decree of the Jerusalem apostles and elders. "When they read it, they rejoiced at the exhortation" (15:31). These two men remained in Antioch until they decided to make a return visit to the churches they had established on their first journey. Barnabas wanted to take Mark on the second journey, but Paul was strongly insistent that they not take with them this one who had turned back on the first trip. "There arose a sharp contention, so that they separated from each other; Barnabas took Mark with him and sailed away to Cyprus, but Paul chose Silas and departed" (15:39). No further reference to Barnabas is made in Acts, but tradition has it that he later established churches in Egypt.

Paul now went back through the regions of Syria and Cilicia until he reached either Derbe or Lystra (the text is not evident), where he took Timothy into his company. Timothy's mother was a Jewish woman who had become a believer, while his father was a Greek who had not circumcised Timothy according to Jewish custom. That Paul had Timothy circumcised does not indicate Paul's concession to the Judaizers; rather it signifies he recognized that this was a necessary step to make Timothy accepted in the Jewish synagogues where they should hope to preach the gospel.

The New Wine Reaches Europe (16:6 to 19:20)

Unnoticed to the reader of the English translation is a certain degree of ambiguity that surrounds the Acts account at this point. "They went through the region of Phrygia and Galatia, having been forbidden by the Holy Spirit to speak the word in Asia. And when they had come opposite Mysia, they attempted to go into Bithynia, but the Spirit of Jesus did not allow them; so, passing by Mysia, they went down to Troas" (16:6-8).

Two possibilities exist: The "North Galatian" theory affirms that this passage suggests a mission by Paul into the region of Galatia in the ethnographic sense, near the southern shore of the Black Sea, where he would perhaps have preached in the cities of Ancyra,

Tavium, and Pessinus. To be sure, Luke does not include all the regions wherein Paul preached, but it seems fair to state that he would have left the reader with more than an ambiguous remark if he were intending to incorporate into his account a record of Paul's preaching in this region.

The "South Galatian" theory, suggesting the region immediately west of Antioch in Pisidia, finds support from at least two observations. (1) The text of 16:6 might be rendered, "They went through the Phrygian-Galatian region," which would mean the part of the ancient region of Phrygia lying in the Roman province of Galatia. (2) No valid support for a Pauline mission in this northern region can be reconstructed from the Pauline epistles. Thus Paul's group would have moved westward from Antioch and then north to the border of the Roman province of Bithynia, which they were forbidden to enter. Turning westward again, they would have traveled along the region close to the border separating Bithynia from the province of Asia and then along the Mysian region of northwest Asia to the city of Troas.[17]

From Asia to Europe.—During the course of their stay in the coastal city of Troas, "a vision appeared to Paul in the night: a man of Macedonia was standing beseeching him and saying, 'Come over to Macedonia and help us' " (16:9). Quite possibly this vision was evoked through Paul's encounter with Luke in Troas, since the author of Acts for the first time includes himself in the company of Paul: "When he had seen the vision, immediately *we* sought to go on into Macedonia, concluding that God had called *us* to preach the gospel to them" (16:10).

From Troas the society of missionaries sailed to the island of Samothrace, departing on the next day for Neapolis in the province of Macedonia. By foot they would have traveled to the city of Philippi along the Egnatian Way, the great Roman road reaching across Macedonia from Neapolis to Dyrrachium. Near Philippi was the plain on which Antony and Octavian in 42 B.C. had defeated Brutus and Cassius. In honor of this victory the two conquering generals made Philippi into a Roman colony, and some of the retired Roman soldiers became its first citizens. Because there was no syna-

---

[17]For an opposing viewpoint cf. Paul Feine and Johannes Behm, *Einleitung in das Neue Testament* (twelfth ed. by Werner Georg Kümmel; Heidelberg: Quelle & Meyer, 1963), pp. 191-93.

36. Athens, Areopagus (Mars' Hill)

gogue within the city of Philippi, Paul and his companions searched along the narrow river for a possible Jewish gathering. When they had found the place of worship, Paul preached to them the gospel, with the result that Lydia, a Jewish proselyte originally from Thyatira, became the first convert in Europe.

Shortly thereafter Paul encountered a semidemented slave girl whose ability at ventriloquism was being exploited by her owners. This young woman followed Paul and his companions crying, "These men are servants of the Most High God, who proclaim to you the way of salvation" (16:17). Publicity of this type was doing the Christian message no good; therefore Paul healed her so that she lost her ability at soothsaying, which ability was possessed only when she was in a state of frenzied emotionalism. Her owners, discovering that their livelihood had vanished, hailed Paul and Silas before the magistrates with the accusation, "These men are Jews and they

are disturbing our city. They advocate customs which it is not lawful for us Romans to accept or practice" (16:20-21). Paul and
Silas were immediately beaten and cast into prison.

About midnight the prison into which Paul and Silas had been
placed was shaken by an earthquake. The jailer, because he was
responsible for the security of the prisoners, thought the men were
escaping and started to take his life rather than face the judgment
of the court. "But Paul cried with a loud voice, 'Do not harm
yourself, for we are all here' " (16:28). Overtaken by superstitious
fears, prompted by the realization that these men had been imprisoned as "servants of the Most High God," the jailer cried out,
"Men, what must I do to be saved?" (16:30). Paul supplied him
an answer he did not expect and had opportunity to explain further
the meaning of his answer, after the jailer had taken him and Silas
to his home for treatment of their wounds.

On the next day the magistrates sought to exonerate themselves
of their swift judgment, which had been prompted by the insistence
of the mob, and sent word that Paul and Silas could be released.
Realizing the implications it might leave if they were released secretly
after having been sentenced publicly, Paul said to the representatives
sent by the magistrates, "They have beaten us publicly, uncondemned,
men who are Roman citizens, and have thrown us into prison; and
do they now cast us out secretly? No! let them come themselves
and take us out" (16:37). With formal apology the disciples were
released, after which they revisited their converts in that city and
then departed westward toward Thessalonica.

En route to Thessalonica the travelers would have gone through
Amphipolis, residence of the Roman proconsul of Macedonia, then
through Apollonia to Thessalonica. The gospel received a favorable
hearing in Thessalonica until the jealousy of the Jews incited a
mob against the congregation, which was meeting in the home of
Jason.

A peace bond was required of Jason by the city authorities and
the disciples immediately sent Paul and Silas by night to the neighboring city of Beroea, lest their lives be in jeopardy. Enthusiastically
the Jews of Beroea responded to the good news. "But when the
Jews of Thessalonica learned that the word of God was proclaimed
by Paul at Beroea also, they came there too, stirring up and inciting
the crowds" (17:13).

To Athens and Corinth.—"Then the brethren immediately sent

Paul off on his way to the sea, but Silas and Timothy remained there" (17:14). Paul's escorts accompanied him as far as Athens, and then they returned with the instructions for Silas and Timothy to come to him as quickly as possible.

Overwhelmed by the idolatry of the Athenians, Paul felt constrained to declare to them the grace of this unknown God who had created all nations that "they might feel after him and find him." The negative response that Paul received in this city of culture was not induced by a change in his message—Paul's message apparently was essentially the same here as elsewhere—but by a change in the makeup of his congregation. Hitherto Paul had spoken basically to congregations oriented to the Jewish hope and familiar with the Jewish doctrine concerning the resurrection of the dead. But not so at Athens, as is signified by the fact that those responsible for Paul's preaching on the Areopagus were philosophers of the Epicurean and Stoic schools, who did not think in terms of a bodily resurrection but in terms of the soul's immortality.

Furthermore, the thinking of these men was conditioned by the teachings of the manifold "mystery religions" of their day in which was portrayed, in various forms, the drama of a god's triumph over death and his attainment of immortality through the help of his female consort. Because of this background the Athenians felt that Paul was preaching to them a new kind of mystery religion in which were two divinities, Jesus and Resurrection (17:18). Hence the Athenians judged that Paul had merely gathered together fragments from other, more ancient, religions and had simply renamed the god and goddess of the redemptive drama. To them this was ridiculous and they refused to waste their time with such a common message. However, some did come to understand what Paul meant, among whom were "Dionysius the Areopagite and a woman named Damaris" (17:34).

First Thessalonians 3:1-10 presupposes a journey not mentioned in Acts. Evidently Timothy did soon arrive in Athens while Paul was still there. But the apostle was so concerned about the welfare of the Thessalonians that he sent Timothy back to strengthen their faith amidst their afflictions. On this return trip Timothy would possibly have taken with him Paul's first correspondence to the Thessalonians. Only after Timothy's return to Thessalonica does Paul then travel to Corinth (Acts 18:1), where Silas and Timothy finally rejoin him (18:5).

At Corinth, Paul met two Jews, Aquila and his wife Priscilla, who were of the same trade as he and who had been expelled from Rome by the edict of the Emperor Claudius (A.D. 49 or 50), commanding all Jews to leave Rome. Paul managed more success with these two persons than with the majority of the Corinthian Jews who "opposed and reviled him" (18:6). Rejected by his own race, Paul now turned to the Gentiles, setting up his headquarters in the home of Titus Justus adjoining the synagogue. This move was not without effect upon the Jews for Crispus, leader of the synagogue, was converted, along with the remainder of his household.

A rather firm date may be fixed for Paul's stay in Corinth through the mention of his appearance before Gallio, the proconsul of Achaia. An inscription known as the twenty-sixth Delphic Inscription fixes the proconsulship of Gallio as having begun in July of A.D. 51.[18] Since the Jews would have interpreted the early days of the new proconsul's term to be his most vulnerable moment, it is quite rea-

---

[18]Adolf Deissmann, *Paul, a Study in Social and Religious History,* trans. William E. Wilson (New York: George H. Doran Co., 1926), pp. 235-60. Cf. Feine and Behm, *op. cit.,* p. 178.

37. The Acropolis from Mars' Hill

sonable to assume that the accusation against Paul was made about mid-July of A.D. 51. After this experience Paul stayed "many days longer" before sailing to Syria. What Luke intends by "many days" is quite indefinite, but the autumn of A.D. 51 is a satisfactory suggestion for the terminus ad quem of the Pauline ministry at Corinth.

Paul's sojourn at Corinth was fruitful, not only for the people of Corinth, but also for people of other churches to whom he wrote communications from Corinth. Apparently 2 Thessalonians was written from Corinth and many believe that Paul wrote 1 Thessalonians in Corinth rather than in Athens, as was earlier suggested. Furthermore, among those who assume a date subsequent to the Jerusalem conference for the writing of Galatians, Corinth is one of the strongest contenders for the place of origin.

Return to Ephesus.—Before sailing for Syria, Paul had his hair cut at Cenchreae, the eastern port of Corinth, in partial fulfilment of a vow. Aquila and Priscilla accompanied him to Ephesus, where Paul stayed for a brief while before going to Antioch via Caesarea and Jerusalem. From Antioch, Paul initiated his "third journey," traveling overland through the Phrygian-Galatian region until he reached Ephesus, the central city of this journey.

Prior to Paul's arrival in Ephesus, the Jews of that city had been amazed by the eloquence and wisdom of Apollos, an Alexandrian Jew who had spoken in their synagogue. Evidently he lacked a thorough knowledge of the Christ event, because "he knew only the baptism of John" (18:25). Fortunately he was willing to listen to the instruction of Aquila and Priscilla, who doubtless informed him of the tradition relating to the passion and resurrection of the Lord. Paul arrived in Ephesus, but not until Apollos had gone to Corinth.

In Ephesus, Paul met a dozen disciples of John the Baptist to whom he testified concerning the Lord Jesus. When these men believed, they, too, recognized the presence of the Holy Spirit as the token of their faith, and expressed this experience in a manner not uncommon among religionists of the east, that is, through ecstatic utterances (19:1-7). For three months Paul spoke boldly in the synagogue. "But when some were stubborn and disbelieved, speaking evil of the Way before the congregation, he withdrew from them, taking the disciples with him, and argued daily in the hall of Tyrannus. This continued for two years, so that all the residents of Asia heard the word of the Lord, both Jews and Greeks" (19:9-10).

Certain persons in the city, attracted by the external manifestations of power wrought through the hands of the disciples, took it upon themselves to secure this power for their own selfish advantage. Among those who made such an attempt were the seven sons of Sceva, a Jewish high priest.   These men believed, in accord with the thought patterns of their day, that certain names possessed magical powers in themselves and could be pronounced for the sake of exorcising demons.   Luke records a humorous episode in which this attempt to use the name of Jesus in such a manner backfired on these seven men and caused many inhabitants of the city to become responsive to the gospel of redemption.

This became known to all residents of Ephesus, both Jews and Greeks; and fear fell upon them all; and the name of the Lord Jesus was extolled. Many also of those who were now believers came, confessing and divulging their practices. And a number of those who practiced magic arts brought their books together and burned them in the sight of all (19: 17-19).

The New Wine Reaches Rome (19:21 to 28:31)

Trouble and delay.—Paul had originally intended to travel to Jerusalem via Macedonia and Achaia, but was prevented by an unexpected uproar prompted by Demetrius, whose idol trade was endangered by the Christian proclamation.   Angry at Paul, the mob which Demetrius and his fellow craftsmen had incited dragged Gaius and Aristarchus, Paul's companions in travel, before the public assembly.   Paul was warned by some of his friends among the Asiarchs (members of the provincial council) not to enter the assembly. Finally, the town clerk managed to convince the mob to act orderly and bring their grievances before the court in the accepted manner, lest the Romans should interpret their gathering as an insurrection and send troops to deal with them.

From Paul's letters to Corinth, written from Ephesus, it can be surmised that Paul evidently endured more conflicts in Ephesus than are intimated by the Acts account.   In 1 Corinthians 15:30, Paul indicates that he was "in peril every hour," which might be only a general allusion, except for some more specific references elsewhere

38. The Acropolis from the Agora (market place)

in the Corinthian correspondence. Second Corinthians 1:8-9 refers to the extreme difficulties fared by Paul and his colleagues while in Asia: "For we were so utterly, unbearably crushed that we despaired of life itself. . . . we felt that we had received the sentence of death."

This passage in 2 Corinthians is intensified when one interprets it in light of 1 Corinthians 15:32, where Paul mentions that he "fought with beasts at Ephesus." According to Acts 20:18-19, Paul was endangered by the "plots of the Jews," which befell him in Asia; while, according to Acts 21:27, it was through the accusations of the Asian Jews in Jerusalem that Paul was almost killed by mob violence. And Romans 16, which may originally have been a portion of a letter of Ephesian destination,[19] mentions both Priscilla and Aquila, who "risked their necks" for Paul, as well as Andronicus and Junias, Paul's "fellow prisoners." Indeed, from the sources available, some have concluded that Paul's "prison epistles" were more naturally written from Ephesus than from Rome.[20]

Paul's stay in Ephesus was culminated in the spring of A.D. 54 or 55, when he appears to have left the city soon after Pentecost (1 Cor. 16:8). Leaving Ephesus, Paul traveled through the region of Macedonia and then returned to Greece (Corinth). Here he spent three months, during which time he wrote Romans.

Roundabout journey.—From Corinth, Paul intended to sail to Syria. But it was discovered that a plot was set against him when he was about to sail, so he hastily rerouted himself through Macedonia. That such a number of traveling companions from various churches were present with Paul at the precise moment the Jews were plotting against him suggests more than a plot against the life of Paul. Evidently the Jews also wanted the money he had collected from the Gentiles for the Jerusalem church.

Paul had hopes that this collection would be significant in unifying the Gentile and Jewish elements within the church, and it seems as if the apostle spent approximately two years of his ministry in this undertaking. In the thinking of Paul, no action could be more effective in bringing unity within the church than an offering from the Gentiles to the Jerusalem church, in recognition of their spiritual indebtedness to that congregation from which the gospel had come to the Gentile world.

---

[19]Cf. the discussion on Romans in the next chapter.
[20]Cf. the discussion of the prison epistles in the next chapter.

Several of Paul's company went directly to Troas, the point of rendezvous, while Paul and Luke (the "we" sections again) delayed at Philippi until after the days of unleavened bread. At Troas, Luke records the miraculous recovery of life by Eutychus, who had fallen from a second story window during Paul's prolonged exhortation. From Troas they traveled down the coast to Miletus, where Paul summoned the leaders of the Ephesian church to his side for one last word of instruction before he sailed to Jerusalem for the Passover. It is difficult to discern how much of Paul's speech (20: 18-35) represents his actual words and how much represents the situation at Ephesus as it had developed by the time Luke composed his record.

En route to Jerusalem, Paul made an effort to visit several places where Christian disciples were located. Among these stops were Tyre, Ptolemais, and Caesarea, where Philip, one of the seven, now resided. It was in Caesarea that Agabus, the prophet, predicted the dangers that Paul would face if he went to Jerusalem. Yet Paul determined that he must go there.

To Jerusalem and prison.—Upon Paul's arrival in Jerusalem he was instructed that many of the Jerusalem converts were still "zealous for the Law," and that these persons had been informed that Paul was deliberately teaching Gentile Christians to ridicule the scruples of Jewish Christians. Once more Paul undertook to demonstrate his willingness to expend himself for the sake of unity within the church. Therefore, he accepted the challenge to fulfil a vow in the Temple along with four other men. As the seven days of the vow were almost completed, several Jews from Asia appeared with vehement, but inaccurate, accusations against the apostle (21:28). And it was all that the Roman soldiers could do to secure Paul's release from the mob and to take him to their barracks.

Doubtless the tribune's haste in securing Paul was conditioned by his belief that Paul may have been the Egyptian Jew who recently had been responsible for an attempted insurrection. But when Paul spoke in the Greek language, the tribune was convinced that he had the wrong man and granted Paul an opportunity to address the Jews. The Jews listened to Paul as he spoke to them in Hebrew of his background and conversion, but when he mentioned his call to the Gentiles, they reacted with violence and said, "Away with such a fellow from the earth! For he ought not to live" (22:22).

Apparently the tribune had taken all he could, for he now prepared to have Paul beaten and then cast into prison. Not eager to endure the unjust punishment, Paul reminded the tribune that he was a Roman citizen about to be imprisoned without having been tried according to Roman law. This changed the complexion of the situation.

On the next day Paul was allowed to present his case before a gathering of Jewish leaders, consisting both of Pharisees and Sadducees. When the question of the resurrection came up, the gathering was suddenly divided, with the result that the Roman tribune was unable to reach any satisfactory decision with respect to his prisoner. Unable to destroy Paul by way of legal procedure, the Jews decided upon a plan of murdering Paul, which plan was revealed to the tribune by the son of Paul's sister. As a precaution to safeguard his prisoner, Claudius Lysias, the tribune, secretly removed Paul to the prison at Caesarea.

Two years of waiting.—Almost immediately after Paul was secured in the Caesarean prison, the Jews arrived with Ananias, the high priest, and Tertullus, their "prosecuting attorney." Caesarea was the residence of the Roman procurator and so Paul's formal hearing was made in the presence of Felix, who held the office from A.D. 52 to 60. Felix, playing the role of a politician, announced to the Jews that he could give forth no final decision on Paul until he had conferred with Lysias.

Some days later Paul had an informal audience with Felix and his wife Drusilla, a Jewish woman and the sister of Agrippa II, who had forsaken her first husband in order to become the third wife of Felix. Since this was no formal hearing, Paul spoke to them concerning faith in Christ and matters of personal morality, which seems to have availed naught. Felix kept Paul in prison for the final two years of his procuratorship.

When Porcius Festus succeeded Felix as procurator (A.D. 60), Paul was still in prison, having been retained there by Felix as a gesture of goodwill towards the Jews. If anything, Festus was a more despicable person than Felix; therefore, Paul appealed to Caesar, a right he possessed as a Roman citizen. With a prisoner on his hands who had appealed to Caesar and with no stable charges against this prisoner, Festus was in a dilemma.

Hence, when Agrippa II visited in the city, Festus asked his advice on the prisoner's situation. In this hearing Agrippa II was accompanied by his wife Bernice, who was also his sister. Paul realized his situation would not be changed through this interview, so he took this as an occasion to preach to Agrippa II, who, as a Jew, knew the Jewish hope. Though Festus did not thoroughly understand all that Paul was saying, Agrippa finally realized that Paul was attempting to reach him with the gospel (26:24-29). Both Festus and Agrippa ultimately agreed that Paul could be set free had he not appealed to Caesar.

To Rome at last.—On the voyage to Rome, Paul was allowed the companionship of his friends, Luke and Aristarchus of Macedonia. When they reached Fair Havens on the southeastern shore of Crete, Paul suggested that they spend the winter there, since the better part of the sailing season had already passed. Although the centurion in charge of the prisoners was especially amicable to Paul, he did not heed the apostle's advice on this occasion and had the captain set sail for Phoenix, a port city west of Fair Havens which was more attractive for wintering.

Suddenly the ship was taken by a storm which had set in from the northeast and which would have wrecked the vessel against the reefs of Syrtis, off the shore of North Africa, had not the crew acted with all swiftness. After being adrift for more than two weeks, the vessel grounded near Malta and all persons were safely taken ashore. Because Paul healed the fever of the father of Publius, the "chief man of the island," the native population received the unexpected guests with honor during their stay of three months.

Early in the next sailing season, Paul and the others embarked toward Italy, landing at Puteoli. Here the group stayed for seven days, during which Paul was permitted to visit with the Christian congregation within the city as well as with those who had come from other cities to see him. When in Rome, the Jews continued to do as they had done elsewhere, and so turned their backs on the gospel. Although the Jews hindered themselves from entering the kingdom of God, Paul continued in Rome for two years, "preaching the kingdom of God and teaching about the Lord Jesus Christ quite openly and unhindered" (28:31). Correctly, Frank Stagg has emphasized the word "unhindered,"[21] because this is the message of Acts: the gospel is now offered to all peoples, unhindered by the limited outlook of Judaism.

---

[21]Frank Stagg, *The Book of Acts* (Nashville: Broadman Press, 1955), pp. 4-18.

Part Three
The New Wine

I am the vine, you are the branches (John 15:5).

For the Christian community Jesus Christ is at once the new wine and the *only* wine. As the branches cannot live apart from a vital attachment to the vine, neither can the Christian community live and be productive apart from the unity with their Lord experienced through his Spirit. To this truth the literature of the New Testament bears a variegated but constant witness. Already this fact has been emphasized in the survey of the Gospels and Acts; it remains now to unfurl various implications of this reality contained in the remainder of the New Testament.

Paul's epistles herald the presence of the new wine through the declaration that the righteousness of God has been revealed, and this through the redemption of man from the present evil age. In accord with the steward at the wedding in Cana, the author of Hebrews announces that God has kept the best wine until last, and he has given this wine in the person of his Son. Bread and wine, symbols of life's daily necessities, characterize the contents of the general epistles, wherein are given doctrinal and practical help for daily living. Revelation reminds the believer of something he already knows, though it yet remains to be manifest to the world: "The kingdom of the world has become the kingdom of our Lord and of his Christ, and he shall reign for ever and ever" (11:15).

6

The Pauline Epistles

—THE WINE OF GOD'S RIGHTEOUSNESS

Various patterns of study are possible for the examination of the Pauline epistles. One may undertake them chronologically so as to trace the progressive development of Paul's thought, or else one may study them in units determined either by theological, historical, or literary considerations. The methodology pursued in this chapter will purpose: (1) to direct attention to the necessary historical-literary questions related to each letter or group of letters; (2) to present an outline and brief exposition of each letter individually with emphasis upon the theological content; and (3) to classify the Pauline letters loosely in conjunction with Paul's basic doctrine of "the righteousness of God." However, it should be acknowledged at the outset, that the divisions as suggested are arbitrary, for it is realized that each letter could easily be classified otherwise, since each possesses content related to more than any one of those divisions offered below.

Romans

Romans and Galatians may be viewed together as setting forth God's righteousness revealed in Christ.

Background

Authorship, destination, and integrity.*—No consequential denial of Pauline authorship has ever been made against Romans or against its briefer companion volume, Galatians. Nor does the fact that at least one manuscript omits "in Rome" from 1:7 and "to you also who are in Rome" from 1:15 speak strongly against the Roman destination of the epistle. However, valid questions exist concerning the position of the benediction (16:25-27) and the original destination

---

*"Integrity" is normally the term used in discussing the unity of a piece of literature.

of Romans 16:1-23. These two problems are so related that a consideration of one requires an evaluation of the other. Basically the problem consists in two factors. (1) Some interpreters have long since felt that the sixteenth chapter is much more suited to an Ephesian destination, though no manuscript evidence exists to omit this chapter from Romans. (2) The benediction appears in no less than three positions in manuscripts of the epistle (after 16:23, 15:33, and 14:23), which again raises questions regarding the original ending of Romans.

Several factors tend to weigh the evidence in favor of deleting Romans 16 as an integral portion of the letter, although the evidence is in nowise conclusive. (1) The best papyri manuscript includes the benediction after 15:33. (2) Internal evidence of Romans 16 makes the content of that chapter seem more suitable for Ephesus than Rome. (3) Elsewhere in the Pauline correspondence (e.g., 2 Corinthians), letter fragments are rather evident, despite the lack of external manuscript evidence. If Romans 16 were not an original part of the epistle, the following is offered as an alternate possibility: Paul wrote more letters, both to churches and individuals, than have been preserved; and the possibility exists that Romans 16 represents all that remains of a brief Pauline letter fragment, which was attached to Romans for fear that on its own it might otherwise be misplaced.

Date and purpose.—As was indicated in the previous chapter, Romans was written by Paul from Corinth during his final visit there in the year A.D. 54 or 55 (Acts 20:2-3). Recognizing the crucial significance of this period in the ministry of Paul, interpreters have customarily understood Romans to have been penned for one of two reasons.

(1) *Historical.* Paul was planning a journey to Rome whence he hoped to travel to the regions of Spain for the further proclamation of the gospel (15:23). If he is to accomplish this task, Paul must have the support, spiritual and material, of the Roman church; and this is the goal that the Roman epistle is designed to achieve.

(2) *Doctrinal.* Because he was under grave suspicion by a large segment of the Christian church, Paul wrote Romans as a definitive expression of his faith, with the conviction that this statement would tend to make his position evident and more acceptable to all Christians. Perhaps Paul wrote with both ideas in mind, and with other personal reasons, known only to himself.

Makeup of the Roman church.—Was the Roman church primarily
Gentile or Jewish? In a modest, but scholarly work, William Manson
has formulated a satisfactory judgment with the suggestion that there
were three distinct groups within the church. (1) "The Roman Christian community is Jewish (i.e., Jewish-Hellenist) in the main. (2)
This Jewish-Hellenist community includes a 'Hebrew' minority (regarding which we have fuller light in the Epistle to the Hebrews).
(3) There is also an observing Gentile-Christian section."[1]

Introduction (1:1-15)

Salutation (vv. 1-7).—The first several verses are similar to the
initial verses of Paul's other letters, whereby he identifies himself
as a bond slave of Jesus Christ, set aside as an apostle for the proclamation of the gospel. Basic to the Pauline concept of apostleship
is that of the prophetic office in the Old Testament by which God
calls a man and *commissions* him with a mission and a message.[2]
This message (gospel) concerns God's Son whose earthly heritage
was Jewish and who, through his resurrection, was exalted to the
Heavenly Lord.

Thanksgiving and hope (vv. 8-15).—As with the churches he
founded, so with the Roman church, Paul is constant to remember
them in his prayers. For a long time he had intended to visit their
congregation, and now, by the grace of God, he hopes to fulfil this
desire so he and the church might be mutually strengthened by their
common faith. Paul's intention to preach in Rome is conditioned
not only by his desire of sharing mutual experiences with the Roman
church but by his willingness to preach the gospel to everyone, for
this is the calling he has received from God.

Theme: The Righteousness of God (1:16-17)

In the Christ event is manifest the power of God, effecting salvation
for all who believe. Through the proclamation of this event the
"righteousness of God" is presently being revealed, although one
cannot see this revelation apart from faith. By the "righteousness
of God" Paul does not mean a negative or static quality of a God

---

[1]William Manson, *The Epistle to the Hebrews* (London: Hodder & Stoughton,
1953), p. 183.
[2]See J. Morris Ashcraft, "Paul's Claim and Concept of Apostleship: Concept
in the New Testament" (Doctor's thesis, The Southern Baptist Theological
Seminary, Louisville, Kentucky, 1955).

who sits enthroned in isolated goodness, apart from the sin and evil of the world. Rather the "righteousness of God" is a positive and active quality of a God who seeks to impart himself to a world which, without him, destroys itself. The righteousness of God is God's sovereign grace actively redeeming man, and at the same time annihilating every human attempt to achieve redemption and righteousness on human merits or through human efforts.

The Righteousness of God's Wrath (1:18 to 3:20)

No more is the wrath of God a negative quality than is his righteousness. Indeed, the wrath of God must be understood in the perspective of the righteousness of God. All that God does is for the redemption of man. God does not delight in the punishment of man, and the wrath of God must not be interpreted as God's attempt to "punish" or 'o "get even with" man for his sin. God's wrath is necessarily involved in his righteousness: it is God's attempt to reveal to man an indication of the eternal destruction that man brings upon himself through sin and unrighteousness. Every manifestation of the wrath of God is a token indication of the final outcome for one who habitually sets himself against the will of God, confronting him in judgment and grace. Each expression of the wrath of God is an act of his grace, calling men away from themselves and to God. Therefore, the righteousness of God and the wrath of God are but the "recto" and "verso" sides of God's redemptive grace.

God's wrath and the Gentiles (1:18-32).—God did not leave himself without witness, even in the Gentile world, "for what can be known about God is plain to them, because God has shown it to them." Paul does not hint at any redemptive value in the revelation of God in creation and in man's conscience; he only points out the corruption of life that exists because this revelation is rejected.

When men reject the true God, they construct gods of their own choosing and attribute to their pseudo gods certain "moral standards," through which the lives of their worshipers are corrupted. Despite the repulsion all this is to God, he continues to honor man's decision of rebellion, and constantly speaks to man the word of grace through his "redemptive wrath." The ultimate revelation of man's rebellion—and of God's wrath—among the Gentiles is expressed in the concluding verse: "Though they knew God's decree that those who do such things deserve to die, they not only do them but approve those who practice them."

39. Road at Corinth

God's wrath and the Jews (2:1 to 3:20).—The Jew is no less guilty than the Gentile. Consequently, the wrath of God is as active among the Jews as it is among the Gentiles, although it may not be as immediately apparent. Disobedience to the Mosaic law is no better than disobedience to the law of conscience; each induces the judgment of God. Paul calls upon the Jews to search themselves and discover that they are guilty of the same sins of which they are accusing the Gentiles. He points out that an obedient Gentile is superior to a disobedient Jew; that circumcision of the heart is more valid than circumcision of the flesh (2:1-29).

Paul now raises a question regarding the advantage of the Jews, a question to which he never really gives an adequate answer, unless the answer is to be found in 9:1-6, which is extremely doubtful. Even the custodianship of the "oracles of God" provides no advantage for the Jew should he reject these oracles, as he has, indeed, done (3:1-20).

The Righteousness of God in Justification (3:21 to 4:25)

Achieves what man could not (3:21-26).—Beginning in 3:21 a radical transition in the chain of thought is indicated by the strong adversative, "But now!" Before this point the apostle had endeavored to demonstrate that all human efforts—Gentile and Jewish alike —only result in the wrath of God, because all human efforts, even those directed towards effecting righteousness with God, are preconditioned by sin. What man in his sin could not do for himself, God has done apart from any sort of law, although the Law and the Prophets attest to this deed of God in Jesus Christ. Faith makes this deed available for all in their need, and the need is universal, "since all have sinned and are falling short of the image of God," whose likeness they were created to bear.

Three figures are used to describe the significance of God's action for the human race. (1) Justification—God pronounces the guilty "not guilty!" and offers him the grace of a new beginning without the barrier that formerly separated him from God. (2) Redemption— he whose only freedom was the "freedom to sin" is now granted the freedom to live in righteousness, not a pseudorighteousness which one imposes upon himself, but a genuine righteousness bestowed by the grace of God. (3) Mercy—the terms "propitiation" (KJV) and "expiation" (RSV) are attempts to incorporate into one word the mercy given to man by God at the new "mercy seat," the cross.

Excludes in boasting in human accomplishment (3:27 to 4:25).— God, who is one, has excluded boasting both from the Jew and the Gentile alike because he makes righteousness available to all men through faith (3:27-31). Even Abraham, forefather of the Jewish people, was not able to boast before God, since "Abraham believed God, and it was reckoned to him as righteousness." Abraham's faith, which came about before he was circumcised, makes him the father of all who, like him, commit themselves to God in faith. Thus, the promises God gave to Abraham carry over to all who accept God's grace in faith and do not attempt to place God in their debt (4:1-25).

The Righteousness of God in Salvation 5:1 to 8:39[3]

In this rather extended passage, Paul brings out various implications of God's righteousness manifest in the community of faith. Therefore,

---

[3]The outline for Romans 5-8 is adapted from Anders Nygren, *A Commentary on Romans,* trans. Carl Rasmussen (London: S.C.M. Press, 1952).

since God has accomplished all this for us through his "redemptive righteousness," we have—

Salvation from death (5:1-21).—Utilizing sacrificial terminology, Paul depicts the victory over death made possible for mankind through the death of Christ. Two sets of synonymous parallelism speak of this event, with each figure of the parallelism expressing one facet of the total saving event:

> justified by his blood, . . . saved by him. . . .
> reconciled by [his] death, . . . saved by his life.

Against the background of the sacrificial concepts current in his day, Paul interprets Christ's death as the medium through which Christ's life is released and made available for all who will receive it. Expressed otherwise, the death of Christ is the primary event whereby God reveals and actualizes his love for sinful humanity, making possible man's reconciliation to God (vv. 1-11).

Through Adam's sin, death received its entrée into human history. And death has subsequently been the lot of all men, because all men have sinned after the pattern set by Adam. One recognizes immediately that Paul does not declare all men guilty because of Adam's sin, but Paul does make the history of each human life synonymous with the history of Adam, which may be summarized in two words: *sin* and *death* (vv. 12-14). In sharp contrast to the deed of Adam stands the deed of Chirst. Adam's deed wrought sin, followed by its due recompense of death; Christ's deed effects righteousness, accompanied by its gift of life eternal (vv. 15-21).

Salvation from sin (6:1-23).—Identity with Christ in baptism is the confession of one's identity with the way of Christ, the way of righteousness rather than one's former way of sin. Christ's resurrection means he will nevermore die, because he lives unto God. Likewise, the Christian's resurrection-confession, signified in his baptism, affirms that his life must be dominated by the life of God which destroys the authority of sin (vv. 1-14). True freedom consists in the freedom *not* to sin. But one does not know this freedom unless he enslaves himself to God, by whose grace the freedom to effect righteousness is freely given (vv. 15-23).

Salvation from the Law (7:1-25).—Codified and externally induced rules of life are unnecessary for the Christian, whose manner of life is determined by the will of God, mediated inwardly through the "new life of the Spirit" (vv. 1-6). The purpose of the Law is not to provide a way of salvation but to serve as a "sounding board" for sin. Through the testimony of the Law, one is able to recognize sin, which recognition is calculated to draw one to God. Yet, the human heart—and Paul believes, his heart in particular—is so sinful that even when it recognizes sin and desires emancipation from sin, it cannot resist sin. How then does one become free from the sin which keeps screaming at him through the Law? God himself provides that answer via his Spirit (vv. 7-25).

Salvation through the Spirit (8:1-39).—The secret of Christian salvation is the Spirit of God, who accomplishes within the man of faith what Christ accomplished outwardly through his resurrection. As the resurrection of Christ is the seal of his triumph over death, so the Spirit's presence is the believer's surety of his personal victory over sin and death. And this final victory over death, which includes the transformation of the believer's mortal body, is currently validated by the internal witness of the Spirit. But the reality of the Spirit's abiding within must be evidenced by one's manner of life (vv. 1-17).

Man's fallen condition is ultimately responsible for the corrupt condition of the universe in which man resides. In this passage Paul gives some insight into his understanding of the problem of evil, moral and natural. Basically, Paul affirms that man lives in a world that is in harmony with his nature as a fallen creature, though Paul does not speculate concerning the "historical" or "prehistorical" moment of the fall. If the reader will recall, this is the same answer given to the problem of evil in Genesis 2-3: when man falls away from God, the entire created order, over which man exercises dominion, also falls away from its original intent. Bound up with the final redemption of mankind is the redemption of the world in which man lives.

Presently the world is in "birth pangs," awaiting its new birth which God's Spirit will make possible. In anticipation of this final transformation of himself and of his world, the believer lives in hope (vv. 18-25). And he can live in hope because God's Spirit, who knows both the heart of God and of man, aids the believer in accommodating his will to the will of God (vv. 26-27). For in all situations of life, whether they be the outcome of God's activity or of human sinfulness, God is able to redeem the situation so that something good is able to result from it for the man of faith. Furthermore, because the believer has already seen the absolute revelation of God's love in the cross, he is confident that no external circumstances in life can separate him from that love (vv. 28-39).

The Righteousness of God in the History of Israel (9:1 to 11:36)

Romans 9-11 may represent one of Paul's sermons, inserted in its present position because it was felt by him to have elaborated the truths expressed in the passage immediately preceding.

Paul's lament for Israel (9:1-5).—Deeply distressed by Israel's rejection of Christ, Paul wishes that he could be set aside as a minister to his own people rather than as a "light to the Gentiles."

Israel's rejection and God's sovereignty (9:6-29).—Paul attempts to "justify" the present status of Israel—rejection of God and rejection by God—through three premises, the first of which is God's sovereignty. God has been sovereign throughout all history and the present condition of Israel is but one expression of God's absolute command of history, wherein he either "chooses" or "rejects" whom he will. Although this answer may be academically sound, Paul recognizes that for one who is passionately concerned about the redemption of his own people, this is an empty and cold reply. Upon the basis of this recognition a second premise is introduced.

Israel's rejection and Israel's freedom (9:30 to 10:21).—Although God's election of the Gentiles was within the scope of divine sovereignty, the particular moment of this election was occasioned by the exercise of Israel's freedom in rejecting God. But even amidst Israel's rebellion, God has not utterly forsaken them, because he stands always with his hands held out "to a disobedient . . . people."

Israel's rejection and God's grace (11:1-36).—Evident in God's rejection of Israel is not only his severity but his grace which Paul underlines by three observations. (1) Israel's rejection is neither final nor absolute, as may be witnessed in the conversion of Paul and of others like him (vv. 1-10). (2) An immediate consequence of Israel's rejection is the salvation of the Gentiles, who otherwise would not have known the grace of God so soon (vv. 11-22). (3) In like manner, that the rejection of Israel effected the redemption of the Gentiles, the acceptance of the Gentiles is intended to effect the return of Israel. And Paul *hopes*—he does not predict—that in this fashion, "all Israel shall be saved." However, all human insights and aspirations have their limitations and must ultimately be subject to the wisdom of God (vv. 23-36).

The Righteousness of God in Christian Living (*12:1 to 15:13*)

Each of Paul's epistles may be divided into two major divisions: doctrinal and practical. Customarily the apostle will emphasize certain doctrinal and theological concepts, after which he will elaborate practical applications of these truths and exhort the Christians to abide by them. Generally the hortatory passages are much less difficult to understand than the doctrinal, although in some places (e.g., Rom. 13:1-7) manifold ramifications are possible. Nevertheless, in the present work only a few observations will be made regarding the hortatory sections of the Epistles, with the feeling that the man of faith will often find these passages self-explanatory.

Romans 12 is very similar to 1 Corinthians 12-13. The Christian is called upon to acknowledge his oneness with all believers and to express the oneness through unselfish love.

The next passage, dealing with aspects of the Christian's attitude toward the state (13:1-7), reminds one of the words of Jesus (Mark 12:14-17) and should be interpreted in light of those words. The passage affirms two truths: (1) All authority comes ultimately from God, although no specific authority (government) should be looked

40. Temple of Apollo at Corinth

upon as divinely established; and (2) even an inferior government is superior to anarchy and should be supported by the Christian so long as he can do so in good conscience.

In matters of personal scruples, where right and wrong are not the issue, one should not seek to impose his feelings upon another. One should not injure the faith of another by a constant bickering over issues unrelated to the life of faith. Finally, Paul urges Christians to please others rather than themselves, to the degree that such actions may have redemptive value (13:8 to 15:13).

Concluding Personal Remarks (15:14-33)

Paul again reminds the Roman church of his calling to the Gentiles, reiterates his plans to visit their church, and enlarges upon his reason for coming.

Galatians

Background

Destination, date, place of origin.—The preceding chapter supported the theory that Galatians was written to the churches in the cities of "South Galatia" visited by Paul on his first and second journeys. However, the date and place of origin one assigns to Galatians are dependent upon the conclusion one reaches with regard to the relationship between the Jerusalem visits of Paul mentioned in Galatians 1:18 to 2:10 and those Jerusalem visits listed in Acts (9:26-30; 11:27-30 and 12:25; 15:1-30; 19:21; 21:17 ff.).[4] With reasonable certainty the Jerusalem visit of Galatians 1:18-24 may be identified with the visit of Acts 9:26-30. But with which of the other four visits in Acts should the visit of Galatians 2:1-10 be equated? Neither of the last two visits (19:21 and 21:17 ff.) has strong support, so the interpreter is left with the alternate possibilities of Acts 11:30 (12:25) or 15:1-30. And in the final analysis the question becomes, Did Paul write the epistle before or after the Jerusalem conference mentioned in Acts 15:1-30?

In favor of the theory that the epistle was written *after* the Jerusalem council, it is argued that Galatians forms the natural link between Paul's thought in 2 Corinthians and Romans.[5] But it is

---

[4] Caird, *op. cit.,* pp. 200-209, provides an excellent summary of the various alternatives.

[5] R. H. Lightfoot, *St. Paul's Epistle to the Galatians* (London: Macmillan & Co., 1910), pp. 123-28.

rather precipitous to assign an epistle its place in Paul's career on the basis of development in the mind of Paul, when so few of the apostle's letters are extant. Furthermore, it is argued that the word in Galatians 4:13 translated, "at first," literally means, "the first of two times," indicating that Paul had already completed his second journey before Galatians was written. However, this word appears to have lost its original classical meaning during Hellenistic times and may simply have meant, "formerly," signifying only one previous visit to their region. For those who support this post-Jerusalem conference date, either Corinth (Acts 20:1-3) or Ephesus (19:1-10) is said to have been the city of origin.

Although it may, though not necessarily, presuppose an early date for Paul's conversion (ca. A.D. 30), it is best to contend that Galatians was written *before* the Jerusalem council, unless the decision of that council was without monument for the early church. At the time he writes Galatians, Paul is waging a life-death struggle for the acknowledgment of his apostleship and message. Hence it is quite unlikely that he would have failed to have alluded to the decision of the council or to have mentioned accurately *all* his previous contacts with the Jerusalem church, neither of which he did, if Galatians was written subsequent to the conference. For those who choose this latter alternative, it is advocated that Galatians was written sometime between the conclusion of the first journey and the Jerusalem conference, likely from Antioch, about A.D. 48.

Purpose.—A band of heresy-hunting Jews from Jerusalem had taken it upon themselves to undermine the ministry of Paul among the Galatians. These Judaizers had made the accusation that Paul was not a true apostle and his message was neither genuine nor did it share the approval of the Jerusalem church. To this accusation these men added the affirmation that the Gentiles must evidence their faith by accepting circumcision. Hearing of this intrusion and its shaking effects upon the Galatians, Paul straightway penned Galatians to validate both his apostleship and his gospel and to undo the confusion now in the minds of those persons with whom he had labored so earnestly.

*41. Roman market place
at Corinth*

Introduction (1:1-10)[6]

Contained in this opening section are the predominant themes of the letter: the validity of Paul's apostleship (vv. 1-2), the content of his gospel (vv. 3-5), and the problems raised by the invasion of the false brethren from Jerusalem (vv. 6-10).

Evidences for Paul's Apostolic Status (1:11 to 2:21)

First, it is necessary for the apostle to refute the erroneous claims reporting him not to be a genuine apostle, since neither Paul's message nor the salvation experience of the Galatians is valid unless Paul himself is a true apostle of Jesus Christ. For this purpose Paul presents an aggregate of five evidences validating his apostolic status.

Paul's gospel (1:11-12).—Paul's gospel came to him by way of a special revelation of the risen Lord, an appearance equivalent to the resurrection appearances to the other apostles.

Paul's past history (1:13-17).—The past history of Paul's life, both before his conversion and after his conversion, attest the validity of his apostleship. This one, who had previously been so zealous for his Jewish religious heritage, did not seek out any human agents to approve the call given him by God.

Paul and the visit with Peter (1:18-24).—It was not until three years after his conversion and subsequent to his meditative experiences in Arabia that Paul even went to Jerusalem; and this was but a brief stay of fifteen days, during which time he saw only Peter and James, the Lord's brother. Others of the Judean churches, knowing Paul only by reputation, also attested to the genuineness)f his ministry.

Paul at Jerusalem (2:1-10).—Paul's attitude toward the "noted" leaders of the Jerusalem church further evidences the validity of his apostleship. One cannot be certain whether "after fourteen years" (v. 1) should be calculated from the moment of Paul's conversion or from the time of his initial visit to Jerusalem. Assuming the visit referred to in verse 1 is the famine visit of A.D. 46/47, this could date Paul's conversion either A.D. 33/34 or A.D. 30/31, dependent upon the manner in which the "fourteen years" are calculated. In either case the significance of Paul's visit is clearly docu-

---

[6]The argument and outline of Galatians largely follows Ernest DeWitt Burton, *A Critical and Exegetical Commentary on the Epistle to the Galatians* ("The International Critical Commentary" [Edinburgh: T. & T. Clark, 1952]).

mented: none of the earlier apostles either added to or took from the content of his preaching, nor did any one of them insist that Titus, Paul's Gentile companion, be circumcised.

Paul at Antioch (2:11-15).—Not only did Paul exercise the freedom of an apostle while at Jerusalem, but he even dared to correct Peter, the apostle par excellence, when Peter failed to exhibit an adequate understanding of the gospel's universal implications. Formerly both Peter and Barnabas shared in table fellowship with the Gentile Christians at Antioch, but when a deputation from Jerusalem arrived, both these men gradually withdrew from fellowship with the Gentiles—a basic denial of the gospel which caused Paul to correct them with fervor.

Crucified with Christ (2:16-21).—Verses 15-21 serve as a climax to the first set of Paul's arguments and as a transition to his second series of arguments. Drawing a conclusion from his experiences at Antioch, Paul reminds his readers that not even the Jews, much less the Gentiles, can hope to establish themselves righteous before God through the keeping of the Law. Any attempt to merit one's salvation through an identity with the regulations of the Law automatically nullifies the grace of God. Conversely, to identify oneself with the grace of God manifest in the cross voids the power of the Law to keep one from God.

Evidences for Paul's Gospel of Justification by Faith (3:1 to 4:31)

The entirety of this section consists of a series of propositions designed to demonstrate that salvation is realized through faith, not through the meritorious keeping of the Law.

Experience of the Galatians (3:1-5).—Paul's thesis, justification by faith, is shown to have applied to the experience of the Galatians themselves, who were given the Spirit as the guarantee of their salvation received through their response of faith. On this premise it would be illogical to conclude that the life begun in faith could possibly discover its goal in the keeping of the Law.

Experience of Abraham (3:6-9).—Abraham's status with God resulted from his response in faith. Consequently all who experience God in faith are the legitimate "offspring" of Abraham and heirs of the promises God made to Abraham.

The Law and the relation between faith and law (3:10 to 4:21). —Having denied the validity of the Mosaic law as a means of salvation, the apostle now ventures to explicate the purpose of the Law and to contrast the consequences of faith salvation with those of Law salvation.

(1) The initial illustration (3:10-14) is extremely difficult to master. It appears that Paul intended to demonstrate that the Law was designed to bring a "curse" (judgment) upon those who broke its regulations rather than to justify men before God. Every man stands under the "curse" of law, because every man has committed a breach of its commandments. To these observations the apostle introduces a "proof text" to indicate that the "curse" of the Law fell upon Christ because of his crucifixion (v. 13). By joining these two Old Testament passages, Paul is able to interpret the death of Christ as the means whereby others might be delivered from the "curse of the Law." To modern ears this methodology of argumentation sounds strange. For the hearers of Paul it was an accepted mode of debate that enabled him to demonstrate the relevance of Christ's death and the necessity of faith.

(2) Since the covenant between God and Abraham antedated the giving of the Law, the Law cannot nullify the promise of faith without a new agreement between the original founders of the covenant; and no such agreement between God and Abraham exists to void the original covenant (vv. 15-18).

(3) By now Paul can hear in his mind the response of his opponents, "Why then the Law? Is it against the promise of God?" To these supposed questions Paul provides some concrete answers. The Law is not contrary to the promises of God; it was given that the promises of God might be effectual. Apart from the intervention of the Law and its "curse" against sin, one could not realize his need of faith to receive the promises of God (vv. 19-29). Even an heir cannot receive his "promise" until the time designated by his parents. Thus it is with the Law and faith: the Law was a disciplinarian to keep men conscious of their sin until the "fulness of time," when through faith in Christ men could receive the promise of God and live in freedom from the power of sin (4:1-7).

(4) Again Paul returns to the experiences of the Galatians themselves, inquiring why they are willing to exchange their present gains for their previous losses. He reminds them that to accept the message of Judaism virtually returns them to their former state, wherein they superstitiously venerated supposed demonic powers of the universe (vv. 8-10). Paul follows this inquiry with a spontaneous outburst of his deep concern for the Galatians (vv. 11-20).

(5) A final description of the relationship between faith and the Law is given in the allegory of Sarah (the free woman, typifying faith) and Hagar (the slave woman, typifying the Law), which tells the Galatians that faith frees a man for the service of God while the Law binds a man for judgment (vv. 21-31).

Implications of Justification by Faith (5:1 to 6:10)

As is customary with the apostle, he derives from his doctrinal statements applications and exhortations relevant to the specific needs of the church or churches addressed.

Hold fast to freedom in Christ (5:1-12).—There exists no middle ground: one either depends upon his own achievements or upon the grace of God for salvation. Any attempt to supplement faith with human merit immediately destroys the redemptive value of the cross and reduces one from the freedom of God's grace to the bondage of the Law.

Liberty and license (5:13-26).—Christian liberty means love, not licentiousness. One must not permit his freedom from the "curse" of the Law to become a base of operations for immorality. Paul speaks here, as in many other places, of the battle raging between the "flesh" and the "Spirit." He is neither making man into a dichotomous being nor is he speaking of a natural evil attached to the physical aspect of human personality. For Paul, "flesh" takes on overtones far outreaching the connotations commonly conveyed by that term.[7]

"Flesh" is the totality of the unregenerate man in his rebellion against God, who is Spirit. The physical side of human personality is not necessarily involved in Paul's use of "flesh," except as the body becomes the medium through which one expresses his rebellion against God. Furthermore, the apostle realizes that one's faith commitment does not straightway destroy one's sinful nature, so that a constant struggle exists between one's natural proclivity toward self-love and one's devotion to God, prompted by God's Spirit.

Freedom and forgiveness (6:1-5).—Divine forgiveness is a gift to be shared within the community of faith; but one who offers the forgiveness of God to others must not act in a spirit of haughtiness and pride.

---

[7]Rudolph Bultmann, *Theology of the New Testament*, trans. Kendrick Grobel (New York: Charles Scribner's Sons, 1951), I, 232-56, is the best discussion available on the Pauline concept of "flesh."

The ministry: spiritual and material aspects (6:6-10).—Verses 7-10 must be taken together with verse 6. In verse 6 the church is exhorted to share its material possessions with the one who exercises a spiritual ministry in their midst, while the next verses describe the issuances arising from the neglect or fulfilment of this ministry with regard to one's material possessions.

Concluding Personal Remarks (6:11-18)

A final review of Paul's thesis is hastily offered, followed by the reminder of his own love for the Galatians.

1 Corinthians

Just as Romans can be related to Galatians, 1 Corinthians can be related to certain other letters of Paul. These are 2 Corinthians, 1 and 2 Thessalonians, Philippians, and Philemon. The unifying theme is God's righteousness revealed in the Christian life.

Background

Paul's correspondence with Corinth.—Included within 1 and 2 Corinthians are indications that Paul wrote at least four letters to the church at Corinth.[8] And it is primarily upon the internal evidence of these two epistles themselves that the following reconstruction of the Pauline Corinthian correspondence is suggested.

The previous letter.—Alluded to in 1 Corinthians 5:9 is a letter in which Paul warned the church not to intermix its fellowship with persons who were not believers and whose lives were immoral. From the context in which this allusion occurs, it seems as if the Corinthian church must have understood this letter as a demand for them to have no contact or association whatsoever with the unchristian element of their society, a demand which would have been impossible to fulfil. Now Paul is writing 1 Corinthians 5:9 ff. to correct this wrong impression and to emphasize again the necessity of separation from immoral persons within the church.

Second Corinthians 6:14 to 7:1 suits the character of this "previous letter."

(1) The content is the same as one would expect from the

---

[8]Moffatt, *Introduction*, pp. 109-10. The reconstruction offered by Moffatt represents a rather well-accepted approach. Walter Schmithals, *Die Gnosis in Korinth. Eine Untersuchung zum den Korintherbriefen* (Göttingen: Vandenhoeck und Ruprecht, 1956) represents a much more extreme reconstruction.

allusion in 1 Corinthains 5:9. In 2 Corinthians 6:14, the command, "Do not be mismated with unbelievers," has reference to the purity which must be maintained within the fellowship of the church, as the remainder of the passage makes exceedingly evident. In this passage the apostle is not dealing with "mixed marriages," but with the need for separation of the church from persons whose immoral character does not manifest the grace of God.

(2) This small segment represents a digression in the context. One can skip this passage and have no disconnection in the continuity of the letter. For example, 6:13 bids the Corinthians to "widen your hearts", while 7:2 continues, "Open your hearts to us." Obviously this previous letter was written sometime before 1 Corinthians, as is indicated by 1 Corinthians 5:9, and quite likely from Ephesus, soon after Paul had left Corinth (Acts 18:18).

The purpose of 1 Corinthians.—First Corinthians was occasioned by two factors: (1) news from the household of Chloe concerning the factions and immorality within the Corinthian church had reached the ears of Paul (1:11 ff.); and (2) correspondence from the Corinthian church had come to Paul, requesting his guidance about certain issues (7:1). It is probable that Stephanas, Fortunatus, and Achaicus had conveyed this letter to Paul (16:17-18). First Corinthians was written from Ephesus in the spring of the year that Paul left Ephesus (16:8,19), perhaps A.D. 54 or 55. Possibly Titus and others accompanied this letter to Corinth.

Introduction (1:1-9)

Paul's universal outlook is immediately reflected in his recognition that the Corinthian congregation is a local expression of the total "church of God" and in his identity of the Corinthian Christians with "all those who in every place call on the name of our Lord Jesus Christ." God's faithfulness to his people is revealed and the Corinthians' faithfulness to God is invoked in Paul's prayer.

Factions Within the Church (1:10 to 4:21)

After Paul rebukes the partisan spirit within the church, he exhorts them to unity.

Rebuke of the factions (1:10-17).—The believer is called upon to be united with the Lord, not with a particular minister whom he likes or whose preaching is eloquent. Such dissensions were not induced by the ministers to whom the Corinthians appeal; none of these ministers baptized in his own name or claimed to have been crucified for the Corinthians.

Exhortations to unity (1:18 to 4:21).—On several grounds, each of which is essential to the heart of the Christian faith, an appeal is made for unity. (1) The "word of the cross," God's message to man, may divide the world, but it unifies the people of God, who otherwise possess no wisdom or power (1:18-31). (2) The one Spirit of God, who effected demonstrations of his power through the hands of the apostles, presently operates within the lives of those who are spiritual, granting them the grace to overcome party spirit and strife (2:1 to 3:4). (3) A proper conception of the Christian ministry demands unity. Each minister performs for the church that which God has called him to do, and unless it is God who "gives the growth," no minister's service is valid. Each minister can only build upon the foundation, Jesus Christ; and should any-one attempt to destroy this temple (the church), he destroys him-self, because he separates himself from the community of faith wherein abides the Spirit of God (3:5 to 4:21).

Problems Necessitating Church Discipline (5:1 to 6:20)

The Corinthian religious background was tainted with immorality and it was only natural for some of them to carry over certain elements of their pre-Christian heritage into their church life. This does not justify, it only explains, their actions. One example will aid the reader to understand the gross immorality present at Corinth. The temple of Aphrodite at Corinth provided a thousand priestesses who were temple prostitutes for the constant service of the "wor-shipers." And this was but one of the many religious systems in Corinth that promoted immorality in the name of religion. Hence one can readily understand Paul's constant struggle to aid the Gentile Christians in understanding the moral implications of their new religion.

Incest (5:1-13).—One member of the Corinthian congregation was living in incest with his young stepmother. Paul rebukes the Corinthian church for its laxity in discipline and tells the church to exclude such a person from its fellowship, thereby consigning him to Satan. Paul's demand to "deliver this man to Satan" reflects the New Testament concept that the Spirit of God abides only within the church, and outside the church is the realm of Satan, where one can be harmed by Satan's power. One notices that Paul's ultimate intention in this matter is to redeem the man rather than to destroy him, which again indicates Paul's understanding of God's "redemptive wrath."

Litigation before pagan judges (6:1-11).—Instead of resolving their personal problems within the context of the church, some of the congregation were taking their grievances against fellow Christians before the pagan courts. This not only placed the Christian congregation in a bad light among the pagans, but it both denied the ability of the believers to discern what was right and expressed an attitude of revenge on the part of those who went before the pagan courts. To permit oneself to be wronged is better than to wrong the entire Christian community at Corinth by reflecting a vengeful spirit before the eyes of the world.

Sexual immorality (6:12-20).—The declaration that "all things are lawful" must be taken *cum grano salis,* because it certainly does not apply in matters of morality.[9] Paul was writing to persons who felt that they were so "spiritual" that physical involvements could not affect their spirits. However, the apostle reminds them that there is no valid severance between one's body and spirit. Consequently, sexual union with a prostitute signified a union of their spirits as well. Furthermore, such a union was the expression of a selfish love which destroys human personality, rather than the expression of a redemptive love.

Questions the Corinthians Raised (7:1 to 11:1)

Questions pertaining to marriage (7:1-40).—The reader should note that the apostle is not writing an essay on marriage; rather he is answering specific questions raised by the Corinthian church.

(1) *Marriage and celibacy* (vv. 1-9,17-38). As a reaction against the rampant immorality of their pagan background, some of the Corinthians had begun to wonder about the propriety of marriage itself. Paul answers that marriage and celibacy alike are proper; neither is superior to the other. If a couple is married, they should continue their sexual relations with one another as a normal and wholesome aspect of the marriage union. Should they refrain from their marital union, this must come about only by mutual agreement and for a brief season. Otherwise, one member of the marriage might be tempted to find sexual fulfilment outside marriage.

---

[9]Schmithals, *op. cit.,* p. 197.

In verses 8 and 9, Paul turns to the question regarding the "unmarried [widowers?] and the widows," and relays his opinion that these people are better off if they remain single as he himself. Customarily, though not necessarily so, a Jewish man of Paul's station would have been married, which raises the question regarding what Paul meant by "single as I am." Had Paul never married or was he a widower? No final judgment may be given.

In either circumstance Paul's suggestion that they not marry was based upon two presuppositions. First, the end of the world was at hand, so that one should not add extra burdens to himself that would cause him added anxiety when the sufferings of the last days approached (vv. 17-31). Second, the unmarried person would not be disturbed by the affairs of married life and would be able to devote himself fully to the Lord (vv. 32-38).

It is in light of this second observation that verses 36-38 should be understood. These verses may describe either the passion felt by one toward his fiance or else the convictions of a father who was holding back his daughter from getting married so she could devote herself "full time" to the Lord. In either case, there is reflected indirectly the influence of Paul's feeling—whether he was right or wrong—that marriage was a potential threat to the spiritual devotion of the individual.

(2) *Marriage and separation* (vv. 10-16). Paul appeals to the teaching of the Lord to convey his conviction that separation should not come about between Christians wed to one another. Nevertheless, in case this should occur, they are either to be reunited or else to remain single. At Corinth a unique situation had arisen because of the coming of the Christian proclamation. On occasion one member of a marriage union had become a Christian, but the other had remained in his unconverted state. Should one who becomes a Christian automatically leave the other marriage partner because that one would not become a Christian? Paul answers, "No!" As long as the pagan marriage partner sees fit to continue the marital relationship in such a manner that the conscience of the Christian marriage partner is not injured, the Christian should remain within the relationship.

Questions concerning idols (9:1 to 11:1).—Related issues dealing with the problem of idolatry are discussed in 1 Corinthians 8 and 10, while chapter 9 represents a digression in which Paul applies to himself the principle of love stated in the previous chapter.

(1) Should a Christian, who recognizes that idols are nonentities, purchase and eat meat which had been sacrificed to idols? This was a very practical question to the Corinthians, for meat sacrificed to idols was not only abundant but inexpensive. Paul affirms that one is free to exercise this privilege, only so long as he does not injure the conscience of the weaker Christian, who may yet not fully have overcome his previous conviction that idols do have a real power behind them and who may stand on the verge of going back into heathenism.

(2) Should a Christian, who recognizes that idols are nonentities, participate in idolatrous feasts? Whereas, Paul's answer to the first question is beset with certain qualifications, his answer to this second question is an unqualified, "No!" Paul's reason for this dogmatic retort was based upon the concept, prevalent in his society, that eating meat in an idolatrous feast was a confession of the

participant's identity with that deity represented by the idol. How could one in good conscience participate at once in the table of the Lord and in the table of demons?

Problems Related to Church Fellowship and Worship (11:2 to 14:40)

In general the Corinthians were to be commended for keeping the "traditions" of Christian fellowship and worship mediated to them through the apostle. However, there were certain laxities.

Conduct of women in worship (11:3-16).—The Christian message had heralded the equality of both sexes before God. But there was danger that the Christian women might be misunderstood if they permitted their newfound freedom to grant them too much boldness in the public assembly. In Paul's day it was customary only for improper women to conduct themselves boldly in a mixed congregation. Thus Paul suggests that the Christian women at Corinth take care that their conduct be not misinterpreted, even if it meant relinquishing some of their freedom.

Lord's Supper (11:17-34).—Participation in the Christian meal must not be patterned after the manner of participation in the suppers dedicated to "Lord Caesar" (v. 20), in which drunken debauchery and overindulgence were the orders of the day. In strong contrast the Christian suppers must confess the oneness and equality of each participant with the other, whether he be slave or master. Therefore, the Corinthians are warned not to conduct this meal in such a manner that open abuse is heaped upon some brother, who himself is a member of the body of Christ.

Spritual gifts (12:1 to 14:40).—Spiritual gifts are all gifts of the ᴊne Spirit. No one gift is superior to the others, although one gift may have a more illustrious appearance than the others. Each gift is necessary and makes its own unique contribution, without which the Christian "body" would lack completeness (12:1-31). The ultimate test of Christian character relates not to these external gifts, but to the inner core of life, where love must reign supreme. Because self-giving love is the very essence of God's nature, it is a quality that remains when all gifts have outlived their usefulness (13:1-13). An indication of the Corinthian's inferior value judgments is seen in their supreme appraisal of the gift of "tongues," which has only negative effects, unless someone is able to interpret the meaning of the experience. And even then, there is some doubt as to its value (14:1-40).

Problems Concerning the Resurrection of the Believer (15:1-58)

The comparative length of this section concerning the resurrection attests its primal significance in the mind of the apostle. Likely the questions concerning the believer's resurrection had been raised by a group of persons who were indoctrinated with the belief in the natural immortality of the soul and who could not bring themselves to accept any concept of a physical resurrection, which to them was signified by the Christian teachings concerning a bodily resurrection. Remaining in the main stream of his Jewish-Christian heritage, Paul staunchly denies the natural immortality of the soul and qualifies what he means by a bodily resurrection.[10]

Reality of the Lord's resurrection (vv. 1-11).—Since the resurrection of the believer is contingent upon the resurrection of his Lord, Paul begins with an article concerning the reality of the Lord's resurrection. The resurrection of Christ, an essential element in the Christian tradition, had been transmitted to the Corinthians through the teachings of the apostle. He had declared to them the redemptive significance attached to the death-resurrection event and had affirmed the reality of this event by an enumeration of reliable witnesses, himself included. And the Corinthians had not only heard, but they had accepted, the reality of this event as the basis of their faith.

The Lord's resurrection and the resurrection of the Christian (vv. 12-34).—Unless the resurrection of Christ is a reality, the believer is without hope, because he has placed his faith in one who is yet dead. Furthermore, the Christian tradition is a fraudulent misrepresentation of God, if Christ has not been raised from the dead (vv. 12-19). But the fact of the matter is that Christ has been raised from the dead, and through his resurrection has made life a reality as Adam made death a reality. And the resurrection of Christ is the seal of his final victory, when death will be altogether vanquished and his victory shared with the believing community.

All of this is achieved through the resurrection of Christ in order that all men might properly honor God, who has made the victory possible (vv. 20-28). Indeed, both the Corinthians and the apostle

---

[10]For a discussion of the Christian doctrine of resurrection as opposed to the non-Christian concept of immortality, Oscar Cullmann, *Immortality of the Soul or Resurrection of the Dead?* (New York: The Macmillan Co., 1958). On this passage in particular, M. E. Dahl, *The Resurrection of the Body* (Naperville, Ill.: Alec R. Allenson, 1962).

believe in this reality and have so given witness by their actions. Otherwise the testimony of baptism [11] is invalid and the sufferings of the apostle are useless (vv. 29-34).

The believer's resurrection body (vv. 35-58).—Not all bodies are of the same nature because the nature of any given body is dependent upon the nature of the realm in which God has designed that body to exist (vv. 35-41). This truth may be seen in the analogy between the physical body and the spiritual body. One's natural body is designed to exist in the realm of the earthly, where all is perishable, whereas one's spiritual body is designed to exist in the realm of the heavenly, where all is imperishable. The resurrection body is no longer flesh and blood; it is a spiritual body designed for existence in the realm of the eternal (vv. 42-50).

One must never forget that this victory over death is not achieved by some supposed natural immortality of the soul, but by a creative act of God, who shall raise from the dead all who believe, as he raised from the dead their Lord (vv. 51-56).

Concluding Remarks (16:1-23)

Collection for the Jerusalem church (vv. 1-4).—The Corinthians are exhorted to have their contribution ready when Paul arrives so that he might send it forthwith to Jerusalem through the hands of persons whom the Corinthian church had approved.

Personal plans (vv. 5-23).—Customary concluding remarks, combined with several personal allusions relevant to the specific situation, form the final portion of 1 Corinthians.

2 Corinthians

The Harsh Letter (10-13)

Two observations combine to suggest that 2 Corinthians 10-13 may comprise part of a "harsh" or "sorrowful" letter that Paul wrote to Corinth. (1) These four chapters make a drastic break in the continuity of the epistle. Chapter 9 is overflowing with praise

---

[11]For the history of the interpretation rendered 1 Corinthians 15:29, cf. Martin Rissi, *Die Taufe für die Toten. Ein Beitrag zur paulischen Taüferlehr. Abhandlungen zür Theologue des Alten und Neuen Testaments 42* (Zurich: EVZ Verlag, 1962), who deduces that the Corinthians appear to have exercised a vicarious baptism in behalf of the dead as a visible witness to the coming resurrection. A similar conclusion is rendered by James Moffatt, *The First Epistle of Paul to the Corinthians* ("The Moffatt New Testament Commentary" [London: Hodder & Stoughton, 1951]), pp. 252-53.

for the Corinthians, whereas in the next chapter Paul quite un-expectedly takes up the rapier of a combatant which he wields mercilessly throughout the remaining chapters. (2) Evidence from within the Corinthian epistles speaks for a sorrowful visit Paul made to Corinth, to which 2 Corinthians 10-13 may well be the sequel. According to 1 Corinthians 4:19-21 the apostle's authority was challenged by persons who were leading the Corinthian church astray, and he promised that he himself would make a visit there to remedy the situation.

From 2 Corinthians 2:1; 12:14; and 13:1 there is a fair inference that Paul made this disciplinary visit. After this brief visit he must have returned to Ephesus sad and baffled because he believed he had failed in his mission (2 Cor. 10:10; 12:21; cf. 2:5-6). But what he was unable to accomplish in person he sought to effect by means of this "harsh letter" (2 Cor. 2:3; 7:8 ff.). What can be assumed as the content of this "harsh letter" (e.g., matters of im-morality and the challenge of Paul's apostleship) is contained in 2 Corinthians 10-13. In light of these observations it is suggested that these chapters contain at least part of the "harsh letter." Titus was either the bearer of this letter or else traveled to Corinth not long after Paul sent the letter.

Paul's authority and mission[12] (10:1-18).—False apostles within the Corinthian church had accused Paul of cowardice and weakness. In reply, Paul indicates that on his arrival there he would demon-strate to them both his boldness (vv. 1-6) and his strength (vv. 7-11). Moreover, Paul himself was the first to reach the Corinthians with the gospel; these false apostles have come only recently for the sake of selfish advantage (vv. 12-18).

Conditions at Corinth necessitate Paul's boasting (11:1 to 13:14). —In order to destroy the strength of these pseudo apostles Paul must demonstrate his own powers as an apostle. This he will ac-complish by "boasting" of his personal achievements among the Corinthians (11:1-6).

(1) Paul may boast because he refused to accept maintenance from the Corinthian congregation, although his ministry merited their help. These false apostles cannot make similar claims (vv. 7-15).

---

[12]The outline of 2 Corinthians is adapted from Alfred Plummer, *A Critical and Exegetical Commentary on the Second Epistle of St. Paul to the Corinthi-ans* ("The International Critical Commentary" [Edinburgh: T. & T. Clark, 1948]).

(2) Paul's sufferings, in behalf of the Corinthian church in particular and in behalf of his mission in general, are sufficient grounds to exhibit his dedication to his calling. How much have these false apostles endured for the faith?

(3) Do these false apostles boast because of feigned revelations they supposedly received through special endowments of the Spirit? Paul received such a genuine and exalted revelation through the Spirit that he was given a bodily limitation so he would not boast of this experience (12:1-10).

(4) Paul's apostleship was confirmed to the Corinthians by those signs which accompany a true apostle, a claim these intruders cannot boast for themselves (vv. 11-18).

(5) Although, in reality, neither Paul nor the false apostles possess any grounds of boasting because of special powers, Christ is powerful and will demonstrate his strength through the hand of Paul on Paul's arrival at Corinth (13:1-14).

The Joyful Letter (1-9)

Rather soon after sending the "harsh letter," Paul departed Ephesus for Troas, intending to meet Titus, who would inform him of the further developments at Corinth. When Titus did not arrive in Troas, Paul went to Macedonia (2 Cor. 2:12-13), where Titus found and comforted Paul with good news concerning the Corinthians' change of heart (7:5-16). Overcome with joy, Paul responded immediately with this "joyful letter" (2 Cor. 1-9 minus 6:14 to 7:1).

Introduction (1:1-11).—In unison Paul and Timothy express their love for the Corinthians, reminding them of the sufferings joyfully endured by them for the sake of the church.

God's will and God's strength (1:12 to 2:17).—Paul's change in plans, by which he refused to visit the Corinthians in anger a second time, was dictated by the will of God rather than by Paul's vacillation (1:12 to 2:4). In like manner the Corinthians ought to conduct the disciplinary matters of their church according to the will of God, who gives grace and strength to his servants (2:5-17).

Paul's evaluation of the Christian revelation (3:1 to 5:21).— First, the Christian revelation is contrasted with the Mosaic revelation (3:1-11). The presence of the Lord's Spirit in the Christian congregation effects a more confident approach to God for the believer than was possible during the pre-Christian period. And this abiding Spirit of God constantly transforms the life of the worshiper into the likeness of God as revealed in Christ.

Second, hope and encouragement are provided through the Christian revelation (4:1 to 5:21). Amidst the blind rebellion of the world (4:1-6) and the frailty of human life (vv. 7-12) the Christian disciple is sustained by the weight of those things unseen, which are permanent (vv. 13-17). Even if death should intervene, the Spirit of God is the believer's guarantee that God will transform his mortal body into a body designed to live in the realm of the eternal. Consequently, hope is the essence of a faith which prompts the believer to bear witness (5:1-11). As in Christ God was reconciling the world to himself, so presently in the church God is actively addressing the world through his ambassadors, the apostles (vv. 12-21).

Finally, the Christian revelation is related to apostleship and discipleship (6:1-13; 7:2-16). The sufferings of Christ, revealing the heart of God to the church, continue in the lives of the apostles and are called for in the lives of the Corinthian disciples.

The collection for the impoverished Christians of Jerusalem (8:1 to 9:15).—Although beset with many afflictions, the Macedonian churches have already contributed according to the full extent of their ability. An involvement of this type in the needs of others is necessitated through one's commitment to the Lord. Hence the Corinthians are urged to complete the collection which they initiated over a year ago.

1 and 2 Thessalonians

Background of 1 Thessalonians

Authenticity.—A few denials of Pauline authorship have been leveled against 1 Thessalonians, but with little consequence. Both from the external evidence (e.g., the presence of 1 Thessalonians in the earliest known collection of Paul's letters) and from the content of the letter itself an almost unanimous voice is raised in favor of Pauline authorship.

Occasion and purpose.—Having departed Thessalonica under negative circumstances, Paul was deeply concerned about the future of his converts at Thessalonica. Thus when Timothy arrived at Athens with news from Thessalonica (1 Thess. 3:1-2), Paul sent him on a return trip with this letter. Through this epistle the apostle offers the Thessalonians encouragement and hope: encouragement because of the example their faith has set, and hope for their loved ones who have died in faith.

The Thessalonians and Paul (1:1 to 3:13)

Almost the entirety of this first section concerns a review of Paul's ministry at Thessalonica and his consequent anxiety for their welfare in combination with his praise for their constant firmness in the faith.

The Thessalonians and Their Lord (4:1to 5:28)

No inconsistency is involved in Paul's following up his praises with admonitions. Even though the Thessalonians had made many strides in their Christian faith, they had not reached maturity in certain areas.

The Lord and daily life (4:1-12).—Marriage is a sacred relationship which must not be defiled by adultery. Adultery becomes a sin against God, who designed the marriage relationship and whose Spirit has revealed the holiness of marriage to the Christian community (vv. 1-8). Discipline in daily living is demanded by one's faith commitment: Be "busy," rather than a "busybody," is Paul's exhortation (vv. 9-12).

The Lord and the departed (4:13 to 5:11).—Evidently the eschatological outlook of the Thessalonians was conditioned by Jewish apocalyptic expectations which had been taken over as a part of the Christian message. Bound up with this outlook were expectations of an earthly reign which would be initiated by the eturn of their Lord and which would by participated in by those of his followers who were still alive at that time. Some of the Thessalonians had died since Paul's ministry there and their loved ones were anxious about the future of these departed ones. Would the departed believers be at a disadvantage when the Lord returns?

Paul's answer indicates that the departed believers will actually have an advantage over those who are still alive at the Lord's return for "the dead in Christ shall rise first."

In the discussion of 2 Thessalonians 2:1-12 further elaboration will be given the particular coloring of the apocalyptic outlook of the Thessalonians. But, for the present, a word of caution is in order. The reader should be careful lest he become overly literalistic in his interpretation of these apocalyptic passages dealing with the second coming. In the New Testament the second coming is a very basic doctrine and ought not be so tremendously distorted by placing the emphasis upon the mode or time in which this event will transpire.

Primarily the second coming has a double importance. (1) It is the affirmation that the same God who in the beginning created the universe and who has declared himself in Jesus Christ will be openly acknowledged by all peoples as the Lord of creation 'and of history. (2) From this recognition the church receives hope and encouragement for its temporal witness to the Lord of the church, who, in reality, determines the destiny of all men.

The Lord and the congregation at Thessalonica (5:12-28).— The Thessalonians are enjoined to follow their leaders in a responsible manner, evaluating honestly all men who profess to speak in the name of the Lord, and expressing proper appreciation for those whose work evidences the power of the Spirit.

Background of 2 Thessalonians

Authenticity.—This companion volume of 1 Thessalonians has also been set upon with charges against its authenticity.

(1) Differences in eschatological outlook between the two epistles is said to deny the genuineness of 2 Thessalonians. But one should recall the many impossible contradictions that can "logically" exist side by side in apocalyptic literature. In this particular case, there appear to be no basic contradictions: 2 Thessalonians merely elaborates and supplements the apocalyptic-eschatological presentation of 1 Thessalonians.

(2) Nor is there any necessary difference between the presupposed recipients of these two letters. Apocalyptic elements would have been just as intelligible to Gentiles as to Jews; especially if the Gentile Christians had previously been Jewish proselytes, which is not at all an impossible conclusion. McNeile's evaluation is correct: to preclude the integrity of 2 Thessalonians "raises difficulties as great as those which it solves."[13]

Occasion.—Somehow Paul received the intimation that the first epistle had not achieved its anticipated end and the situation at Thessalonica had grown rather severe. More Christians were be-

---

[13]*Op. cit.,* p. 131.

coming lax and idle because of false impressions concerning the second coming. With much more strictness and with some less personal warmth, Paul hopes to restrain this misinterpretation of the Christian's role during the interval before the close of the age.

Salutation and Warning (1:1-12)

A second time the Thessalonians are commended for their steadfast faith, especially in a community influenced by the Jewish prejudice against the Christian message. Suffering is no more than the followers of Christ can expect from the Jewish society, since their Lord also experienced ignominy at the hands of the Jews. But God will requite those who pervert his will.

The Return of Christ (2:1-12)

Apocalyptic terminology is used by Paul to demonstrate that the end of time was not upon them. In apocalyptic thought the world was to grow progressively worse until immediately before the close of history the power of evil would attain its apex. At this moment a final "rebellion" would be led against God by one variously called

43. Paul's voyage to Rome

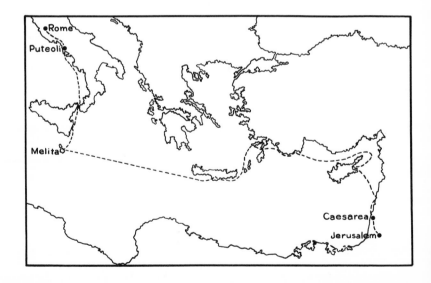

the "man of lawlessness," the "son of perdition," or the "lawless one." When this rebellion had reached its final proportions, God would intervene, whereupon the power of evil would be destroyed and an earthly kingdom of peace and righteousness established. One can perceive the logic of Paul's argument: the "man of lawlessness" has not arrived and the "rebellion" has not begun, therefore, the end of the world cannot be in the immediate future. On this basis the Thessalonians are enjoined to readjust themselves to their normal routine of life and to conduct themselves as Christian disciples. Did Paul accept this apocalyptic outlook himself, or was he simply accommodating himself to the thought patterns of the Thessalonians? Apparently he did accept it as he wrote 2 Thessalonians, although he later seems to have modified his thinking.

Conduct During the Interval (2:13 to 3:17)

Christian conduct is a more valid and authentic witness to the grace of God than is the pretension to foretell the end of history. The Thessalonians are encouraged to follow the example of the apostles who served in their community and who demonstrated that work rather than laziness was the proper manner in which to conduct oneself during the interval.

Philippians

Background

Roman or Ephesian origin?—Four epistles, Ephesians, Philippians, Colossians, and Philemon, have in common the affirmation that Paul was in prison during the period of composition. For this reason these epistles have become known as the "prison epistles." Each epistle has special problems of its own, but from their joint witness to a Pauline imprisonment arises the difficulty of deciding what imprisonment was meant. The problem resolves itself into two possibilities: Rome and Ephesus. In favor of Rome is the certain knowledge that Paul was imprisoned in Rome, a conclusion which cannot be argued so affirmatively for Ephesus, though a great deal of evidence points towards the possibility of an Ephesian incarceration.[14] Most of the other arguments favoring Rome also favor Ephesus,

---

[14]For a critique of a Roman origin and for further evidence in favor of an Ephesian origin, see J. Hugh Michael, *The Epistle of Paul to the Philippians* ("The Moffatt New Testament Commentary" [New York: Harper & Bros.,) n.d.]) pp. xii-xxi.

while the weightiest contentions against a Roman origin are the implied journeys mentioned in Philippians (especially of Epaphroditus), which presuppose a more ready access of the Philippians to Paul than would have been possible at Rome.

The unity of Philippians.—Philippians 3:2 inaugurates a change in tone within the epistle that has caused many to assume Philippians contains two (or more) Pauline letter fragments welded into one. Some who hold to this theory feel that both parts (1:1 to 3:1 and 3:2 to 4:23) were addressed to Philippi,[15] while others maintain these fragments were sent originally to separate readers.[16] Moffatt, accepting the essential unity of the epistle, notes, "The hiatus is striking, but it need not denote the place at which two notes have been joined." For this reason Moffatt looks upon 3:1 to 4:1 and 4:2-9 as two postscripts attached to the original letter, with 4:10-23 rounding off the topics interrupted by the excursus begun at 3:1.[17]

Purpose of Philippians.—Several considerations were in Paul's mind when he wrote Philippians, but the primary consideration appears to have been that of informing the Philippians concerning Epaphroditus, whom they had sent to undergird Paul during his imprisonment. Evidently, the Philippians were upset with Epaphroditus because news had reached them that it had fallen Paul's task to minister to Epaphroditus, who had become ill after his arrival and was currently planning to return home. The apostle reminds the Philippians that Epaphroditus had ministered well in their behalf, even to the point of involving his own safety. Secondary reasons for the letter may be listed as follows: (1) to inform the Philippians of Paul's own situation and personal plans; (2) to address the problems within the church; and (3) to thank the readers for their con- 'tribution to the gospel.

Introduction (1:1-11)

Including Timothy along with himself, Paul addresses the church and their leaders, "the bishops [overseers] and deacons." Mention of these two classes of church officials has been suspected by some

---

[15]Edgar J. Goodspeed, *An Introduction to the New Testament* (Chicago: University of Chicago Press, 1953), pp. 90-92.

[16]McNeile, *op. cit.*, pp. 179-80, believes that 3:2 to 4:1 is foreign to the passages which precede it, and so concludes that this fragment was sent to other readers.

[17]*Introduction*, pp. 175-76.

to be a later interpolation; but this is in nowise a necessary conclusion, unless one feels these titles must be understood in their later, more technical sense.

A prayer concludes the introduction.

Paul's Personal Situation (1:12-26)

Paul's incarceration has served to propagate the gospel. Through his imprisonment, opportunity has been provided to witness to his guards, and boldness has come to other disciples who have heard of Paul's steadfastness. Despite his desire "to depart and be with the Lord," Paul is willing to accept the impoverishment and deprivation and suffering of a continuing earthly ministry for the sake of the Philippians.

Exhortations, Plans and Warnings (1:27 to 3:2)

Exhortation to a proper confession (1:27-30).—The Philippians are exhorted to keep their manner of life in harmony with their confession of Christ's lordship. Such a commitment will permit them the joy of suffering for the gospel, an experience that identifies them more closely with Paul and their Lord.

Exhortation to humility (2:1-11).—How should one interpret the frequent Pauline phrase "in Christ" (v. 1) and its companion phrases "in Jesus," "in the Lord," and "in him"? Paul evidently intends no mystical absorption of the believer into the person of the Lord by which the believer's individual identity is lost in a "beatific vision." This interpretation would be contrary both to the Jewish and Christian understandings of God and human personality. Paul's usage of these terms must be rendered in light of his presentation of the church as the "body of Christ." To be in Christ is the equivalent of being in his body, the church, wherein resides or dwells the Spirit of God.

In Philippians 2:6-11 Paul appeals to a hymnic description of Christ as an example of Christian humility which the Philippians are called upon to follow.[18] Beyond a doubt this hymn is one of the most profound and beautiful passages in all the New Testament. Originally it appears to have been arranged into six strophes, the first three demonstrating the humiliation and the last three declaring

---

[18]Ernst Lohmeyer, *Kyrios Jesus, Eine Untersuchung zu Phil. 2:5-11* (Heidelberg: Carl Winter, Universitätsverlag, 1961), pp. 5-6, 12-13.

the exaltation of Christ.   Lohmeyer's strophic arrangement is pursued.

(1) Who, though he was in the form of God,
        did not conspire
        to grasp after equality with God;
(2) But he emptied himself,
        when He took the form of a servant,
        when He came in the likeness of men;
(3) And because He appeared in human form,
        He emptied himself,
        becoming obedient unto death.
(4) Therefore God highly exalted him,
        and gave to him
        the Name above every other name;
(5) That at the name of Jesus,
        every knee should bow,
        in heaven, on earth, and under the earth;
(6) And every tongue should confess
        "Jesus Christ is Lord!"
        to the glory of God the Father.

Miscellaneous exhortations (2:12-18).—Most significant among this series is the exhortation for the Philippians to carry out the full implications of their redemptive experience with "fear and trembling," because God himself is the one who grants them both the will and the power to approach this goal.

Plans and explanations (2:19-30).—Paul indicates his plans to send Timothy to Philippi. Then he explains the status of Epaphroditus.

Warnings (3:1-21).—Whether Paul's opponents were one or several is difficult to ascertain from the context. Walter Schmithals[19] believes they were one: Jewish libertine Gnostics[20] who placed a symbolic interpretation upon circumcision as a seal for the annihilation of the

---

[19]*Op. cit.,* p. 174, fn. 1.

[20]For a more detailed explanation of the term "Gnostic," cf. below pp. 270-72. Hermut Koester, "The Purpose of the Polemic of a Pauline Fragment (Philippians III)," *New Testament Studies,* 8 (April, 1962), 317-32, reaches a different, but somewhat related, conclusion when he suggests that these opponents are "typical of early Christian gnosticism," p. 331.

44. Puteoli (modern-day Pozzuoli), where Paul landed in Italy

flesh. F. W. Beare[21] interprets these opponents as several: Judaizers emphasizing the value of circumcision (3:2-16); and antinomians, perceiving no necessity for morality (3:17 to 4:1). Whatever the actual situation may have been, Paul's answer nullifies the significance of circumcision and attacks those who do not perceive that the Christian commitment involves morality. In addition he points out that their distorted claims of "spiritual maturity" are founded upon false premises, which invalidate the meaning of their Christian confession.

Conclusion and Thanks (4:1-23)

Paul concludes his appeal for humility and unity with a special reference to the friction existing between Euodia and Syntyche, two of the more prominent women in the Philippian congregation. He summarizes the position taken in the main body of the letter and gives thanks to the Philippians for their material possessions supplied in his behalf.

Philemon

Several indications hint at a common place of origin for Colossians and Philemon: Paul's imprisonment, inclusion of Timothy in the introduction, and the same persons mentioned in the greetings.[22] The least complicated theory is to assume that the letter was written for the sake of encouraging Philemon to receive Onesimus, his runaway slave, in the same spirit of love and gratitude that he would have received Paul himself. Philemon possessed the legal authority to exact the death penalty from Onesimus, but Paul reminds Philemon of the useful service that Onesimus has rendered the gospel and calls upon Philemon to receive him "no longer as a slave but more than a slave, as a beloved brother."

How may one best account for the presence of this brief and personal note in the Pauline collection? C. L. Mitton points out that a certain Onesimus was bishop of Ephesus toward the end of the first century when Ignatius journeyed through that city on his

---

[21]*A Commentary on the Epistle to the Philippians* ("Black's New Testament Commentaries" [London: Adam and Charles Black, 1959]), p. 101; cf. pp. 100-141.

[22]Martin Dibelius, *An die Kolosser, Epheser, an Philemon.* Third edition by D. Heinrich Greeven ("Handbuch zum Neuen Testament" [Tübingen: J. C. B. Mohr (Paul Siebeck), 1953]), pp. 10-12.

route to martyrdom in Rome. As Ignatius writes back to the Ephesian church he includes an unusual number of indirect reflections on Paul's letter to Philemon, a letter he never once alludes to in his other known correspondence. Mitton conjectures that this is the same Onesimus referred to in the epistle to Philemon and that he has subsequently become bishop of Ephesus. He further argues that about A.D. 90 Onesimus undertook to collect Paul's letters and included among them Philemon, because it possessed a unique relevance for his own personal life.[23]

Colossians

Background

Colossians and Ephesians deal with the theme, God's righteousness revealed in creation, in history, and in the church.

Authenticity of Colossians.—Arguments against the Pauline authorship fall into two classifications: (1) *Language and style.* But the problems are not as insurmountable as some would presume. The number of new words and phrases is not extreme, and the stylistic variations may well be attributed to the polemical situation and to the content of the liturgical materials incorporated into the letter. (2) *Content and opponents.* One need no longer assume that the incipient Gnostic dangers combatted by the epistle were post-Pauline. There is a strong possibility that certain of the problems faced by Paul at Corinth and at Philippi were preconditioned by Gnostic viewpoints similar to those opposed in the Colossian letter.

The Colossian heresy (definition of gnosticism).—Behind the heresy at Colossae lay a type of cosmological speculation determined by the presuppositions of a form of Jewish gnosticism.[24] Details of the specific Gnostic heresy at Colossae will be mentioned throughout the exposition; but before proceeding any further it is necessary to offer a brief definition of gnosticism. All the numerous Gnostic sects known to have existed were founded on the same basic presuppositions, regardless of the unique external expressions and paraphernalia of any particular sect.

(1) *Dualism.* It is believed that there exists a permanent con-

---

[23]*The Formation of the Pauline Corpus of Letters* (London: Epworth Press, 1955).

[24]Dibelius, *op. cit.,* p. 39.

tradiction between the world below and the heavenly world. The former is the world of darkness, imperfect and doomed for decay, while the latter is in the world of light, eternal and perfect.

(2) *Redemption.* This dualism carries over among the world of men: some are "natural" (or "earthly"), belonging completely to the world of darkness, and cannot be saved; others are "spiritual," with their souls temporarily imprisoned in a body of flesh, longing for their return to the world of light. To these who are "spiritual" belongs the gift of *gnosis* (an innate spiritual "knowledge"), which grants them an understanding of their true origin and nature, as well as the mystery of redemption.

(3) *Freedom.* Since the Gnostic is of the heavenly world, he cannot be subject to the "powers" of the earthly realm in which he lives; he must express his freedom with respect to the world of flesh and material. This Gnostic concept of freedom expresses itself in one of two diverse patterns: Asceticism—the Gnostic may demonstrate his superiority over the world of flesh by overcoming all the natural desires of the flesh, or else he may elect a contrasting route of freedom—libertinism. The latter view holds that the physical world can in no way contaminate the Gnostic's pure spiritual being, leaving him free to indulge in all the sins of the flesh, especially in immorality and idolatrous feasts.

Occasion and place of origin.—No definite judgment can be made with respect to the place from which Colossians was written, but the choice lies between Rome and Ephesus. From the content of the letter several deductions may be drawn concerning the occasion which invoked the correspondence. Paul had never visited Colossae nor the neighboring city of Laodicea (2:1), though he knew their ministers (1:7) and perhaps had been indirectly responsible for the Christian mission into the cities of the Lycus Valley. For some reason Epaphras, the Colossian minister, had felt himself incompetent to encounter further the heretical invasion of Colossae and had called upon Paul to address the congregation, which he did in this letter.

Introduction (1:1-14)

After mentioning his concern for the Colossians and his high regard for Epaphras, Paul advances directly to his basic premise (v. 14). The Gnostic leaders at Colossae had claimed the believers' relationship with Christ insufficient to deliver them from the power of the demonic forces surrounding the earth and to gain them access into the world of light. Therefore the Colossian Christians had been cautioned to venerate these demonic forces through various ascetic practices and to seal their veneration through the acceptance of circumcision (2:11-23).[25] Paul's response was to the contrary: Christ has already delivered the believer from the sway of all demonic forces, real or imagined, and has made effective, even in the present, the kingdom of his Son, in whom is complete redemption.

The Significance of Christ (1:15-23)

In order to demonstrate the superiority of Christ over all other powers, Paul quotes a Christological hymn consisting of two stanzas, the former emphasizing the cosmological and the latter the soteriological (redemptive or saving) function of Christ. Whether the hymn was originally written about Christ or taken over from a Gnostic hymn and subsequently applied to Christ, the effect remains the same: all events, past, present, or future, find their meaning only in Christ.

Christ and creation (1:15-17).—Evidently the Colossians had fallen into the error of limiting the redemptive activity of Christ to the forgiveness of sins and had overlooked his total cosmological significance.[26] Hence this initial stanza of the hymn defines Christ in his relationship to God and the universe. (1) Christ, the visible manifestation of the invisible God, existed before all creation. (2) He is the mediator between God and the visible world below, and is the one through whose creative power all else has come into being. And this comprehensive creative work of Christ includes the creation of all "powers" ("thrones, lordships, principalities, and authorities") existing in the realm between heaven and earth, powers which the Colossians feel constrained to venerate. Through Christ all creation continues to be sustained, and he is the goal toward which creation and history are moving.

Christ and the church (1:18-20).—Christ's triumph over death enabled him to inaugurate a new creation, his body, the church. Inasmuch as Christ shares the "fulness of God" (a technical term

[25]In Jewish gnosticism circumcision gained a different meaning from that which it held in Judaism, where it was a token of the covenant relationship. For the Gnostic it symbolized one's conquest of the material world.

[26]Dibelius, *op. cit.,* pp. 10-12.

with many overtones, emphasizing the absolute relationship between Christ and God), his redemptive activity includes the totality of the created order in its estrangement from God. With this passage might be compared Romans 8:18-19, where also the entire created order is conceived of as affected by the saving work of Christ.

Christ and the Colossians (1:21-23).—Through their own faith the Colossians have enjoyed the salvation offered by Christ; only Paul warns them, lest they be led astray by these false teachers.

The Divine Mystery and Paul's Ministry (1:24 to 2:7)

Again the New Testament motif of lordship-discipleship comes to light: the sufferings of Christ are carried over into his body, the church. Because Paul is a member of Christ's body, he himself endures the sufferings of Christ. That God's intention includes the salvation of the Gentiles is a "mystery," once hidden, but now revealed to the church. Only in Christ does one then become "mature" (a term used by Gnostics to characterize themselves), because it is in him alone that this "mystery" is known (1:24-29). The next verses (2:1-7) are transitional.

Truths Derived from the Cosmic Significance of Christ (2:8 to 3:4)

Since Christ's work is cosmic in its effects, it accomplishes for men not only the forgiveness of sins but emancipation from the "elemental spirits of the universe" (equivalent to the "thrones, lordships, principalities, and authorities" of 1:16). From this axiom Paul derives two truths: (1) No longer need the believer fear or venerate these "powers" (2:16-23) because their influence was destroyed through the work of the cross (v. 15). (2) The believer must direct his gaze toward Christ, who sits enthroned above all "powers" (3:1-4). By means of the diagram provided below the reader can conceive more accurately the premise from which Paul derived these truths.

CHRIST—"Heavenly World," "World of Light"

authorities
principalities } "ELEMENTAL SPIRITS" or "POWERS"—"WORLD OF DARKNESS"
lordships
thrones

EARTH

The "powers" were thought to determine man's fate on earth, to prevent his soul from traveling to the "World of Light." In opposition to this view, Paul taught that:

1. Christ is the *Creator* of all that exists.
2. Through his death he *conquered* the entire fallen creation, including the rebellious "powers."
3. Therefore, the believer must look beyond all "powers" to Christ, who is enthroned "Lord of all."

Exhortations to Christian Living (3:5 to 4:6)

Introduced at 3:5 is the hortatory section of the epistle, dealing with various areas of the Christian life: All believers must avoid immorality (3:5-11) and develop positive Christian virtues, especially love (vv. 12-17); they must demonstrate Christian grace in all aspects of the family relationship (vv. 18-21). Slaves and slave owners alike must act with equanimity toward one another (3:22 to 4:6).

Personal Greetings and Conclusion (4:7-18)

Greetings are sent from Paul and his fellow ministers who are with him at the time of writing. Mention of the "letter to Laodicea" (v. 16) has caused no little debate. The most frequent suggestion is that the reference is to a letter, similar in content to Colossians, but which is now lost. John Knox has advanced the theory that the letter referred to is the canonical book of Philemon, which was actually addressed to Archippus, owner of Onesimus and host to the Laodicean church. If this is the case, the words of verse 17 are to encourage Archippus to conduct himself properly toward his returning slave, Onesimus.[27]

Ephesians

Background

Authenticity of Ephesians.—On several accounts Pauline authorship has been brought into question.[28]

(1) *Language and style.* No final judgment may be leveled against the authenticity of Ephesians on the linguistic and stylistic evidence alone, since to some degree the purpose and emphasis of a writing will determine its language and style.

(2) *Contrast between Colossians and Ephesians.* It is denied that the same author could be responsible for Colossians and Ephesians because different interpretations are given the place of the church and the significance of Christ's person and death. Although different emphases are made in these areas of thought, this factor does not necessarily militate against a common authorship, for the specific emphases in any writing are determined by its anticipated goal.

(3) *Literary affinities.* Literary dependence upon some of the later New Testament literature (e.g., Luke-Acts, John, 1 Peter) is argued. Yet this argument is far from conclusive, and the evidence presented in its behalf is often quite subjective.

(4) *Form.* All of Paul's other writings are genuine "letters,"

[27]*Philemon Among the Letters of Paul* (London: Collins, 1960).
[28]The following summary is indebted to McNeile, *op. cit.*, pp. 166-75 and Moffatt, *Introduction*, pp. 375-89.

including salutations and benedictions, while Ephesians is apparently more general, without attachment to a particular letter situation. In rebuttal the proponents of a Pauline authorship appeal to the personal allusions incorporated into Ephesians as indications of its authenticity.

(5) *Doctrinal.* Several doctrinal features are believed to be difficult to account for unless Ephesians is post-Pauline. Two such doctrinal problems will be mentioned. (a) References to the "holy apostles and prophets" (3:5) and to the "apostles and prophets" (2:20) as the foundation of the church intimate a period when "the apostles" were looked upon quite objectively and on equal par with the Old Testament "prophets." The only other New Testament counterpart to this usage is found in Revelation 21:14, written toward the close of the first century. (b) The claim of Ephesians 3:4 ("When you read this you can perceive my insight into the mystery of Christ"), which is probably intended to elevate the status of Paul, is said to read more like a Pauline disciple than like Paul.

Destination of Ephesians.—Omission of "in Ephesus" (1:1) from a number of manuscripts has opened the door for several different opinions regarding the destination of Ephesians.

(1) Many have theorized that Ephesians was originally written by Paul as a circular letter, with a copy sent to each of several Asian churches. According to this theory the "in Ephesus" present in some manuscripts merely attests that these particular manuscripts were produced from the copy of the circular letter received at Ephesus. But this thesis is confronted with two objections: (a) Omission of place-names appears not to have been the methodology of ancient letter writers. (b) If other churches received copies of this circular letter, why is it that Ephesus is the only name to occur in any of the extant manuscripts?

(2) This letter was originally sent to Ephesus, but for some reason or other a later scribe omitted "in Ephesus" from his manuscript. A major flaw in this assumption is that it offers no satisfactory reason for the scribal deletion.

(3) It is put forward that Ephesians was written by a Pauline disciple in Ephesus as a preface to the Pauline letter collection.[29] But an outstanding weakness of this theory is that no known collection of Paul's letters places Ephesians at the forefront.

---

[29]Goodspeed, *Introduction*, pp. 222-26.

One can immediately recognize that no single theory of authorship and destination is without its difficulties; so the student of Ephesians will accept as a "working hypothesis" the particular conclusion he feels to be most adequate. Although the major topics of discussion relevant to Ephesians have customarily centered about the question of authenticity, the reader should be reminded that the basic reason for the study of this epistle—as for the study of any biblical writing—is to uncover the *message* of the author, whoever he was.[30] Discussions of date, authorship, destination, and related issues are relevant only to the degree that such discussions contribute to the understanding of the book's message.

Purpose of Ephesians.—Assuming that Paul wrote Ephesians, what was his purpose? Answers to this question generally follow one of two viewpoints, polemical or doctrinal. Some interpret Ephesians as a continuation of Paul's polemic against heresies similar to those at Colossae. Others understand Ephesians as the exposition of Paul's concept of the church and/or his philosophy of world

---

[30]Henry Chadwick, "Die Absicht des Ephesesbriefes," *Zeitschrift für die Neutestamentliche Wissenschaft,* 51 (1960), 145.

46. Coin of Nero

history in light of God's purpose as revealed in Christ. For those who do not support the Pauline authorship, it is generally maintained that a close disciple of Paul's, familiar with his outlook and endowed with his spirit, wrote this summary statement of Pauline theology as a tribute to the "apostle of the Gentiles." Whether by Paul or another, whether polemical or doctrinal, the main theme of Ephesians in the church—one, holy, universal, and apostolic.[31]

Prayer of Thanksgiving and Praise (1:3-14)

Ephesians begins with a solemn and profound prayer of thanksgiving to God for all he has provided "in Christ." The liturgical and hymnic traits of this passage have long since led interpreters to look upon these verses as a prayer composed for public worship, perhaps designed to be offered in conjunction with a baptismal service.

Chosen in Christ (vv. 4-6).—The "election" of the church, realized in union with Jesus Christ, God's "Elect One," is in accord with the eternal purpose of God. "In Christ" the believers already experience the benefits and values of the heavenly world, since God has chosen to create "in him" a new humanity, destined "to be his sons" and to share the divine image and glory.

Redemption in Christ (vv. 7-10).—Although the forgiveness of sins can in no sense be minimized, the reader is again reminded (as per Romans and Colossians) that the redemptive scope of Christ's mission includes the entire universe. Indeed, this recognition tends to magnify the work of forgiveness, without which the universe would remain in its corrupted condition. Yet only in the church ("in Christ" of v. 9) is this revelation of God's intention for the universe proleptically experienced and proclaimed.

Inheritance in Christ (vv. 12-14).—"In Christ" both Jews (*we*, v. 12) and Gentiles (*you*, v. 13) are united in anticipation of the full inheritance promised the people of God. For the present the Spirit's dwelling in the life of the church is the divine attestation to the complete inheritance toward which God is directing his church.

God's Purpose Revealed in Christ (1:15 to 2:22)

Prayer for the understanding of God's purpose (1:15-19).—No event has ultimate relevance for the life of a people unless they are

---

[31]*Ibid.,* 146.

able to perceive the meaning involved in the event. Consequently, Paul prays for spiritual perception on the part of the church, that they might have insight sufficient to discern the true character of their inheritance revealed in Christ's work.

God's purpose revealed in Jesus Christ (1:20 to 2:10).—Christian salvation, prepared for all mankind, is not without its historical roots in the triumphant death-resurrection event; nor is this salvation event without its concrete realization in the body of Christ, the empirical church (1:20-23). This salvation has been revealed to the Gentiles so that in the present, as in the future, God might of his own grace bestow upon them the benefits of his goodness (2: 1-10).

God's purpose shared "in Christ" (2:11-22).—Before the historical moment of God's revelation through Christ, the Gentile world neither knew of nor shared in the promised salvation. But "in Christ" Jews and Gentiles are united, both participating together in the divine grace. The "dividing wall of partition" may refer either to the division within the Jewish Temple or to the Gnostic concept of a wall (guarded by the "principalities and powers") designed to prevent man's entrance into the heavenly world.[32] However one interprets this wall, the conclusion is essentially the same: "In Christ" the powers of evil are defeated and all men, Jews and Gentiles alike, are given free access to God.

The Call of God and the Unity of the Church (3:1 to 4:16)

God's call and Paul's mission (3:1-21).—God's call has revealed to Paul the mystery of the church: "the Gentiles are fellow heirs, *members of the same body,* and partakers of the promise *in Christ Jesus* through the gospel" (v. 6). For the proclamation of this mystery Paul was called to be an apostle; for the knowledge of this mystery Paul bows in praise before God; and for the church's growing comprehension of this mystery Paul constantly prays.

One God—one church (4:1-16).—Correlative with the oneness

---

[32]It is tempting to interpret this passage, and many others in Ephesians, as a rebuttal to the Gnostic presuppositions. Cf. Petr Pokorný, "Ephesierbrief und gnostic Mysterien," *Zeitschrift für die Neutestamentliche Wissenschaft,* 53 (1962), 160-94, especially 180-91.

47. The Appian Way, traveled by Paul on the way to Rome

of God is the oneness of the church—the *one* Spirit dwells in all "the body," the *one* Lord is confessed by all "the body," and the *one* God is Father of all "the body." The poetic parallelism of this affirmation possibly reflects a hymnic confession offered at baptism and may be so formulated:

> One Spirit . . . one body
> One Lord . . . one confession
> One God . . . one Father

A further concomitant, arising from the oneness of God and the oneness of the church, is the oneness of the Christian ministries. All spiritual ministries, no matter how diversified in their function, are gifts of the one Lord whose Spirit is striving to bring the church **to full maturity** so that the *ideal* oneness of the church shall ultimately become an *actual* oneness. This actual oneness is not achieved through mystical identity with Christ, but through the developing of a mature love within the family of God. To paraphrase a Pauline figure of speech, "Now the church sees in a mirror dimly; now the church sees in part. But when love is finally matured, the church will know its Lord, even as it is known by its Lord." Only then will the church truly become at one with itself and with its Lord.

The Call of God and the Holiness of the Church (4:17 to 6:20)

Not only does the oneness of God determine the oneness of the church, but the holiness of God underlies the holiness of the church. To use an Old Testament parallel: "Because I am holy, you shall become holy." In a Christian context holiness involves a twofold significance: (1) separation to the worship and service of God, and (2) participation in the divine image and character. God's holiness, which defines the nature of the holiness to which the church is called, is most adequately described by unselfish and redemptive love. In keeping with these truths, the hortatory section explicates the meaning of redemptive love in various avenues of the church's relationship with itself and with the world.   These exhortations, semipoetic in form, are almost self-explanatory, but should be read with much deliberation and care.

1 Timothy

Three of Paul's letters, 1 and 2 Timothy and Titus, have long been grouped together under the designation Pastoral Epistles.

Their unifying theme is God's righteousness revealed in the worship and ministry of the church.[33]

Background

Problem of the Pastorals. In recent years the Pauline authorship of the Pastorals has been challenged.[34] Many have concluded that these letters were written after Paul's lifetime by a faithful disciple who felt the church of his day needed someone to speak in the spirit and name of the apostle. This Pauline disciple combined some of Paul's genuine letter fragments along with his own spiritual insights into what he felt would be a practical guide for the church and ministry of the post-Pauline era. A conclusion of this nature is not designed to deny the divine authority behind these letters. Proponents of this view realize that divine inspiration is not limited to any given theory of authorship, whereas the contemporary relevance of these letters is dependent in large measure upon a proper knowledge and understanding of the circumstances and occasion of their writing.

Challenges to the Pauline authorship come from several directions. Four of these are of a literary character: (1) *Lack of early manuscript witness.* The Pastorals appear neither in the Chester Beatty papyri (the earliest papyri collection extant) nor in the collection of Marcion (a heretic of the mid-second century who made the first known collection of New Testament writings). (2) *Problem of Paul's release and second imprisonment.* To support the Pauline authorship one must assume that Paul was released from his initial imprisonment, carried on further missionary activities in the East (rather than in Spain as was his stated intention in Romans), and finally was reimprisoned. Beyond the Pastorals themselves no other New Testament literature intimates these journeys. (3) *Language and style.* Many of Paul's favorite expressions are absent; while some of the favorite expressions in the Pastorals do not occur in the other

---

[33]P. N. Harrison, *The Problem of the Pastoral Epistles* (Oxford: The University Press, 1921) pp. 13-16, points out that the earliest known designation of these letters as "Pastorals" goes back to Thomas Aquinas, while the "modern application of this term to these epistles collectively as a technical designation" is traced back to Paul Anton in lectures delivered at the University of Halle (1726-27).

[34]Harrison, *op. cit.;* Moffatt, *Introduction,* pp. 395-420; McNeile, *op. cit.,* pp. 188-200; Goodspeed, *Introduction,* pp. 327-44; Burton Scott Easton, *The Pastoral Epistles* (New York: Charles Scribner's Sons, 1947), pp. 1-35.

of Paul's epistles. And the feeling of spontaneity and vitality, so apparent in the other Pauline letters, is noticeably lacking in the Pastorals. (4) *Method of dealing with the heresies and problems.* Whereas, in his other writings Paul uses logic and argumentation to refute the heretical doctrines, in the Pastorals the heresies are merely condemned apart from the presentation of reasoned bases.

Four other problems grow out of content. (1) The ecclesiastical organization is more complex and developed than the fluid organization of Paul's day. Bishops, presbyters, and deacons, along with their qualifications and organizational responsibilities, are mentioned in some detail. Widows, in order to receive church support, must have been faithful to the church throughout the full course of their married life. (2) A *completed* body of Christian doctrine is assumed and may be referred to as "the faith" (in contrast to Paul's concept of "faith" as a living and dynamic experience), "the truth," "the deposit," "the teaching," or "the commandment." (3) The Christological and theological affirmations, though not contrary to Paul, are never used by him in his other epistles, and represent developments away from the traditional Pauline thought patterns. For example, God, not Christ, is spoken of as "Saviour"; and the familiar Pauline echo, "in Christ," is hauntingly absent. (4) The character of the heresy combatted suggests developments after Paul's time. Apparently the Gnostic problem has become more acute than it was in Paul's day; and there is a possibility that the injunction to avoid the "contradictions (antitheses) of the false knowledge (gnosis)" may be a reference to Marcion's heretical book entitled *Antitheses.*

These challenges to the authenticity of the Pastorals have in turn received rebuttal from the proponents of the Pauline authorship.[35]

It is pointed out that the exclusion of the Pastorals from the Marcionite collection speaks neither for nor against their acceptance by the early church. Their absence from the Beatty Papyri is explained from the fact that the last part of the Beatty collection, where the Pastorals would have been included, is not intact. Furthermore, their use in the early church is attested by Polycarp of Smyrna (*ca.* A.D. 110-17), who supposedly alludes to at least three passages from the Pastorals.

---

[35]Donald Guthrie, *The Pauline Epistles* ("New Testament Introduction" [Chicago: Inter-Varsity Press, 1961]), pp. 198-246; Alfred Wikenhauser, *New Testament Introduction,* trans. Joseph Cunningham (Freiburg: Herder-Druck, 1958), pp. 445-52.

The problem of Paul's release and second imprisonment is not insurmountable unless one assumes that *all* of Paul's activities are mentioned in Acts, an unwarranted inference indeed. Acts itself, both through reference to the words of Agrippa (26:32) and through the allusion to Paul's freedom in teaching (28:31), intimates that the Roman imprisonment was not the final curtain to Paul's ministry. Then too, the early church tradition assumes Paul's release. Clement of Rome (A.D. 95) tells of Paul's preaching mission to Spain, as does the apocryphal Acts of Peter.

One cannot fairly decide against the authenticity of the Pastorals on the basis of linguistic statistics. Admittedly, the style and vocabulary are peculiar, but these peculiarities are explained from the unique nature and intention of these epistles.

Paul's treatment of the heresies is not so different from his earlier epistles, where he sometimes condemns the heretical or immoral person without offering a full explanation of his reasons.

The ecclesiastical and doctrinal developments are not so late as is often imagined. Philippians 1:1 (cf. Acts 20:17) mentions the bishops and deacons side by side, while Acts 6:1-6 alludes to the church's concern for the widows. With respect to the alleged later doctrinal developments, it is noted that Paul did speak of "the faith" in the same manner that this phrase occurs in the Pastorals (Phil. 1:27; Col. 2:7; Eph. 4:5); and one is reminded that the other doctrinal developments reflected in the Pastorals are incipient in Paul's earlier epistles.

Finally, very few interpreters, it is said, presently maintain that the heresies opposed in the Pastorals are later than the last years of Paul's life.

The date assigned the Pastorals is dependent upon one's decision with regard to the authorship. For those who designate these epistles post-Pauline, dates anywhere from A.D. 90-125 have been suggested. On the other hand, if Paul himself wrote the letters, an acceptable period would run from A.D. 62-65. On this latter assumption 1 Timothy and Titus were written under the shadow of Paul's encroaching martyrdom, while 2 Timothy was composed almost immediately prior to the dark event.

Purpose of the Pastorals.—Assuming a non-Pauline authorship, these letters were composed by a disciple of the Pauline circle who attempted to make relevant Paul's message for a later generation. If Pauline authorship is acknowledged, the purpose of these letters is quite manifest. First Timothy was written for guidance in the proper conduct of church order and to give moral support to Timothy's ministry. Titus, closely related in form and content to 1 Timothy, was written to encourage Paul's fellow minister to meet Paul at Nicopolis. According to 2 Timothy, Paul is now in prison, expecting death, and he writes with anticipation of his victory to be achieved through death and with warnings to Timothy about the false teachers.

Occasion of 1 Timothy (1:1-20)

Into the first two verses is incorporated a predominant theme of the Pastorals: "The teaching that Timothy receives from Paul has *divine authority*—and so is forever unalterable."[36] On the basis of this divine authority Timothy is encouraged to oppose the false teachers and their perverted teachings.[37] (1) These false teachings are discontinuous with the gospel (1:3-11). No value for Christian discipleship may be realized from the mythological speculations concerning the demonic forces that supposedly surround the world and are said to exercise control over human fate.[38] Such speculations generally are prompted by persons who have no vital faith and whose lives are profligate. (2) As Paul, the worst of all sinners, received divine power for his ministry, so will God's power be provided for Timothy (1:12-17). In verse 15 is the first appearance of a formula ("The saying is sure and worthy of full acceptance") frequently utilized in the Pastorals to introduce an accepted confessional statement (cf. 3:1; 4:9; 2 Tim. 2:11; Titus 3:8). (3) Compliant with the testimony of his ordination, Timothy is exhorted to stand firm and not to pursue the example of those who have wrecked their confession (1:18-20).

---

[36]Easton, *op. cit.,* p. 30. Emphases added. Easton makes this observation with reference to the opening verses of 2 Timothy, but the same judgment may be made with reference to 1 Timothy 1:1.

[37]The outline of this section is dependent upon Walter Lock, *A Critical and Exegetical Commentary on the Pastoral Epistles* ("The International Critical Commentary" [Edinburgh: T. & T. Clark, 1952]), pp. 3-4.

[38]In light of Titus 1:14, where these "myths" are specifically defined as Jewish, and Titus 3:9, where "genealogies" are united with questions concerning the Law, it is tempting to understand these as some sort of Jewish-Gnostic speculation. For a different interpretation, E. F. Scott, *The Pastoral Epistles* ("The Moffatt New Testament Commentary" [London: Hodder & Stoughton, 1948]), pp. 8-9, who connects the teachings with the methodology of Jewish rabbis, without any reference to gnosticism.

General Regulations for Church Life (2:1 to 3:13)

Regulations for public worship (2:1-15).—(1) The church's prayers are to incorporate a concern for all people, within and without the community of faith, for God wills the redemption of all men (vv. 1-7). (2) Men are to be the dominant leaders in public worship and women are to assume a secondary role (vv. 8-15). The reason for this instruction is perhaps the same as that connected with the injunction of 1 Corinthians 11:3-16, but the method of validating this procedure is interesting. Paul interprets the fall as the responsibility of the "woman [who] was deceived and became a transgressor." A number of choices are possible for the interpretation of 1 Timothy 2:15. However, in light of the context, it is probable that this is an expansion of the two previous statements: Men, not women, are to be the public worship leaders; women are to be quiescent and find their ministry in the proper rearing of their families, which will establish them faithful in the sight of God.

Qualifications for church leaders (3:1-13).—All biblical terms used to describe the church leaders (bishop, elder, deacon) are beset with various connotations colored by the particular ecclesiastical background of the reader. To the degree that one can, it is best to dismiss from one's mind the current connotations attached to these designations and to note the qualifications and duties presented in 1 Timothy itself.

(1) *Bishop* (vv. 1-7). According to Titus 1:5-9, bishop and elder are equivalent terms. Perhaps the former depicts the responsibility and the latter the maturity of the churchman. Most of these qualifications are self-explanatory. But what is meant by the requirement that "he be the husband of one wife"? This regulation is best understood in the broadest sense possible, that the bishop should be a man of absolute purity, whether married or single. Among the implied duties of the bishop are presiding, teaching, regulating finances, and witnessing to the non-Christian society.

(2) *Deacons* (vv. 8-10, 12-13). Etymologically the word "deacon" means to "minister" or to "serve," and such is the intimation of this passage for the duty of the office. Verse 10 may imply a probationary period that the candidate is to undergo before being instated, or else it may simply imply that his life must previously have given evidence of his steadfast Christian character.

(3) *Deaconesses* (v. 11).—A question looms about this verse. Are the "women" wives of deacons, or are they "deaconesses," who

minister to areas of the church life wherein it would be extremely difficult for the deacons to do so in all modesty? In light of the fact that the early church is known to have recognized the office of deaconess a few years later, the latter interpretation is more probable.

The Mystery of Faith (3:14-16)

This brief passage, transitional by location, contains a Christological hymn which calls for special attention. In the hymn the redemptive work of Christ is described in relation (a) to the world of men and (b) to the heavenly world.

He was manifested in the flesh [a],
vindicated in the Spirit [b],
   seen by angels [b],
preached among the nations [a],
believed on in the world [a],
   taken up in glory [b] (v. 16).

Warnings and Instructions to Timothy (4:1 to 6:21)

Danger of false asceticism (4:1-5).—Upon the Gnostic assumption that the entire material world was essentially evil, certain pseudo-Christian teachers were forbidding marriage and setting regulations on what foods could be eaten without spiritual defilement. Timothy is reminded that marriage, if kept pure, and all foods, if eaten with thanksgiving, are within the creative intention of God. Furthermore, the presence of so many false teachers is abundant evidence that the time is approaching when Satan's full power will be released.[39]

Instructions for proper self-discipline (4:6-16).—In opposition to the false values of asceticism and mythological speculations, godliness (Christian character) has a genuine and permanent value. If Timothy strives for godliness it is an indication that he has his hope set on the living God, who is the Savior of all men, especially of those who believe" (v. 10). The description of God as the "Savior of all men" is a direct affront to the insidious Gnostic pretensions that God is the Saviour only of those few persons who possess gnosis.[40] Although God is potentially the Saviour of all men, he is the Saviour of the Christian in a unique sense.

Instructions for various life situations (5:1 to 6:21) This section of 1 Timothy provides guidelines for various life situations and

---

[39]Cf. above, p. 228-29.
[40]Cf. above, 236.

applies the Christian ethic of love to several avenues of personal relationships. Also included are instructions regarding the manner in which the church should conduct itself toward widows (5:3-16) and toward their spiritual leaders (vv. 17-22). Verse 23 is a further attack against those who affirm that the body is innately evil. In rebuttal to this attitude Paul instructs Timothy to take proper care of his body, avoiding the extremes of asceticism.[41]

Titus

Inasmuch as Titus is almost synonymous in temperament and content with 1 Timothy, only a few remarks will be made concerning its interpretation. According to Titus 1:5, Paul and Timothy had labored together in Crete for some while, and Titus had remained after Paul's departure. Titus is to join the apostle in Nicopolis, as soon as Artemas or Tychicus arrive to assume Titus' duties in Crete (3:12). Chapter 1 deals with the responsibilities of church leaders in light of the antinomian teachers; chapter 2 concerns matters essentially the same as were discussed in 1 Timothy 5:1 to 6:2; and the last chapter explicates certain Christian ethical principles and reveals Paul's wishes for Titus.

2 Timothy

Greetings and Exhortations to Timothy (1:1 to 2:13)

Noticeably formal are Paul's words of greeting and thanksgiving (1:1-5) offered immediately prior to his exhortation for Timothy to sacrifice himself loyally in the service of the gospel (1:6 to 2:13).[42] (1) Patterning himself after the example of Paul, Timothy must exercise boldness and steadfastness so he will receive the "reward" of Christian service, as men in other walks of life (soldiers, athletes, farmers) receive their "rewards" through perseverance (1:6 to 2:7). (2) As the words of the hymn declare, service to the gospel involves identity with the way of the Lord:

If we have died with him, we shall also live with him;
if we endure, we shall also reign with him;
if we deny him, he also will deny us;
if we are faithless, he remains faithful—
for he cannot deny himself (2:8-13).

---

[41]Easton, *op. cit.,* p. 160.
[42]Wickenhauser, *op. cit.,* p. 443.

Guidance in Confronting False Teachers (2:14 to 4:8)

Timothy is warned to avoid the Gnostic cosmological speculations (2:14-16) whereby only a symbolic interpretation is placed upon the Christian resurrection hope (v. 18); he must stay in the main stream of Christian teaching by dealing properly with the basic Christian truths (v. 15). Timothy must also shun immorality, but at the same time attempt to be redemptive toward those who have gone astray (vv. 20-26). The presence of so many who pervert the truth indicates, as was previously stated (1 Tim. 4:1-5), that these are the "last days" (2 Tim. 3:1-9). According to Jewish tradition, Jannes and Jambres were the names of the Egyptian magicians who opposed Moses (Ex. 7:8 ff.).[43]

---

[43]Martin Dibelius, *Die Pastoralbriefe,* third edition by Hans Conzelmann ("Handbuch zum Neuen Testament" [Tübingen: J. C. B. Mohr (Paul Siebeck), 1955]), pp. 87-88, supplies a listing of the primary sources in which these names appear.

Paul's example, as the example of other ministers of the word, should inspire Timothy to conduct himself with integrity, whether the moment is favorable or not (2 Tim. 3:10 to 4:5). Paul's faithfulness, which gives him confidence of victory, serves as a witness to the victory to be achieved by Timothy, if he maintains "the faith" against the false teachers (4:6-9).

Concluding Personal Remarks (4:9-22)

If this section of 2 Timothy was written by Paul, the following observations suggest that it was written at a later imprisonment than that mentioned in Acts. (1) Verse 13 indicates a later imprisonment, unless the cloak and parchments had been at the home of Carpus for almost five years. (2) Acts 21:29 states that Trophimus accompanied Paul to Jerusalem; while 2 Timothy 4:20 tells that Paul had left Trophimus ill in Miletus. (3) Contrary to the intimations of Acts 28, Paul feels that he may soon be executed (2 Tim. 4:6) and requests Timothy to hurry to his side before the navigation seasons ends (vv. 9,21).[44]

------

[44]Wickenhauser, *op. cit.,* pp. 444-45.

7

Hebrews

—THE BEST WINE AT LAST

Background

Authorship.—Originally the book of Hebrews was taken into the New Testament canon under the auspices of a Pauline authorship; yet even at the moment of its acceptance into the canon many realized it was not written by Paul. Nothing in Hebrews is contrary to Pauline theology, but the language and style, and especially the thought patterns of Hebrews, are altogether other than Paul's.

Before presenting different views of authorship, it will be of value to note several characteristics of the author that are generally acknowledged by most schools of thought. (1) Evidently the author knew well the Old Testament in Greek, especially the Law and the Psalms, as well as other Jewish-Alexandrian literature (e.g., the Wisdom of Solomon). (2) Through the mention of Timothy (13: 23) the author intimates his possible connection with the Pauline circle. (3) The literary style of the author more nearly approximates the format of classical Greek than does the style of any other New Testament literature, with the possible exception of Luke-Acts.

Barnabas is thought by some to have been the author of Hebrews. This tradition apparently goes back as far as Tertullian, the prominent Christian leader of the late second and early third centuries. In favor of this thesis are several recognitions. (1) Barnabas came from Cyprus where relatively excellent Greek was in use. (2) Since Barnabas was a Levite, he may well have interpreted the person of Christ in the framework of the Old Testament ritual. (3) Except for the conflict about Mark, which was possibly soon overcome, Barnabas shared a close affinity with Paul. On the other hand, it is extremely improbable that Paul's name would subsequently have been attached to Hebrews, if the name of Barnabas had been associated with the epistle from its inception.

Since the time of Martin Luther, the earliest known spokesman for Apollos as author, the Apollos tradition has been forcefully propounded.[1] From the New Testament it is known that Apollos, an Alexandrian Jew well-versed in the Old Testament and apparently familiar with the Alexandrian philosophical thought, was able to argue fervently that Jesus was the Christ. And these are, indeed, the traits of the author of Hebrews. But this view, drawn entirely from the internal evidence of the epistle, is immensely weakened through the absence of any early tradition in its favor.

Realizing the impossibility of deciding upon one specific author and relying primarily upon the testimony of Hebrews, William Manson has undertaken to characterize the author, without naming a particular individual. Manson concludes that the author of Hebrews was an Alexandrian Jew who had received his introduction to the Christian faith through the followers of Stephen and whose composition expands the motifs inherent in Stephen's world-mission theology.[2]

Destination, date, and readers.—Three representative views will be presented.

One view maintains that the writing was addressed to Jewish converts of Jerusalem, who, having finally recognized the absolute incompatibility between Judaism and Christianity, were not willing to relinquish their ties to Judaism for the sake of the gospel. A date sometime before the destruction of the Jerusalem Temple, perhaps A.D. 64-67, is commensurate with this view.[3]

Of the arguments in support of this thesis only two are significant: (1) Jerusalem Christianity had many in its congregation who sought to hold fast to the tenets of Judaism; (2) the Jerusalem Temple most nearly approximated the original tabernacle; and the tabernacle worship is constantly in the background of Hebrews. Nevertheless, the disadvantages outweigh the advantages of this view. (1) Unless Hebrews was written to second generation Christians—an extreme improbability for the Jerusalem theory—it is difficult to understand why the author referred to his readers as those who had received the

---

[1]For a recent reworking of this hypothesis in light of the Dead Sea Scrolls, C. Spicq, "L'Epitre aux Hébreux, Apollos, Jean-Baptiste, les Hellénistes et Qumrân," *Revue dè Qumran*, I (1959), 365-90.

[2]*Op. cit.*, pp. 167-72 in particular.

[3]Brooke Foss Wescott, *The Epistle to the Hebrews* (Grand Rapids: Wm. B. Eerdmans Co., 1951), pp. xxxv-xliii.

gospel from "those who heard" (2:3). (2) Hebrews 6:10 and 10:34 mention the charity of the readers, while Jerusalem Christianity was traditionally noted for its poverty. (3) Could it be said of the Jerusalem church that they had not taught others (5:12)? (4) Aramaic, the language of Palestine, would have been more appropriate than Greek for this congregation.

A second view holds that the writer addresses Gentile Christians, domiciled somewhere in Italy, to correct their misconceptions of the Christian faith; to achieve this goal he appeals to their Scriptures, the Septuagint, and says, "Come back to your Bible and see how fully it suggests the positive value of Jesus."[4]

Several arguments are induced to substantiate this theory. (1) It is said that the title, "to the Hebrews," was incorrectly added by a later scribe, whereas the content of the epistle itself attests that the title should have been "to the Gentiles." But it would seem, in opposition to this conclusion, that the overall emphasis of the letter

---

[4]James Moffatt, *A Critical and Exegetical Commentary on the Epistle to the Hebrews* ("The International Critical Commentary" [New York: Charles Scribner's Sons, 1924]), pp. xxiii-xxvii.

49. Medal celebrating Roman victory over the Jews, A.D. 70

more nearly concerns Jewish than Gentile Christians. (2) Appeal is made to the Septuagint, the Bible of the Gentile world. However, one should be reminded that many Jews outside Palestine used the Septuagint, and the Jews of Egypt were initially responsible for the Greek translation. (3) Jews of the first century A.D. were concerned about the Law (as per Paul's epistles), not with the ritual of the sacrificial system. A statement of this nature is inadequate inasmuch as it presupposes that the only Jewish Christianity of the first century was the type reflected in the Pauline epistles. But this is not the case, for there were other Jewish Christian communities which could easily have been greatly concerned about the sacrificial ritual. (4) No mention is made concerning the Jewish-Gentile problem, which would have been mentioned had Hebrews been written to Jews. This argument is based upon the same premise as (3) and assumes that conflict necessarily ensued wherever Jewish and Gentile elements were united in churches. This is an unwarranted assumption, since it is quite likely that many integrated congregations experienced no inner conflicts.

A third possibility incorporates many advantages of these other viewpoints. Recently it has been suggested that the epistle was written to an overly conservative "Hebrew" minority within the Jewish-Hellenist church at Rome. The danger faced by these "Hebrews" was that of "remaining as Christians under the covert of the Jewish religion, living too much in the Jewish part of their Christianity, and so missing the true horizon of the eschatological calling."[5] Among other reasons, the Roman destination is concluded from (1) mention of "those from Italy" (13:24), who send their greetings back to their home church; and from (2) the observation that Clement of Rome (*ca.* A.D. 95) is the earliest known churchman to have quoted Hebrews.

While A.D. 95 is a necessary terminus ad quem for the composition of Hebrews, several data of an internal nature suggest a date about A.D. 60 for the issue of the epistle. (1) The excessive interest in the Jewish cultus is more natural before the destruction of Jerusalem. (2) Chapter 10, verses 32-34 may refer to the edict of Claudius in A.D. 49. (3) The frequent emphasis upon the "forty years" of Israel's probationary period in the desert may suggest that the author was writing about forty years after the initiation of the salvation in

---

[5]William Manson, *op. cit.,* **pp.** 24, 159-62.

Jesus Christ. (4) Finally, as a general recognition, nothing within the epistle innately demands a later date.

Purpose and Outline.—To some degree the purpose of Hebrews has been touched upon in the previous discussions, but a reiteration of several aspects will be helpful. (1) Insight into the author's purpose must be gleaned almost solely from the content of the epistle itself. (2) Interpreters recognize that Hebrews was written to declare that Jesus Christ alone is the adequate and absolute "Word of God" for mankind; if one would know God, he must become obedient to this "Word." (3) No unanimity exists relevant to the outline and development of the epistle. Did the author outline his work on theological or literary grounds? What are the major divisions of the epistle? Perhaps the impression of Moffatt is correct:

> It is artificial to divide up a writing of this kind, which is not a treatise on theology. . . . The flow of thought, with its turns and windings, is best followed from point to point. So far as the general plan goes, it is determined by the idea of the finality of the Christian revelation in Jesus Christ, the Son of God.[6]

Hebrews declares the uniqueness of Jesus Christ as the only mediator between God and man. Jesus Christ, "truly God and truly man," accomplished through his incarnation what could be effected in no other manner: absolute community between God and man. In Jesus Christ is revealed at once the gracious divine condescension and the perfect human response. For the faith of the church Jesus Christ embodies not only the best, but the *all* of God offered freely to man; he is, indeed, the *only* wine of which the church partakes.

Mediator of a Superior Revelation (1:1 to 2:18)

Character of the Mediator (1:1-4).—The essence of the entire epistle is contained in verses 1-4, which in content and function are analogous to the prologue of the Fourth Gospel. Indicated in these verses are both the *theme* and the *methodology* of Hebrews: the superiority of Jesus Christ revealed through his continuity-discontinuity with the religion of Israel. The writer of Hebrews does not deny that God spoke to Israel in times past, nor does he deny the validity of

---

[6]*Hebrews,* pp. xxiii-xxiv.

that revelation *for times past;* but he reminds his readers that *for the living present* the only adequate revelation for mankind has been mediated by God's Son.

This revelation in the Son is neither partial nor temporary; it is complete and absolute, and may be so indicated in a variety of ways. (1) The preexistent Son is the one through whom the entire space-time universe came into being; and since he is the "heir of all things," he is also the one in whom is found the meaning of all existence. (2) Manifest in the Son is the exact reduplication of God's essential character and nature. (3) Because of the redemption achieved for mankind through his death, the Son is exalted to the right hand of God. (4) Thereby the Son is acknowledged to be the superior mediator of revelation among God's messengers.

The Son's superiority evidenced by the Scriptures (1:5-13).— Judaism considered angels to have been the mediators of God's revelation in times past. To evidence the superiority of the Son over all angelic mediators, the author appeals to the Greek Old Testament, accepted as authoritative by him and his readers. The author's methodology shows how the early Christians interpreted the Old Testament so as to apply certain passages to Christ. In many cases the application does not rest on the original meaning of the Old Testament passage but rather on a word or phrase that suggested some truth about Christ. This approach to using the Old Testament was practiced by Jewish rabbis as well as early Christians. (1) Psalm 2:7 and 2 Samuel 7:14 suggest the truth of the Son's unique relation to the Father. (2) Psalm 97:7 demonstrates that the angelic mediators of the old revelation are called upon to worship the Son. (3) Two other Psalms (104:4 and 45:6-7) attest the eternal nature of the Son, while (4) Psalm 102:25-27 asserts that the Son is over the entire universe. (5) Finally, Psalm 110:1 declares again the exaltation of the Son to the Father's right hand.

By way of transition Hebrews 1:14 summarizes the role of the angelic mediators: they function solely for the sake of ministering to the Christian community, who are the heirs of salvation.

Danger of neglecting the revelation mediated by the Son (2:1-4). —Drawing an argument from the lesser (angelic revelation) to the greater (revelation through the Son), the author demonstrates the danger inherent in neglecting the Christian revelation which was given through the Son, witnessed by the church, and validated by evidential manifestations of the Holy Spirit's power.

Revelation, incarnation, and redemption (2:5-18).—God's original intention in creation was for the world to be subjected to man; but man has never realized this ideal, except the one man, Jesus Christ, whose death-resurrection experience achieved God's intention for man (vv. 5-9). Redemptive revelation ultimately involves incarnation—a complete incarnation, including the peculiarly human experience of death—for in this manner alone does God become directly involved in the human situation. Therefore, the Son himself became man, *a man,* who shared life and death in common with every other man in order that he might lead all other men to God and so deliver them from the anxieties associated with finitude and sin (vv. 10-18).

Mediator of a Superior Promise (3:1 to 4:18)

Comparison of Moses with Jesus (3:1-6).—Although both Moses and Jesus were faithful in their respective ministries, Jesus offers a better promise than Moses. Moses was faithful as a *servant within* the household of God *witnessing* to the promise to come, while Jesus was faithful as a *Son over* God's household *bearing* the promise. Hence the promise held forth by Jesus supersedes what Moses offered and establishes as members of God's household all who in hope hold fast to Jesus.

Comparison of Joshua with Jesus (3:7 to 4:13).—God's promise of rest became ineffectual for Moses' generation because the people who followed Moses from Egypt rebelled and died in the desert (3: 7-19). This rebellion did not void the promise of God, although the promise was not fulfilled in the acquisition of Palestine under the leadership of Joshua (4:1-10). Because God lives, God's word (promise) is living; accordingly the promise of rest for God's people is available to the present generation, should they not destroy themselves through unfaithfulness (vv. 11-13).

Mediator of a Superior Redemption (4:14 to 10:18)

Transition to the theme of high priesthood (4:14-16).—This passage is transitional, renewing the theme of Christ's high priesthood (first mentioned in 2:17) which is pursued until 10:18. Because of Jesus' achievement and its significance for humanity, the readers are admonished to persevere in faithfulness. Verse 15 is no less difficult than it is important and offers at least two possible interpretations, depending upon whether the last words are rendered "without sinning" or "without sin." (1) The former rendering emphasizes the *outcome* of Jesus' temptation: although Jesus was tempted like all other men, he endured his temptation "without sinning." (2) The latter rendering emphasizes the *nature* of Jesus' temptation: many temptations experienced by men have their origin in man's sinful nature, whereas the temptations confronted by Jesus were "without sin" insofar as they were never induced by a sinful nature.

Qualifications for the high priest (5:1-10).—Since the function of the high priest is to mediate between God and man, his qualifications are two: (1) He must be able to sympathize properly with human frailty; and (2) he must be appointed to his office by God (vv. 1-4). Christ qualifies as the high priest because Psalms 2:7 and 110:4 validate his divine appointment and his incarnation qualifies him from the human side. God's demand of obedience from his Son during his earthly life was not less than God's demand of obedience from every other man during his earthly sojourn. Jesus' absolute obedience to God caused Jesus to share all human experiences, including death, and so qualifies him to lead into eternal salvation all who will follow him in obedience (vv. 6-10).

Exhortation to maturity and steadfastness (5:11 to 6:20).— Mention of Melchizedek brings to the author's mind a new Christological theme which he desires to elaborate. But before developing this theme, the author feels compelled again to exhort his readers to a more mature grasp of their faith. These frequent exhortations dispersed throughout the epistle must not be looked upon as digressions from the main theme. They reflect the author's purpose in writing, for it is ever his intention to formulate his doctrinal considerations in such a manner that they may serve to call his readers to a firmer commitment. From several angles this exhortation is approached.

The present immaturity of the readers limits their spiritual insight and demands that they go beyond the "elemental doctrines" of their faith to a more mature development (5:11 to 6:3). These 'elemental doctrines" of the faith are listed in a series of three doublets.

(1) repentance from dead works, and faith toward God,
(2) instructions about ablutions, and the laying on of hands,
(3) resurrection of the dead, and eternal judgment.

Wilful failure to realize the full implications of the Christian calling constitutes apostasy from which there is no repentance (6:4-8). Several observations relevant to this passage (and its companion passage 10:26-27) are in order. (1) That the reference is to apostasy is overly evident from the description of the readers as those "who have once been enlightened, who have tasted the heavenly gift, and have become partakers of the Holy Spirit, and have tasted the goodness of the word of God and the powers of the age to come." (2) Whatever the sin that the author equates with apostasy, it constitutes a specific decision by which one wilfully turns his back upon the fulness of the Christian revelation. (3) In the overall context of Hebrews it is tempting to interpret the nature of the sin as an attempt of some Jewish Christians to hold to the security of Judaism after having recognized the absolute incompatibility between Judaism and the eschatological Christian calling. (4) The Jewish faith, rightly understood, leads to its consummation in Jesus Christ; consequently there can be no new beginning (repentance) for those persons who have experienced God's offer in Christ and have decided this to be insufficient compared with their Jewish faith.

Better things than apostasy are expected from the readers because of the manner in which they have manifested their faith in times past (6:9-12). From all indications the author is dealing only with what he feels to be a "potential" apostasy and is "pointing out the danger that threatens a beleaguered community in order to exhort them to steadfastness."[7] God's faithfulness, which cannot prove false, should encourage faithfulness on the part of his people (vv. 13-20).

The priesthood of Melchizedek parallel to the priesthood of Christ (7:1-28).—The few illusive references to Melchizedek in the Old Testament (Gen. 14:17-20 and Psalm 110:4) provide the perfect medium for demonstrating the meaning of Christ's priesthood.

(1) The priesthood of Melchizedek, patterned after the priesthood of Christ, intimates the *character* and *eternality* of Christ's priesthood (vv. 1-3). By translation Melchizedek means "king of righteousness" and Genesis states that he was "king of Salem [peace]." Furthermore, since the Genesis account mentions Melchizedek without reference to his parentage, the author utilizes this omission to indicate that Melchizedek (like Christ) was without parents and so a priest forever.

---

[7]Charles E. Carlston, "Eschatology and Repentance in the Epistle to the Hebrews," *Journal of Biblical Literature*, LXXVIII (1959), 301-302.

(2) Melchizedek's superiority to the Levitical priesthood illustrates the *superiority* of Christ's priesthood (vv. 4-10). Abraham, father of the Levitical priesthood through his offspring Levi, acknowledged his inferiority to Melchizedek when he was blessed by him. This intimates the superiority of Christ's priesthood over the Levitical, since Melchizedek's priesthood was patterned after Christ's.

(3) There is *need* for a priest in the likeness of Melchizedek because the Levitical priesthood proved inadequate for human need (vv. 11-28). Christ's appointment to the high priesthood (confirmed by an oath from God) is adequate for human need because he always lives and his ministry is never beset by his own frailty or sin.

Better provisions in the priesthood of Christ (8:1 to 10:18).— Christ's priesthood, exercised in the true tabernacle located in the heavens, is superior to the Levitical priesthood, exercised in a copy of the real tabernacle. Thereby Christ offers the benefits of a better covenant relationship between God and man, a covenant inscribed within the heart (8:1-13).

The Levitical sacrifices, serving only to remind men of their sin without cleansing their conscience, could not effect what Christ achieved through the offering of himself (9:1-14). Contained in verse 14 is a microscopic view of the Christology and soteriology (doctrine of salvation) of Hebrews.[8] (1) The offering was that of *Christ* himself as opposed to the animal offerings of Judaism. (2) His self-offering was made "through an *eternal Spirit*," which relates this historical event to the eternal purpose of God and affirms that time cannot efface its value. (3) The *fulness* and *perfection* of Christ's dedication is manifest through his offering of himself without sin (blemish). For the human situation Christ's offering is effective, for through this medium (4) *men are brought to God* and (5) the *guilt of sin is removed* from the human conscience.

Motifs already elaborated in earlier passages (especially the completeness and eternality of Christ's sacrifice) are reiterated in 9:15 to 10:10 and a singular emphasis is intended: the power of Christ's life has been released for the benefit of all who will appropriate it for themselves.

The finished work of Christ continues to be effectual, bringing forgiveness and establishing an eternal fellowship with God for all who are set apart by God through the work of the Son (10:11-18).

---

[8]Cf. William Manson, *op. cit.,* pp. 133-38.

Mediator of a Superior Way of Life (10:19 to 13:24)

Although exhortations and admonitions have been interspersed throughout the "doctrinal" portion of the epistle, the author now introduces a special section concerned mainly with the application and appropriation of the truths already presented.

Privilege and peril (10:19-39).—The provision made possible through the priestly work of Christ ought to encourage steadfast faithfulness and to grant courage so that the believing community might grasp the fulness of what God offers in Christ (vv. 19-25). The greater the privilege, the greater the responsibility; apostasy from the Christian revelation invokes a fearful judgment upon the apostate (vv. 26-31. On 10:25-26, cf. above, p. 265). Through their faithfulness amidst the difficulties of times past, the readers have given evidence that they will not cower but will persevere and "keep their souls" (vv. 32-39).

Faith among God's people in the past (11:1-38).—It is the purpose of this entire passage to demonstrate what faith *does* rather than to define what faith is. To be sure, faith involves spiritual insight and perception (vv. 1-3); but the faith of which the author speaks demands an *active* response to the call of God. Abel *offered* a sacrifice; Enoch *pleased* (walked with) God; Noah *constructed* an ark; Abraham *obeyed* . . . he *sojourned* . . . he *offered* Isaac; Sarah *conceived;* Isaac *invoked blessings* upon his descendents; Jacob *blessed* his sons; Joseph *made mention* of the Exodus and *gave directions;* Moses *refused* to be called the son of Pharaoh . . . he *considered* . . . he *chose* . . . he *looked* . . . he *left* Egypt . . . he *endured* . . . he *kept* the Passover . . . he *sprinkled* the blood; the people *crossed* the sea; Rahab *gave* friendly welcome to the spies; to say nothing of what was *accomplished* by many lesser known or unknown men and women of faith (vv. 5-38).

Promise of faith (11:39-40).—Faith has ever held forth its promise to those who share its life; but in their day none of these men and women received the full reward of faith which is waiting to be shared by them and others of this present generation.

Faith demanded in the contemporary life of God's people (12:1 to 13:25).—In biblical thought witnesses are not spectators sitting idly by in a grandstand observing a race; witnesses are persons who themselves actively bear witness to the grace of God. The plea of the author is that God's people of the present generation may be faithful witnesses as those whom he has listed were faithful witnesses in their day (12:1). Most outstanding among the witnesses to God was Jesus Christ, who through his humiliation-exaltation became the initiator and consummator of the salvation offered to God's people (v. 2). The present generation of witnesses has not known the full impact of suffering unto death, and they must interpret their present sufferings as a vital part of their discipleship, designed to perfect rather than to punish them (vv. 3-17).

In Jesus Christ the people of God appropriate everything and more than was offered initially to Israel around the holy mountain (vv. 18-29). These few verses are important because they remind the readers that there is no further need to hold fast to the security of Judaism. In Jesus Christ are present all the spiritual benefits God has promised his people, and in Christ these blessings are no longer earthly and transient, but heavenly and eternal: "Therefore let us be grateful for receiving a kingdom that cannot be shaken, and thus let us offer to God acceptable worship, with reverence and awe; for our God is a consuming fire" (vv. 28-29).

Except for 13:12-14 the remainder is epilogue, rounding out a few moral implications of Christ's redemptive activity. The exhortation to follow Christ *outside* the camp is the author's final appeal to his readers to go forward in Christian maturity, leaving the security of a former life and accepting the full ignominy and stigma attached to the Christian confession.

8

The General Epistles

—BREAD AND WINE

A few of the New Testament letters are usually grouped together as the "General Epistles" because they do not mention a specific place of destination. This group includes James, 1 and 2 Peter, 1, 2, and 3 John, and Jude. These letters have in common that they each deal in some fashion with problems relating to the life of the church in their own time and locale. For this reason their overall message may be characterized by the symbols "bread and wine."

James

Background

Authorship and date.—Tradition as early as A.D. 200 ascribes this epistle to James, the brother of the Lord and leader of the Jerusalem church. Generally those who accept this view tend to date the epistle before the development of the Jewish-Christian conflict (i.e., about A.D. 40-45), since that issue is not mentioned in the letter. Other proponents of this view place its composition in the period A.D. 60-62, when the Pauline letters were being disseminated, because James apparently opposes those who are distorting the Pauline doctrine of justification by faith.

Several objections are often presented against this view. (1) There is nothing within the epistle itself that hints at an intimate tie between its author and the Lord; rather the lack of reference to the death-resurrection event suggests otherwise. (2) The extreme difficulty with which the epistle was received into the New Testament canon militates against this position. (3) Much of the content reflects a background and religious orientation other than would be expected for a Palestinian Jew of the first century.

Rejecting the traditional view, many have assumed that James is pseudonymous, written by an unknown author of the late first or early second century. However, in pseudonymous writings it is customary for the author to belabor the point of his identity with the assumed author, a technique quite noticeably lacking in James.

As an attempt to mediate these two extremes, it has been suggested that the epistle represents teachings originally given by James, the Lord's brother, but which have been reworked and arranged by a later editor. But this approach has nothing positive to commend it and suffers all the weaknesses of the views it attempts to mediate.

A few have maintained that this letter was composed by some other James of the first century whose identity was subsequently forgotten. Later the James of this epistle was thought to have been the Lord's brother. A weak link in this hypothesis is the recognition that anyone named James writing so general a letter must surely have realized that he would ultimately become confused with one of the more noted Jameses of the early church, unless he identified himself more accurately.

Finally, it has been put forth that James (equivalent in Greek to Jacob) actually represents an allegory formulated on the analogy of Jacob's departing words to his sons, written for the purpose of exhorting the readers to pursue the virtues he describes. In support of this theory it is argued: (1) The Christian editor has entitled himself "Jacob, the servant of Jesus Christ" so as to differentiate himself from the Old Testament Jacob, often referred to as "Israel, my servant" (cf. Gen. 32:10; Isa. 41:8; 48:20; Jer. 46:27; Ezek. 28:25); and (2) the various themes of the epistle are based upon the characteristics of persons in Jacob's family (e.g., Isaac is joy, 1:2; Rachel is endurance, v. 4; Jacob becomes mature through trial, vv. 4-12; Levi represents religion, v. 27; Dan is judgment, 2:12 f.).[1] As ingenious and attractive as this theory may initially appear, it is difficult to accept wholeheartedly, because the author, if he intends his work for an allegory, is overwhelmingly vague in expressing this intent.

Josephus places the martyrdom of James in the year A.D. 62, which immediately fixes the terminus ad quem, if written by James, the brother of the Lord. As a rule, those who reject the traditional view of authorship date the writing of the epistle anywhere from A.D. 60-125, with the weight leaning toward the latter period.

---

[1]Hans Windisch, *Die Katholischen Briefe*. Third edition by Herbert Priesker ("Handbuch zum Neuen Testament" [Tübingen: J. C. B. Mohr (Paul Siebeck), 1951]), pp. 2-3, and *passim* in 1-36.

**51. Arch of Titus (Rome),
celebrating Roman victory over the Jews**

Recipients and content.—Neither the description of the readers
as the "twelve tribes of the dispersion" (1:1)[2] nor the mention of
their gathering in a "synagogue" (2:2) demands that the recipients
were Jews and not Christians, especially if the references to the
"Lord Jesus Christ" (1:1; 2:1) are integral parts of the letter. The
mention of these two factors does not even require that the recipients
of this brief communication were Jewish Christians.[3] It is better
to render the word in 2:2, generally, as "assembly," rather than in
the technical sense of "synagogue." And it is more probable that
the address (1:1) "denotes, not Christians of Jewish birth, but

---

[2]"Jews of the dispersion" is the technical description for those Jews living
outside Palestine.

[3]Though Donald Guthrie, *Hebrews to Revelation* ("New Testament Introduction" [Chicago: Inter-Varsity Press, 1962]), p. 84, believes it difficult to
avoid the impression that the Christians have a Jewish background.

271

Christendom in general conceived under the oecumenical symbol of ancient Israel (cf. Gal. 6:16; Rev. 7:4 f.; 21:2)."[4]

The content of James is as varied as the opinions regarding its authorship. Diverse themes are woven together with no apparent connection and with no obvious transition from one series of thoughts to another. This recognition has led to the description of James as a handful of pearls with no evident tie to one another.[5] An overall impression is that the epistle either represents a Christianity that approximates a purified Judaism in which the person, the history, and the redemptive activity of Christ have not attained their full impact, or else the author simply felt no compulsion to speak of these aspects, since they were not expedient to his purpose.[6]

Teaching

Testing (1:2-12).—Through faith and steadfastness the Christian lacks in nothing amidst difficulties; he is mature and possesses all wisdom and knowledge because God fulfils his requests.

The goodness of God and true religion (1:13-27).—Since God is good, he sends men only good and perfect gifts. Therefore, any temptation[7] one faces arises from sinful desires rather than from the activity of God (vv. 13-18). God's goodness determines the nature of true religion, defined as unselfish love (the perfect law), charitable deeds, and moral purity (vv. 19-27).

Rich and poor (2:1-13).—Preference for the rich over the poor in the worship service indicates partiality and puts to shame the Christian community, which generally is despised by the rich (vv. 1-9). The sin of partiality, like all other sins, represents a rejection of God himself, and so establishes one guilty before God (vv. 10-13).

No faith without works (2:14-26).—As the body without the spirit is dead, so faith without works is dead (vv. 17,26). By means of a *chiasmic* arrangement (from the Greek letter, *chi*, formed X) the author compares the body to works and the spirit to faith:

---

[4] Moffatt, *Introduction*, p. 464.

[5] This observation accounts for the disproportionate number of major headings in the outline provided for James. Cf. Windisch, *op. cit.*, pp. 4-36.

[6] *Ibid.*, p. 36.

[7] "Temptation" is the same word rendered "testing" above; but James evidently intends a different emphasis for this word in these two passages.

In all likelihood James's purpose is to refute a misguided or perverted interpretation rendered Paul's doctrine of justification by faith apart from the works of the Law. Whereas Paul interpreted the works of the Law to mean legalistic deeds performed to earn one's salvation, James is confronted by persons who interpret Paul's words to signify any deeds of goodness done in the name of religion. Because of the manner in which Paul constantly speaks of the necessity for Christian love and morality, it is quite likely that he would have redressed this group of false teachers with the same words used by James. There is no difference between Paul and James "so far as the Christian praxis of religion is concerned . . . but each lays the emphasis on different syllables."[8]

Dangers in teaching and in the tongue (3:1-12).—One should not become overly desirous for the teaching office as have the false teachers whose manner of life is contradictory to what they teach. Mention of the "cycle of nature" (v. 6), as the earlier reference to being "brought . . . forth by the word of truth" (1:18), represents a phrase current in the Hellenistic world.

False and true wisdom (3:13-18).—Although the appeal is to interpret other passages in James as an anti-Gnostic polemic, verse 15 reveals the clearest trace of this polemic.[9] James even incorporates into this passage several technical Gnostic terms ("wisdom from above," equivalent to "gnosis," and the classification of mankind into two groups, "spiritual" and "earthly") in order to argue against the false teachers. Through this medium James reverses the claims of the false teachers. They are not "spiritual" but "earthly," while the believers are "spiritual," because they profess the true "wisdom from above," manifested in purity and humility.

Preaching repentance to the worldly-minded (4:1-10).—Inner conflicts with oneself, begotten from a wrong relationship with God, engender strife and produce war. Therefore, humility and repentance are called for. Verse 6 is quoted from Proverbs 3:34, but no satisfactory hypothesis has been suggested for the quotation in verse 5, which breathes heavily of a Pauline influence, as does 1:12.[10]

---

[8]Moffatt, *Introduction*, p. 465.
[9]Hermann Schammburger, *Die Einheitlichkeit der Jacobusbriefes im anti-gnostischen Kampf* (Gotha: Leopold Klotz, 1936), p. 33.
[10]W. E. Oesterley, *The General Epistle of James* ("The Expositor's Greek Testament," ed. W. Robert Nicoll [Grand Rapids: Wm. B. Eerdmans Publishing Co., n.d.]), IV, 459.

Against slander and judging (4:11-12).—Slander against one's brother is slander against the Law (cf. Lev. 19:16) and consequently against God, who gave the Law.

Against the impiety of businessmen (4:13-17).—The readers are called upon not to forget that all undertakings are dependent upon the grace of God. Verse 17 does not directly concern the topic discussed in verses 13-16 and must be taken alone.

Against the rich (5:1-6).—God's coming judgment upon the rich, who have not paid their laborers and who have violated the innocent, is vivified as if it were a present reality.

Words of comfort for the faithful (5:7-12).—Christians must be patient and set their mind upon God, who will suddenly appear as the Judge of all men. Verse 12 (like 4:17) actually deals with a separate subject from verses 7-11 and so forms a major topic in itself.

Regulations for various situations (5:13-20).—The ill-treated ought to pray, the healthy ought to sing, and the sick should call upon their spiritual leaders to pray in their behalf. Anointing the sick with oil was customary among the Jews, and this passage indicates the manner in which this custom was taken over into the early church. Also indicated is the Jewish concept that illnesses were often the result of sin; consequently, healing denoted forgiveness (vv. 15-16). It is debatable whether the multitude of sins covered over by recalling an erring brother (vv. 19-20) refers to the one who has erred or to the one who has kept him from sinning further, since both teachings have their counterpart in Jewish thought.

1 Peter

Background

Authorship and date.—In the letters of Polycarp exist evident allusions to 1 Peter, and Irenaeus openly ascribes this epistle to Peter. Furthermore, the author entitles himself, "Peter, an apostle of Jesus Christ" (1:1), and makes reference to his being a witness to Christ's sufferings (5:1). If the Petrine authorship be accepted, the date A.D. 62-64 is most probable because (1) Peter, according to tradition, was martyred in the Neronian persecution of A.D. 64, and (2) the content of this epistle is said to reflect the developing animosity of Nero and Rome toward the Christian movement.

Some have conjectured that Peter did not write the epistle, and their arguments are several.

1. *Language and style.* The Greek style of 1 Peter is comparatively good and the author constantly cites the Septuagint for his Old Testament references. But E. G. Selwyn has aptly demonstrated that these factors do not speak against a Petrine authorship; for it is quite likely that the apostle granted Silvanus (Silas of Acts), his learned amanuensis, freedom to formulate in his own words the teachings given through him (5:11).[11]

2. *Literary dependence upon the Pauline epistles.* However, it is more likely that Paul and Peter have utilized materials from the common stock of early Christian tradition than it is that 1 Peter is dependent upon the Pauline epistles.

3. *Historical situation.* First Peter is believed to reflect the intensive persecutions under the Emperor Domitian (A.D. 81-96),

[11]*The First Epistle of St. Peter* (London: Macmillan & Co., 1955), pp. 9-17.

52. Rome, Colosseum

rather than the local problems incited by Nero's hatred of the Christians. This is an extremely tenuous argument because it has never been established that the Domitian persecutions were of any more severity or any more widespread than the local reprisals under Nero. Nor is a date during the Emperor Trajan's reign (A.D. 98-117) any more satisfactory; because even Trajan advised Pliny the Younger, governor of Bithynia, not to seek out the Christians for punishment. Moreover, the sufferings endured by the Christians in the geographical regions mentioned in 1 Peter 1:1 require no general persecution for their source; these may well represent nothing more than the popular disfavor in which the Christians' movement was held generally.

4. *Doctrinal*. First Peter is said not to reflect any of the burning issues prevalent during the apostle's lifetime and to contain doctrinal developments of the late first century. On the other hand, proponents of a Petrine authorship explain the omission of certain issues by the intention of the author and affirm that the teachings of the epistle are not post-Petrine.[12]

In light of the available evidence the following judgments are tentatively reached. (1) First Peter was written from Rome. It was in Rome where the apostle exercised the last years of his ministry and the reference in 5:13 ("in Babylon") could readily be a cryptogram for "in Rome." (2) Either Peter himself wrote the letter toward the last years of his life, or the letter was written soon after his death by the Roman church, which desired to circulate some of the apostle's teachings as a memorial to him. (3) In either instance, whether by Peter himself or by the church he served, the epistle incorporates not only the teachings of the apostle but reflections of liturgical materials used in the Roman church's worship.

Destination.—It has been suggested that the names listed in 1 Peter 1:1 occur in such an order that one would expect a bearer of the letter to visit the provinces of Asia Minor, beginning at Sinope, and then making a circuit through the four provinces, finally returning to Bithynia.[13] But why did the author delete mention of Lycia, Pamphylia, and Cilicia? One suggestion is that Peter omitted Lycia because there were no significant churches in that region; while

---

[12]Ibid., pp. 363-466; cf. Phillip Carrington, *The Primitive Christian Catechism* (Cambridge: The University Press, 1960), *passim*.

[13]F.J.A. Hort, *The First Epistle of St. Peter 1:1-2:17* (London: Macmillan & Co., 1898), pp. 17, 157-84.

Pamphylia was intended to be included in Galatia, and Cilicia in Syria.[14] Another way to explain the "blank spots" in 1 Peter's geography is to conclude that Peter is addressing only those communities which acknowledge his authority, and that the other areas were not included because the churches in those regions no longer permitted his mixing in their church life, perhaps because they were under the influence of heretical teachers.[15]

Form and content.—Through the application of *form history* to a study of 1 Peter many excellent insights have resulted and several diverse opinions have come forth regarding the form and content of the epistle. Two of these theories will be outlined and a third followed in the exposition.

B. H. Streeter outlines the epistle in two major sections: (1) 1:3 to 4:11 representing a bishop's address to some newly baptized believers, with (2) 4:12 to 5:11 incorporating the bishop's words to his entire congregation (or else a letter written later by the bishop in light of a forthcoming trial to be faced by the church).[16]

Frank L. Cross, perceiving in 1 Peter a series of references to the Exodus and interpreting the epistle against the backdrop of a baptismal service performed at Easter, comes forward with this outline:

(1) 1:3-12—The Bishop's opening prayer.
(2) 1:13-21—The Bishop's formal charge to the candidates (after which baptism takes place).
(3) 1:22-25—The Bishop's welcome to the new converts.
(4) 2:1-10—The Bishop's address on the fundamentals of sacramental life.
(5) 2:11 to 4:6—The Bishop's address on Christian duties.
(6) 4:7-11—Final admonitions and doxology.[17]

The exposition below is developed on the assumption that 1:13 to 4:11 contains an early Christian baptismal service climaxed by the worship service of the entire church (4:12 to 5:11). If this

---

[14]Windisch, *op. cit.*, p. 51. So also D. G. Wollenberg, *Der Erste und Zweite Petrusbriefe und der Judasbriefe* (Leipzig: A. Diechert'sche Verlagsbuchhandlung Werner Schol, 1915), pp. xv, 3-4.

[15]Walter Bauer, *Rechtglaubigkeit und Ketzerei in Ältesten Christentum* (Tübingen: J.C.B. Mohr [Paul Siebeck], 1934) pp. 92-93.

[16]*The Primitive Church* (New York: The Macmillan Co., 1929), pp. 121-36.

[17]*I Peter: A Paschal Liturgy* (London: A. R. Mowbray & Co., 1954), pp. 38-41. But to the contrary cf. T.C.G. Thornton, "I Peter, a Paschal Liturgy?" *Journal of Theological Studies*, 12(1961), 14-26.

impression is accurate, 1 Peter represents the earliest record of a Christian worship service.[18]

The Baptismal Service (1:13 to 4:11)

The service begins with a prayer-psalm (1:3-12).—This opening hymn unfolds an emphatic eschatological attitude ("living hope . . . resurrection of Jesus Christ . . . imperishable inheritance . . . salvation ready to be revealed in the last time . . . the revelation of Jesus Christ . . . the outcome of your faith . . . salvation of your souls") which stipulates the reason for rejoicing (vv. 3-9). Assuming that the readers of 1 Peter were Gentile converts, verses 10-12 may be paraphrased thus: "The Christian prophets [preachers] have diligently searched the Old Testament, seeking the proper time when Christ's Spirit would lead them to proclaim to you [Gentiles] the grace of God and the sufferings bound-up with the Christian confession."[19]

The catechetical address (1:13-21).—With the language of liturgy this address calls upon the catechumens to renounce their former way of life and become holy because (1) God is holy (vv. 15-16); (2) God judges each person according to his life (v. 17); and (3) the nature of the Christian life demands holiness (v. 18).[20] Of particular interest is the affirmation of verse 20, whereby Peter relates the redemptive work of God revealed in the historical Christ event to the eternal purpose of God. This confession unifies God's creative-redemptive activity and gives the Christian life more than a transient significance.

The baptismal act.—For several reasons it may be concluded that between 1:21 and 1:22 the baptismal act has transpired. (1) The preceding passage (vv. 13-21) utilizes the imperative to address those about to enter the fellowship of the church. (2) In the following passage (vv. 22-25) the assumption is made that these persons have already purified their souls through obedience to the truth and have already been born anew through the word of God. (3) Chapter 2, verse 3, which is quoted from Psalm 34:8, changes the impera-

---

[18]Herbert Preisker in Hans Windisch, *op. cit.,* pp. 156-62.
[19]E. G. Selwyn, *op. cit.,* pp. 133-39, 259-68.
[20]Hans Windisch, *op. cit.,* p. 52.

53. Interior, the Colosseum

tive of the Psalm ("taste") to the indicative ("you have tasted").

A baptismal prayer (1:22-25).—After the act of consecration (baptism) comes a brief baptismal prayer, exhorting to effectual love. Whoever is received into the fellowship of Christ must evidence the newness of his life through love, the unique characteristic of the Christian life, rather than through ecstatic experiences, as in the Hellenistic religions.

A hymn of the new life (2:1-10).—A three-strophed hymn (vv. 1-3; 4-5; 9-10),[21] derived from the Old Testament, is introduced next, perhaps by a gifted individual, and describes the traits of the new life. The references to those who stumbled "as they were destined to do" (v. 8) relates specifically to the Jewish rejection of Jesus Christ and ought to be interpreted in light of a passage like Romans 9-11.[22]

An exhortation to humility (2:11 to 3:12).—Another minister stands before the congregation for exhortation; and the stylistic change is noted immediately both through the new mode of address ("Beloved") and the new introductory formula ("I beseech"). As the minister approaches his central theme (suffering for the sake of Christ and its subsequent redemptive value) the church speaks forth with a Christological hymn (2:21-24) descriptive of Christ's unselfish love:

> He committed no sin;
> no guile was found on his lips.
>
> When he was reviled, he did not revile in return;
> when he suffered he did not threaten;
> but he trusted to him who judges justly.
>
> He himself bore our sins in his body on the tree,
> that we might die to sin and live to righteousness.
>
> By his wounds you have been healed.

Because the redemptive love of Christ was expressed through his humiliation, the Christian ethic is one of humility in all realms of life. Chapter 2, verse 13 states this as a general principle and the remainder of this exhortation (exclusive of the hymn) applies this

---

[21]Herbert Preisker, in Hans Windisch, *op. cit.*, p. 158, suggests that verses 6-8, introduced by a special formula ("because it is contained in the Scripture") and dealing with a contrast between belief and unbelief, were written for the sake of explanation rather than as a part of the hymn.
[22]Cf. above, pp. 229-31.

ethic to specific life situations. This verse should be interpreted, "Be subject for the Lord's sake to every human creature (i.e., to every human being)."

A revelatory address (3:13 to 4:7a).—This address proceeds from the reality of the church's situation and the speaker reveals: (1) the blessedness of persecution (3:14), (2) the eschatological hope (v. 15), (3) the profit in God-willed suffering (v. 17), (4) the redemptive value in suffering (4:1-2), (5) the seriousness of the final judgment (v. 5), (6) the extent of Christ's redemptive activity (v. 6), and (7) the imminence of the end (v. 7).

First Peter 3:18 to 4:6,[23] a passage most difficult of exegesis, must be examined both by way of *form* and *content*. Obviously the form is kerygmatic in that it reflects the essential elements of the Christian proclamation; and in this respect the passage is similar to Philippians 2:5-11 and 1 Timothy 3:16. Two brief one-line stanzas tie together the two longer stanzas, the former emphasizing the death-humiliation theme and the latter the resurrection-exaltation theme.

> Christ also died for sins once for all,
> the righteous for the unrighteous,
> that he might bring us to God.
>
> Put to death in the flesh.
>
> Made alive in the spirit.
>
> He is at the right hand of God,
> having entered into heaven,
> angels, authorities, and powers subject to him (3:18,22).

Recognition of this hymnic pattern provides a vital clue to the interpretation of the so-called *descensus* passage (3:19-21). It would appear that these verses were appended to the hymn for the sake of explicating where Christ was and what he did during the interval between his death and resurrection. The answer given implies that Christ's death, rather than limiting the effect of his re-demptive mission, instead provided him opportunity to herald the good news to "the spirits in prison." The term "spirits in prison" possibly describes all those persons who had died previous to the

---

[23]For a definitive essay on this passage, Bo Reicke, *The Disobedient Spirits and Christian Baptism* (Copenhagen: Ejnar Munksgaard, 1946); cf. also Selwyn, *op. cit.,* pp. 313-62; Sherman E. Johnson, "The Preaching to the Dead," *Journal of Biblical Literature,* LXXIX (1960), 48-51.

advent of Christ, although the author refers specifically to the men of Noah's day for at least two reasons. (1) These men were typical of the rebellious generations living before the coming of Christ; and (2) the author desired to compare Christian baptism with the waters of the deluge: as Noah was saved from the sin and corruption of his generation through the flood waters, so the Christian is delivered from the sin and corruption of his former life by the confession of baptism. That no meritorious or magical effect is placed upon the rite of baptism is explicitly acknowledged through the words that baptism must be an appeal to God for forgiveness and the confession of the lordship of Christ (vv. 21-22).

Chapter 4, verse 6 is best understood in light of the overall context of 3:19 to 4:5. Following the confession at baptism, the Christians are obligated to live a life commensurate with their confession (4:1-5). This postbaptismal life is analogous to the life offered the dead through Christ's preaching and shares a common recognition: the final value of one's life is decided not by the opinion of men, but by the judgment of God (v. 6).

A concluding prayer (4:7b-11c).—The newly baptized persons now truly belong to the community of God and participate in the Spirit, who grants them the gifts of love and service. A doxology, sung by the entire church, concludes the baptismal service: "to God be the glory and the strength forever. Amen!"

The Worship Service of the Entire Church (4:12 to 5:11)

In the first part (1:3 to 4:11) the sufferings of the Christians are spoken of as only conditional or hypothetical (1:6; 3:17), whereas in the last part (4:12 to 5:11) actual sufferings experienced by the church are mentioned. This change in tone is understood from the thesis that the first part of the epistle pertains to catechumens who as yet do not belong to the fellowship of faith and so have not known persecution. Now that they are baptized they must reckon with the possibility that they will experience suffering in behalf of their faith. Therefore, this last section relates a concluding act of worship on the part of the entire church.

A revelatory address (4:12-19).—Themes enunciated in these verses form the counterpart of the earlier companion passage (3:12 to 4:7a). However, in the present context more maturity in the Christian life is presupposed, because the congregation addressed has known the impact of suffering for the name.

A hortatory address (5:1-9).—In this passage are contained exhortations to the elders (vv. 1-4), the newer church members (v. 5), and the entire congregation (vv. 6-9).

Benediction and doxology (5:10-11).—An elder offers the final benediction (v. 10), followed immediately by the concluding doxology sung by the entire church (v. 11).

The Johannine Epistles

1 John

Authorship and relation to the Gospel.—No attempt is made by the author of 1 John to identify himself. From the earliest references, however, a close kinship with the style and thought of the Fourth Gospel has been acknowledged. To demonstrate this kinship one has only to list a few of the central themes that 1 John has in common with the Gospel: definition of the relationship between the Father and the Son (1:3; 2:22-24; 4:14); the sending of the Son into the world (4:9-10, 14); the incarnation (4:2); water and blood (5:6-8); the Spirit of Truth (4:6; 5:6); the basic contrasts, God and the world (2:15-17); love and hate (2:9-11; 3:13-15); light and darkness (1:5-7; 2:9-11); life and death (3:14); truth and lie (1:6 ff.; 2:4 ff.). These and other considerations lead to the conclusion that 1 John was written either by the author of the Fourth Gospel or else by someone who conceived of Christianity in the same fashion and lived in the same circles as the author of the Gospel.[24] Moreover, this brief volume would seem to have originated about the same period as the Fourth Gospel—that is, toward the last decade of the first century A.D.

Literary character, unity, and purpose.—First John is a Christian tract which appears to be intended for a definite circle of readers (1:4; 2:12-14), but in reality it is directed toward all Christendom. Because the epistle consists of a variegated series of considerations, exhortations, and warnings set loosely beside one another, some interpreters (e.g., Rudolph Bultmann) discern a disturbing disunity within the epistle and assign to it a composite authorship, while others (e.g., Ernst Lohmeyer) perceive an extraordinary unity within the epistle. Neither theory of composition is thoroughly convincing and the final word in this regard has obviously not been spoken. Even though the destination of the epistle is not specified,

---

[24]Hans Windisch, *op. cit.,* pp. 109-10.

from the content it is decided that the author wrote to refute an antinominan gnosticism which denied a genuine incarnation, assigning to the body of Jesus only the semblance of flesh and blood.[25] In rebuttal, 1 John presents two tests of Christian "orthodoxy": (1) an *intellectual* test, which requires the confession of a real incarnation; and (2) a *moral* test, which declares the necessity of Christian love and purity because of the nature of God.[26]

Prologue (1:1-4).—Incarnation!   This is the proclamation of the church: a genuine incarnation, reconciling man with God and effecting community among men.   For the eternal Word of God became a man who was heard, seen, and touched by those who knew him in the flesh.

The first revelation: God is light (1:5 to 2:6).—The terms used in 1 John to characterize God (e.g., light, life, love, truth) were frequently used by the religions of the eastern Mediterranean world to characterize their deities. Especially were these terms prevalent among the Gnostic sects, who used the counterparts (e.g., darkness, death, hate, lie) to describe the power of evil which opposed God. However, the particular meaning that these terms have in 1 John are determined by the Christian revelation of God in Jesus Christ, not by the significance these words may have had in other religious systems. Nevertheless, it is profitable to understand John's use of these terms as a medium whereby he refutes an antinomian Gnostic movement; John uses their terms, but fills them with Christian meaning. (2) God's light nature (equivalent to goodness and holiness) determines that those who worship him evidence their participation in his likeness through confession of sin and transformation of life. Knowledge of God and fellowship with God exist only where there is obedience to God; otherwise one equates the God of truth with the God of lies (evil).

The second revelation: God is love (2:7-17).—The theme of this section is further elaborated in 4:7-12, though it is limited to neither of these passages. God's love, as well as his light, must determine the nature of the Christian life. Hatred of one's brother (experienced in the Gnostic claims of superiority to the "less spiritual" brothers) is evidence that one dwells in the realm of darkness (hate) rather than in the realm of light (love). Those to whom

---

[25]Martin Dibelius, *A Fresh Approach to the New Testament and Early Christian Literature* (New York: Charles Scribner's Sons, 1936), pp. 209-10.
[26]McNeile, *op. cit.,* pp. 300-302.

the author speaks have shown their defeat of the evil one, but they are warned against the danger of developing excessive attachment to the transitory values of life (vv. 15-17).

Christ and the antichrist (2:18 to 3:24).—That it is the "last hour" is witnessed by the apostasy of those who have forsaken the fellowship of the Christian community and have attached themselves to the Gnostic heresy (2:18-20). These false teachers (called antichrist because they oppose the Christian doctrine of Christ) deny the basic fact that Christ and Jesus are one. It was typical of certain Gnostics to declare that the "spiritual Christ" descended upon Jesus at baptism but ascended before the crucifixion, thus denying a real incarnation and destroying the basis of Christian redemption. Failure to acknowledge the unity of Jesus Christ and to confess his absolute relationship with the Father identifies one with the antichrist; but the readers have an anointing (the Spirit of God) which will direct them away from this heresy (vv. 22-27).

The eschatological revelation of the believer's likeness to his Lord is dependent upon his present life. One who has this hope in himself cannot live a life constantly dominated by sin because God's life (nature) abides within him (2:28 to 3:10). Again the necessity of love is indicated so as to attest one's unity with the community of faith and to grant one courage to stand before God (3:11-24).

Incarnation and love (4:1-21).—Better than any other single passage, this section unites the doctrinal and ethical demands of the epistle. (1) The basic doctrinal confession consists in a proper evaluation of the incarnation: Jesus Christ did not *appear* to be a man, he *was* a man, whose body was of *flesh,* as the body of every other man who has lived (vv. 1-6). (2) Love, redemptive and unselfish, is the basic Christian ethic (vv. 7-12). In verses 13-21 these doctrinal and ethical foundations of the faith are interwoven once more.

Incarnation and faith (5:1-12).—Faith makes possible the proper recognition of Jesus' person and so indicates that one is begotten of God. Involved in this proper recognition is the confession that Jesus Christ experienced not only baptism (water) but death (blood).[27] The historical events themselves (e.g., the baptism and crucifixion) bear witness to this confession; and the Spirit in the life of the church also bears this same witness. Failure to accept

---

[27]Cf. Oscar S. Brooks, "The Johannine Eucharist," *Journal of Biblical Literature,* LXXXII (1963), 293-300.

this witness of the Spirit is rejection of God's testimony and thereby the refusal of eternal life.

Epilogue (5:13-21).—A reiteration of the author's basic themes is offered in this brief epilogue. In light of the remainder of the epistle, the "mortal sin" of verse 16 most probably has reference to the denial of the incarnation: there can be no life for one who denies that "the Word became flesh."

2 and 3 John

Quite often the "elder" mentioned in these letters is identified with "John the elder," the disciple of John the apostle in the city of Ephesus. Others attribute these epistles to the apostle himself, while still others hold the epistles to be anonymous. In any respect these letters have been considered members of the Johannine correspondence since the second century A.D. The "elect lady and her children" (2 John 1) is the writer's manner of addressing the Christian community for which his letter is designated. For the most part her "children" are walking according to the truth, despite the presence of many false teachers (antichrists) who deny the reality of Christ's human body (vv. 7-8). The readers are warned lest they be deceived by these false teachers; they must not even receive these teachers into their homes (church? vv. 9-11). Gaius, the otherwise unknown recipient of 3 John, is commended for his hospitality offered to the Christian missionaries; but the church congregation is to reject the assumed authority of Diotrephes, a false teacher, whom the "elder" himself will reproach upon his arrival.

Jude

Authorship and date.—(1) From the writer's description of himself as "Jude, a servant of Jesus Christ and brother of James," it has been concluded that the epistle was written by Jude, the brother of the Lord (Mark 6:3). Eusebius, the church historian, writing about A.D. 325, transmits a tradition which suggests that Jude had died before A.D. 70, since during the reign of Domitian (A.D. 81-96) only the grandsons of Jude were still alive. Therefore, if Jude, the brother of the Lord, wrote this epistle, a date toward A.D. 70 is most probable, considering both the internal and external evidence. (2) Upon the theory that the epistle reflects an orientation other than a Palestinian Jew would have had, others have concluded either that

---

²⁸Hans Windisch, *op. cit.*, p. 45.

Jude is pseudonymous[28] or else the words "brother of James" represent an interpolation by a later scribe who desired to give the letter more authority.[29]

Purpose and content.—Jude is truly a "general epistle," designed for the church at large in its polemic against the false teachers, who, under the guise of Christian prophets, have entered the Christian community (v. 4*a*). These pseudo Christians have both a distorted Christology (v. 4) and a perverted understanding of man (v. 19).[30] They participate in open immorality and in pagan feasts so as to demonstrate that involvements in the deeds of the flesh cannot violate their spiritual nature (vv. 8,10,12). Through a zealous participation in all sorts of blasphemy, these men hope to soar above the powers of the angelic forces which surround the world and enter the world of light (vv. 8-10). But God's judgment is inevitable, as it was with Sodom and Gomorrah and with the generation who sinned in the desert (vv. 5-7). Of interest is the observation that Jude quotes directly from 1 Enoch 1:9 (vv. 14-15) and refers to a passage from the Assumption of Moses (v. 9), as well as to a second passage from 1 Enoch 10:4 ff. (v. 6).

2 Peter

Authorship and date.—The lack of reference to 2 Peter in the early Christian writers and the absence of the epistle from the earliest Christian collections speaks indirectly against the theory of a Petrine authorship. And an even more thoroughgoing argument against the Petrine authorship is raised by the content of the epistle itself. Either Jude is dependent in toto upon 2 Peter 2:1-18 or vice versa.[31] The latter alternative is more probable, because it is unlikely that Jude would simply have rewritten this passage from 2 Peter without

---

[29]B. H. Streeter, *The Primitive Church,* pp. 183-86.

[30]The reference to setting up "divisions" relates to the Gnostic teaching that they are "spiritual" and all other men are "earthly." Jude reverses these categories and characterizes these Gnostics as "earthly" and "devoid of the Spirit."

[31]Hans Windisch, *op. cit.,* pp. 91-92, sets out the relationship between 2 Peter 2:1-18 and Jude:

(1) Description of the erroneous teachers (Jude 4; 2 Peter 2:1-3)
(2) Three Old Testament examples (Jude 5-7; 2 Peter 2:4-9)
(3) Sins against the flesh and against angels (Jude 8-10; 2 Peter 2:10-12)
(4) Voluptuous and seductive activities (Jude 12; 2 Peter 2:13-14)
(5) Old Testament patterns (Jude 11; 2 Peter 2:15-16)
(6) Comparisons from nature (Jude 12; 2 Peter 2:17)
(7) Haughty nature (Jude 16; 2 Peter 2:18*a*)

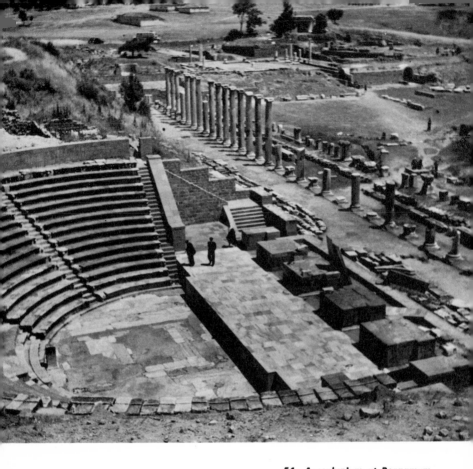

incorporating at least indirect allusions to other portions of the longer epistle; while it is conceivable that the author of 2 Peter would have incorporated the entirety of Jude into his more lengthy composition.

Further indications of a late date are evident. (1) Second Peter 3:16 speaks of "all the epistles of Paul" in such a manner as to presuppose the existence of a collection of scriptures in which the Pauline epistles were a vital part. (2) Second Peter 3:2 ("the holy prophets and . . . apostles") perhaps alludes to a sacred collection of scriptures, including portions of the Old and the New Testaments. (3) From the nature of the reference to "the fathers" (v. 4), it would appear that the first generation of Christians has long since passed away. These considerations contribute to the opinion that 2 Peter was written after the end of the first and before the middle of the second century A.D., perhaps A.D. 125-150.[32]   If this judgment is valid, 2 Peter is the last book of the New Testament to have been written.

Content.—As one would expect from the foregoing discussion, 2 Peter is closely akin in content to Jude. In fact the first of its two sections deals solely with the issue presented in Jude.

(1) *Against antinomianism* (1:1 to 2:22). Like its predecessor, 2 Peter combats the antinomian doctrines of the erroneous teachers who have pretentiously entered the Christian communities, perhaps in the region of Asia Minor.   These false teachers follow self-conceived myths as opposed to the true message of the church (1: 16), misinterpret the Scriptures of the church (1:20-21); have a faulty Christology (2:1); and pursue licentiousness (2:2-3).   Though they promise freedom, their doom is inevitable (2:4-22).

(2) *Against those who deny the meaning of Christian eschatology* (3:1-18). Because of the unexpected span of time that has ensued since the initial promise of Christ's return, many false teachers have decided that the Christian hope is a farce (vv. 1-4). In reality the delay in Christ's return is due to the grace of God, who is extending the time so others may have the opportunity of faith; but this does not preclude the final judgment of God which is inevitable (vv. 5-18).

---

[32]McNeile, *op. cit.,* p. 249.

9

Revelation

—THE GOBLET OF VICTORY

Background

Authorship and date.—Revelation claims to have been written by John, and though it is not clear which John is meant, there is no a priori reason to assume a pseudonymous authorship.[1] Tradition has generally ascribed the writing to the apostle John, who is believed to have written sometime during the years of Domitian's reign (A.D. 81-96) and who is said to have lived until the time of Trajan (A.D. 98-117). Whoever the John of Revelation may have been, he appears to have been well known in the churches addressed by him, and so could speak with authority concerning their church life.

Method of interpretation.—A few of the more prevalent methods of interpretation will be surveyed.

(1) *Continuous historical.* This approach sees in the book of Revelation a symbolic description of the church's history from the writer's day until the end of time. Although this approach receives its initiative from the desire to make Revelation meaningful for the present, it suffers from at least two serious objections. The specific direction of this approach is determined, not by an objective study of the book itself, but by the subjective imagination of the interpreter who attempts to make the details of the book conform to his own preconceived notions. As an example, the antichrist of Revelation has been applied to many different persons in generations subsequent to the author's day (e.g., the Pope, Hitler, Stalin, Khrushchev) without regard to what the *author himself* may have intended *in his own day*. A second major weakness in this view is that it is founded upon a misconception of Christian prophecy. The role of the New Testament writers, including the author of Revelation,

---

[1]Moffatt, *Introduction,* pp. 512-13.

was one of interpreting the meaning and outcome of history upon the basis of God's revealed purpose, rather than one of predicting the exact details of future history.[2]

(2) *History of religions.*[3] This school assumes that many ancient mythological traditions lie at the roots of the imagery used by John, and the meaning of these symbols may be explained by uncovering the source of these traditions. It is not to be denied that a knowledge of the origin of the sources used by Revelation contributes to its understanding. But Revelation is more than a link in a chain and in the final analysis must be understood in light of the unique meaning given these symbols by John himself.[4]

(3) *Liturgical.* Some have supposed that Revelation is formed on a liturgical framework which is dependent, in whole or in part, either upon an early Christian worship service[5] or else upon the liturgy of the Jerusalem Temple.[6] One must acknowledge that parts of Revelation reflect Jewish and Christian liturgical materials, but this should not imply that these materials are the central criteria for the understanding of Revelation.

(4) *Contemporary historical.* The most stable approach is the contemporary historical, which acknowledges that Revelation must be interpreted in the light of its own day. That is, although this writing is relevant for all generations, its relevance must be drawn from the truths that John intended to communicate to the people of his own time. In its usual form this view maintains that Revelation depicts the conflict of the early church with the political-religious power of the Roman Empire: the figure of Babylon represents Rome; the first beast the emperor-cult; and the seven heads of the beast stand for Roman emperors. Since this is the most widely-held view

---

[2]I. T. Beckwith, *The Apocalypse of St. John* (New York: The Macmillan Co., 1919), pp. 291-310, 334-36.

[3]The founder and classic representative of this school is Herman Gunkel, *Schöpfung und Chaos in Urzeit und Endzeit* (Göttingen: Vandenhoeck und Ruprecht, 1895).

[4]Ernst Lohmeyer, "Die Offenbarung des Johannes 1920-1934," *Theologische Rundschau, VI* (1934), 282-84.

[5]Otto A. Piper, "The Apocalypse of John and the Liturgy of the Ancient Church," *Church History,* XX (1951), 10-22; Lucetta Mowry, "Revelation 4-5 and Early Christian Liturgical Usage," *The Journal of Biblical Literature,* LXXI (1952) 75-84.

[6]Joseph Peschek, *Geheimne Offenbarung und Templedienst* (Paderborn: Verlag Ferdinand Schöningh, 1929); Philip Carrington, *The Meaning of the Revelation* (London: Society for the Promotion of Christian Knowledge, 1931).

among New Testament scholars, it will be pursued in the interpretation to follow. However, before the interpretation is entered into, a brief comparison between the book of Revelation and Jewish apocalypses will be made.

Revelation and Jewish apocalypses.[7]—In respect to *form,* Revelation is similar to those Jewish apocalypses which preceded it: the seer relates a series of symbolic-allegorical scenes which he has received in a vision. With regard to *content* Revelation is also related to those apocalypses which antedated it: mythical materials, secret numbers, and visions are the means for revealing heavenly realities.[8] Yet, in areas more significant than peripheral, Revelation differs from these earlier writings. (1) Revelation is apparently neither anonymous nor pseudonymous. The author makes no elaborate attempt to identify himself as some famous noteworthy; and the simple name John is a valid key to the name of the author, no matter which John is meant. (2) This is a "revelation of Jesus Christ" rather than a "revelation of John," immediately differentiating this from earlier apocalypses which claimed to be the "revelation" of Moses, Enoch, or the twelve patriarchs. (3) The events depicted through the visions of this book are not past history described as future; they are visions which refer to the present and immediate future of the author himself. (4) Revelation is a thoroughly Christian writing which affirms the lordship of Jesus Christ no less than any other New Testament book.

Christ and the Seer (1:1-20)

The "revelation of Jesus Christ" is the *theme* of the entire composition. By this phrase John affirms his intention to reveal Christ's significance in God's creative-redemptive purpose for mankind. In this regard it is not to be overlooked that the attributes of the risen Lord portray him in his relationship to the church (vv. 5-6), to the unbelieving world (v. 7), and in his overall significance to the entire created order (vv. 12-18).

Christ and His Church (2:1 to 3:23)

Why were these seven churches of Asia Minor chosen by John?

---

[7]The reader is referred to the earlier discussion of apocalyptic literature, pp. 35-41. "Revelation" is, of course, a translation of the Greek word "apocalypse."

[8]Johannes Behm, *Die Offenbarung des Johannes* ("Das Neue Testament Deutsch" [Göttingen: Verlag von Vandenhoeck und Ruprecht, 1956]), pp. 2-3.

To this question several answers may be given. (1) *Representative of all Christendom.* It is quite possible that his choice was in some measure determined by his preference for the sacred number seven, which to him implied divine completeness. John's message to these seven churches would then be looked upon as his message to all Christendom of his day. (2) *Foremost representatives of the churches in each geographical region.* William Ramsay points out that these seven churches could easily have marked out a postal route followed by the bearer of this letter, and from these seven churches the letter was to be communicated to other nearby churches.[9] (3) *John's authority in Asia Minor.* It may also be that the seer directs himself to these particular churches because they are the major churches in this region (Asia Minor) that acknowledge his authority and will obey his injunctions.

From what information has been gained from archaeological, historical, and literary sources, it is quite obvious that John knew the geography and history of these seven cities, as well as the inner life of the church in each city. This observation directly supports the viewpoint that the author addressed the particular historical situation in which he himself lived, otherwise such references would lose much of their weight.

(1) The church at Ephesus is plagued by false teachers (Nicolaitans) who must not be endured. To those who overcome the temptation to this error a share in the tree of life is promised (2:1-7).

(2) Victory over the "second death" is promised to those believers in Smyrna who will be steadfast amidst the strong opposition from the Jewish population within the city (vv. 8-11).

(3) The church at Pergamum has already had one of its members put to death and faces difficulties from within by the presence of heretical teachers. To the faithful in Pergamum are guaranteed spiritual strength (hidden manna) and divine guidance (white stone) inscribed with a secret name (vv. 12-17).

(4) Jezebel, a false prophetess in the church at Thyatira, will soon be destroyed along with her followers; but those who are not led astray by her immorality and false teachings will be rewarded when the final victory is achieved (vv. 18-29).

(5) Sardis, a city proud of its wealth and other resources, has

---

[9] *The Letters to the Seven Churches of Asia* (London: Hodder & Stoughton, 1909).

within it a church that is almost dead, but the few faithful in the church are promised that they will not have their names erased from the book of life if they continue in their faithfulness (3:1-6).

(6) Jewish opposition is also present in Philadelphia, but those who are steadfast in their faith will become a part of God's new spiritual temple (vv. 7-13).

(7) Laodicea, a city noted for its self-sufficiency, has there a church which seems to reflect this same self-sufficiency, but they are reminded that they need the presence of their Lord who stands always ready to be invited in (vv. 14-22).

Christ and World History (4:1 to 14:20)

Worship and praise to the God of creation and redemption (4:1 to 5:14).—The entire fourth chapter of Revelation is formed upon the analogy of a magnificent enthronement ceremony culminating in a majestic hymn of praise to God for his works of creation *and* redemption.

> To the One sitting upon the throne
>   and to the Lamb,
> Blessing, honor, glory and strength,
>   forever and forever! (5:13)

Much disagreement exists with respect to the form and content of the sealed book of Revelation 5, but it seems most probable that this book was intended to convey God's plan for world history and for world redemption, to which Christ alone holds the key. Through the recognition and confession of Christ's lordship the church gains the proper perspective of God's purpose for mankind; and this purpose is now unfolded in the opening of the seals.

Judgment and grace in world history (6:1 to 14:20).—In several respects the *seal visions* (6:1 to 8:1) and the *trumpet visions* (8:2 to 11:15) are analogous. (1) Each series is determined by the sacred number seven, as are the later bowl visions (15:1 to 16:21). (2) In each series the seventh member serves as a literary technique forming a transition to the following section: the seventh seal introduces the series of trumpet visions and the seventh trumpet, the vision of the ark in the heavenly sanctuary. (3) There is an interlude between the sixth and seventh vision in each series. (4) However, a difference exists in that the seal visions receive their outline from the sevenfold apocalyptic expectation connected with the last days (cf. Mark 13), while much of the content of the trumpet visions (and the bowl visions) receives its cue from the Exodus account of the plagues (e.g., hailstones, locusts, water to blood, sores upon man and beast, darkness on the earth).

Attention should be drawn to the *significance* each sevenfold series of visions (e.g., seals, trumpets, bowls) has in the framework of Revelation. Each series of visions has its own unique emphasis, but the overall meaning of each is essentially the same: the revelation of God's actions in the affairs of mankind. (1) The *seals* contain the summation of all history, past and present, seen in light of God's judicial and redemptive activities. Throughout the course of human history men of faith have endured suffering (6:9-11), but God knows those who are his (7:1-8; cf. also 11:1-2)[10] and constantly brings his judgment upon the unbelieving world, which is not able to perceive in its failures the judgment of God (6:1-8, 12-17). (2) The trumpet visions (8:2 to 11:15) underline God's final action in history, which the seer believes to be imminent, climaxed by the final resurgence of the antichrist (11:15 to 13:18) and the appearance of the Son of man (14:1-20). (3) From the apparent analogy between the trumpet and the bowl visions, it is safe to conclude that the latter visions are intended to be an intensified reworking of the trumpet visions. That is, the seer approaches from another angle the theme of 8:2 to 11:15, only this time in a more climactic and absolute fashion. Thereto the same elements are attached as in the former series: the final defeat of the demonic forces behind the evil of the world (Babylon, 17:1 to 19:10), followed by the appearance of the Word of God and the consummation of all history (19:11 to 22:19).

The description of demonic powers as *beasts* comes into Revelation under the influence of a certain phase of Jewish apocalyptic thought which ultimately owes its origin to the Babylonian tradition of Tiamat, the primeval monster slain by Marduk, god of Babylon, and from whose body Marduk fashioned the universe. In Jewish literature two such monsters are marked off by name: Leviathan and Behemoth. It was believed that in the beginning these were the foes whom God conquered but did not destroy. Presently one of these beasts dwells in the sea and the other in the earth, but at

---

[10]Sealing the believers (7:1-8) and measuring the Temple (11:1-2) both indicate God's watchcare over his people, although throughout history some are called upon to suffer for their faith (6:9-11; 11:3-14).

the end of time they will reappear and oppose the anointed of God.

John takes over this apocalyptic terminology and utilizes it to describe the demonic foes that he sees asserting themselves against God and his Anointed (Christ). The first beast is the antichrist, who tries to usurp the place of the true Christ (13:1-10), the second beast is its prophet (vv. 11-18), while the dragon or serpent is Satan (12:9) from whom the antichrist receives its authority and strength. Since the overall purpose of apocalyptic literature is to offer encouragement to the people of God in their contemporary situation, it is necessary to look for John's application of these symbols in light of his own times. Though other possibilities exist, the most generally accepted interpretation is to understand the dragon as the devil, working through the power of the Roman Empire spread throughout the Mediterranean world. The first beast represents the emperor-cult, which deified the Roman emperors; and the second beast is a symbol for the religious personnel (e.g., prophets and priests) associated with the emperor-cult.

Although this fearsome looking horde of demonic monsters comprise a powerful foe, John indicates that the final victory belongs to God's Chosen One and to those who follow him. This he symbolizes in two ways. (1) The birth of the child by the heavenly mother signifies that the initial coming of Christ has in reality overthrown the power of the devil (12:1-18). And (2) the appearance of the Lamb upon Mount Zion (Jerusalem) with the 144,000 whom he has redeemed looks forward to the final outcome (14:1-20).

Christ and the Consummation of History (15:1 to 22:21)

God's judgment and the consummation (15:1 to 21:1).—(1) The *seven bowls* (15:1 to 16:21). In the same fashion that the previous plagues were preceded by an act of worship (4:1 to 5:14), so these final plagues follow a worship experience (15:1-8). But whereas the earlier plagues pointed to God's judgment throughout history, the bowl visions portray the final revelation of God's judgment by which history is brought to its consummation. That these visions are symbolic of God's *final* judgment upon the sin of the world is indicated by the completeness of their effects as compared with the partial force of the previous plagues, and by the observation that these visions culminate in the absolute overthrow of the world: "the cities of the nations fell, . . . every island fled away, and no mountains were to be found" (16:19-20).

(2) *Babylon* (17:1 to 18:24). Even though all the nations of the earth have fallen, the sin and the strength of Babylon are so enormous that a special judgment awaits her. If the supposition is correct that the Roman Empire was understood by John as the absolute embodiment of the demonic force facing the church of his day, then the figure of Babylon must be interpreted in this light. Babylon symbolizes the imperial city of Rome resting upon the strength of her emperors, who are represented by the seven-headed beast upon which the woman is seated. And, though it is not at all certain which emperors are indicated, it is believed that each of the seven heads represents one in the succession of Roman emperors. That there are seven emperors, and no more, further states that the Roman power has reached its end and the true King is about to appear.

(3) *The King of kings* (19:1 to 20:15). Revelation 19 brings the redemptive drama close to its climax. This chapter opens with two hymns, one looking back to the accomplished victory (19:1-2), and the other anticipating the wedding of the Lamb (19:6-8). With the appearance of the King of kings is initiated the final defeat of all those evil forces which lie behind the sin and evil of the world. The beast and the false prophet are destroyed (vv. 11-21), and this is soon followed by the casting of Satan into the lake of fire and brimstone (20:1-10). Then comes the judgment upon all who have rejected the grace of God (vv. 11-15).

God's grace and the consummation (21:1 to 22:21).—A final manifestation of God's grace is his gift of the "new Jerusalem" to his people. Here those whom God has redeemed will worship him always, and the presence of God and the Lamb will never depart from their midst!

Part Four
New Wine in New Skins

Behold, I make all things new (Rev. 21:5).

Through the apostolic witness to the lordship of Jesus Christ the new wine had begun to flow. But soon it was realized that if others were to "taste and see the Lord is good," this wine must be gathered and placed in suitable skins, else it might become diluted and mixed with impurities.

Though the task was not easy, under the leadership of God's Spirit the church finally decided what was truly wine, and this they have preserved in the New Testament canon.

It is confessed by the church that the new wine is better than he old, for in reality the new wine was "before" the old wine (John 8:58). Therefore, it is the conviction of the church that the witness to God in the new supersedes the witness contained in the old, for in Jesus Christ are all the treasures of God, both old and new.

10

The New Testament Canon

—THE MAKING OF THE NEW WINE

The "What" of the New Testament Canon

The term "canon" is a transliteration of the Greek word meaning reed. In daily life the reed was used as an instrument of measurement and had to be both straight and inflexible. Later this word was taken over and used in a number of ways, concrete and abstract, denoting standards requisite for various vocations, concepts, persons, and things. In a more restricted sense, a canon came to denote a collection of writings acknowledged to possess a definite authority for a given group of people. The word "canon" used in relationship to the New Testament describes that collection of writings accepted by the Christian community as binding and authoritative upon its life and thought. Although historically there has been much variance of opinion regarding the exact limits of the New Testament canon, all Christian denominations, Catholic and Protestant alike, presently acknowledge the same group of New Testament writings as authoritative.

The "Why" of the New Testament Canon

Before surveying the historical process by which the twenty-seven books of the New Testament came to be a part of the Christian canon, one should concern himself with the idea (the *why*) of the New Testament canon. And this consideration immediately brings forth two inseparable issues: (1) Why did the church impose upon itself the authority of a second set of Scriptures, and (2) what should be the attitude of the church toward the Old Testament canon? The second of these questions will be discussed first.

The church and the Old Testament.—Unless the Old Testament has more than a cultural or literary value for the church there is no reason for these writings to maintain their status as sacred Scriptures.

But, indeed, the Old Testament does have permanent contributions to make to the life of the church; these contributions are of such a nature that they render the life of the church unintelligible apart from the Old Testament witness.[1]

The Old Testament is a witness to the mighty redemptive acts of God in times past. God's redemptive activity in the history of Israel is also a part of God's redemptive activity in the history of the church. There is a continuity between what God accomplished in times past and what God is presently accomplishing through the church. The early Christians recognized this continuity and so referred to themselves as the "true Israel," and confessed that God was the same, yesterday, today, and forever.

The Old Testament is a witness to the Lord of the church.

Traditional Christianity has always seen our Lord against the background of the Old Testament; therefore it has added to His human name

---

[1]This present discussion is indebted in part to Floyd V. Filson, *Which Books Belong in the Bible?* (Philadelphia: The Westminster Press, n.d), pp. 43-72, and A. G. Hebert, *The Throne of David* (London: Faber & Faber, 1951), pp. 19-38.

55. Early Christian portrait of
Peter and Paul receiving crowns from Christ

Jesus the Greek word "Christ," which translates the Hebrew word "Messiah," the Anointed, in order to signify that He came as the Saviour of Israel promised of old by the prophets. But in proportion as the Old Testament background is cut away, He is left in lonely grandeur, as a human figure, making an ethical appeal.[2]

By this observation one cannot mean that the Old Testament prophets lived in an isolated vacuum and spoke detailed descriptions of the coming Lord; but one does indicate thereby that the prophetic hope of a glorious future, founded upon faith in the redemptive grace of God, was finally realized in the person of Jesus Christ. In Jesus Christ are fulfilled all the promises of God. He is God's eternal "Yes" to the needs of man; but this is a "Yes" which cannot be understood apart from the hope of Israel expressed in the Old Testament.

The Old Testament is a witness to the self-understanding of the church. Not without reason did the early church read the Old Testament as an integral part of its worship services and address God by the Old Testament titles. Through meditation upon the implications of God's call to Israel, the church was able to interpret in fuller measure its responsibility to God and to invoke from God the promises made to the seed of Abraham. For this reason the writers of the New Testament can appeal to the Old Testament Scriptures as a verification of their relationship with God: "But the words, 'it was reckoned to him,' were written not for his sake alone, but for ours also" (Rom. 4:23). "You are a chosen race, a royal priesthood, a holy nation, God's own people" (1 Peter 2:9).

Moreover, the church's appeal to the Scriptures for clarification of its role receives its pattern from the church's Lord, who came to an understanding of his own role from the reading of such passages as Isaiah 42.

The church and the New Testament.—Since the church had a valid and permanent witness to God in the pages of the Old Testament, why did the church confess its need for a second written authority?

The church recognized in the person of Jesus Christ, the Lord of the church, a unique authority: God was in Christ, the Word became flesh! "Jesus Christ is Lord!" was the earliest Christian confession; and involved in this confession was the recognition that the

---

[2]Hebert, *op. cit.,* pp. 21-22.

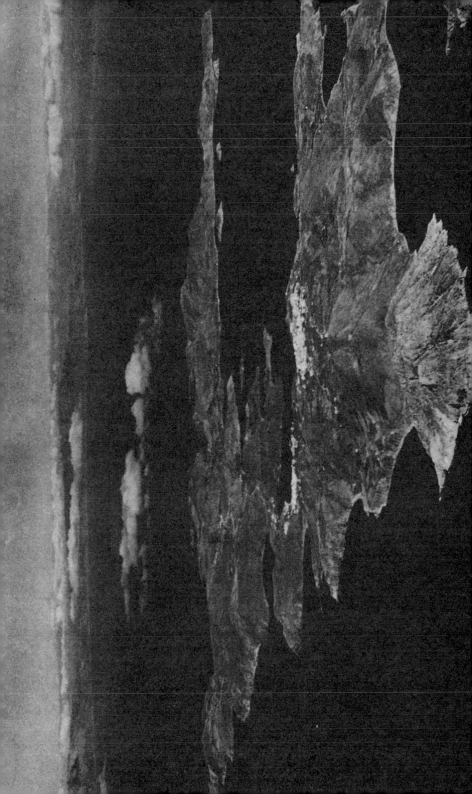

authority of Jesus Christ superseded all other authorities, including that of the Old Testament. Also embodied in this confession was the presupposition that ultimately must lead to a second written authority if future generations were to have a witness to the Lord of the church.

Testifying to the absolute authority of Jesus Christ were the men who had known him in the flesh, the apostles. After the resurrection of Jesus it was only natural, and proper, that the church should depend upon the memory of the apostles for authentic information concerning what the Lord was like and what he had taught. So the apostles gradually assumed, as it were, the same authority that the Lord himself possessed during his earthly life. Soon it was realized that the Lord was not to return within the life-span of the apostles; therefore, something must be done to perpetuate accurately their witness to the Lord. From this realization there dawned the necessity of a transition from the oral (and few disconnected written) traditions to an adequate and more permanent written record of the apostolic testimony.

Guided by the Spirit of God, certain men deliberately set out to incorporate into written records a valid and permanent witness to the Lord (Luke 1:1-4; John 20:30-31). Others, keeping in harmony with the traditions concerning the Lord and under the leadership of his Spirit, wrote letters and other documents which embodied implications of the lordship of Christ (e.g., 1 Cor. 7:40*b*). Nevertheless, none of these men were intentionally contributing to a collection which they believed would someday become regarded as Holy Scripture. Gradually the church came to the conviction that the voice of the Lord spoke to them through some of these writings, and ultimately, from this recognition, developed the *why* of the New Testament canon.

The "When" and "Where" of the New Testament Canon

As one can conclude from the foregoing observations, the *why* of a new canon of Scriptures was incipient in the incarnation itself. But one must raise a kindred question: When, where, and under what circumstances did these twenty-seven writings come to be the authoritative expression of the faith and doctrine of the Christian

56. Patmos

church? Obviously, in a survey book of the New Testament a detailed answer to this question would tend to grow out of proportion to the remainder of the book. Should the student wish to pursue this question further, he is directed to the sources listed below, upon which the present discussion is dependent.[3]

The New Testament writers.—Do the writers of the New Testament express any hopes for the development of a second set of authoritative scriptures? In general it might be answered that the words of Jesus are placed on a par with the testimony of the Old Testament; and when contradictions arise between the teachings of Jesus and the Old Testament, the words of Jesus are followed. As examples of these two observations one might recall both Paul's appeal to the "words of the Lord Jesus, how he said, 'It is more blessed to give than to receive' " (Acts 20:35) and the authoritative claims of Jesus in the Sermon on the Mount, "You have heard it said (in the Old Testament), but I say to you." Elsewhere the finality of Jesus' authority is contrasted with the partiality of the Old Testament (Hebrews); and Jesus is spoken of as the fulfilment of Judaism (John and Matthew).

A few places in the New Testament possibly reflect an appeal to some type of written authority. Paul commends the Christians because they "maintained the traditions" which he had made known to them (1 Cor. 11:2); and he strongly encourages the Thessalonians to follow the traditions which they were taught (2 Thess. 2:15; 3:6). The Colossians are to read their letter as well as the one Paul sent to Laodicea (4:16). In the Pastorals, as in Jude, a written source seems to be presupposed in such expressions as "the faith, which was once for all delivered to the saints." The most overt indication to an authoritative collection of writings are the words of 2 Peter 3:15, which likely refer to at least a partial Pauline collection: "So also our beloved brother Paul wrote to you according to the wisdom given him, speaking of this as he does in all his letters."

In light of these and other indications within the New Testament, the following conclusions are made: (1) The authority of Jesus was

---

[3]Casper René Gregory, *Canon and Text of the New Testament* (Edinburgh: T. and T. Clark, 1907); McNeile, *op. cit.*, pp. 312-372; Oxford Society of Historical Theology, *New Testament in the Apostolic Fathers* (Oxford: Clarendon Press, 1905); A. Souter, *Text and Canon of the New Testament* (London: Gerald Duckworth and Co., Ltd., 1954); Brooke Foss Wescott, *A General Survey of the History of the Canon of the New Testament* (New York: Macmillan & Co., 1889).

recognized above even the Old Testament. (2) There was much fluidity in the use of the traditions referring to Jesus. (3) Some of the New Testament writers referred to what apparently were recognized authoritarian sources for the churches in their particular locale, but this does not imply that these same sources were generally recognized among all other Christian communities. (4) Most of the appeals to written authorities seem to have arisen in polemic situations, and the New Testament writers were not beyond appealing to sources that subsequently have not been accepted by Christendom (e.g., Jude appeals to 1 Enoch). (5) No writer defines the limits of the authority to which he appeals; these sources may have been only a few pages or else several whole compositions.

Apostolic Fathers.—Barnabas, a pseudonymous epistle of the late first or early second century, contains quotes from Matthew, 1 Enoch, and 4 Ezra, all placed on a par with one another and with the quotes from the Old Testament.

The Didache is composed of four sections containing material dating anywhere from A.D. 80-150. In the ecclesiastical section appears a passage that is often thought to be a reference to Matthew 6:9-15, but this may instead represent an oral tradition: "Neither pray as the hypocrites; but as the Lord commanded in His Gospel, thus pray: 'Our Father who art in heaven, hallowed be Thy Name . . . for Thine is the power and the glory for ever' " (8:2).

Clement, bishop of Rome, wrote a letter to the Corinthian church about A.D. 96. When quoting from the Old Testament, his quotations are close and exact, while his references to the New Testament are loose and inexact. Clement introduces his Old Testament quotations with formulas as, "for it is written." Because this formula prefaces a passage (50:6-7) common to Romans 4:7-9 and Psalm 32:1-2, some have concluded that Clement is quoting Paul. But it is more natural to conclude that both he and Paul were referring to a passage from the Old Testament in frequent use by the early church.

En route to martyrdom in Rome (A.D. 110-117), Ignatius of Antioch addressed letters to those churches of Asia Minor which had shown him hospitality. Ignatius produces a very enigmatic passage in Philadelphians 8:2: "For I have heard some saying, If I do not find the Gospel in the archives, I will not believe it. To such persons I say that my archives are Jesus Christ, to disobey whom is manifest destruction. My authentic archives are His cross, and death, and resurrection."

What does Ignatius mean by the "archives"? This word might be rendered "official documents" or "original documents," and in the context probably refers to the Old Testament.[4] This intimates that Ignatius is appealing to the authority of the Christian proclamation as opposed to those who depend entirely upon the Old Testament witness. In Philadelphians 5:1-2, Ignatius mentions "gospel . . . apostles . . . prophets"; however, "prophets" seems to be in opposition with "apostles," thus narrowing down the references to "gospel and apostles." Yet the question must be asked whether Ignatius had in mind oral or written traditions, and the weight must be given to the former possibility, though not altogether excluding the possibility of some written sources as well.

The one extant correspondence of Polycarp, bishop of Smyrna, who was martyred in A.D. 155, is his letter to the Philippians. Polycarp makes two specific references to the words of Jesus, the former introduced by "remembering what the Lord taught, when he said" (2:3), and the latter by "even as the Lord said" (7:2). As with the other sources thus far examined, the likelihood would be that he is referring primarily to an oral tradition.

Second Clement, so-called because it purports to have been written by Clement of Rome, is actually a homily dating from the middle of the second century. In 2:2 the term "Scripture" appears for the first time in conjunction with the New Testament: "And another Scripture also says, 'I came not to call righteous, but sinners!'" On the other hand, in 11:2-4 the author affirms, "The prophetic word also says . . . ," with reference to some unknown apocalyptic source, probably in dependence upon the similar quote in 1 Clement 23:3-4.

What generalizations may be drawn from the use of the New Testament in the Apostolic Fathers? (1) There is a manifest interest in the oral traditions (and in the fragments of written tradition) circulating freely within the early church. (2) None of the Fathers hints at the existence of a universally acknowledged collection of scripture on equal authority with the Old Testament. (3) The presence of quotes from the New Testament does not signify that the New Testament has become recognized as a unique authority, because there are also quotes from apocryphal sources. (4) As yet

---

[4]William F. Arndt and F. Wilbur Gingrich, *A Greek-English Lexicon of the New Testament and Other Early Christian Literature* (Chicago: The University of Chicago Press, 1957), p. 111.

there is no noticeable attempt to determine the value of the sources quoted.

From Marcion through the third century.—The first *known* collection of New Testament writings was that of Marcion, who traveled from Sinope to Rome around A.D. 150. Under the influence of Cerdo, the Syrian Gnostic, Marcion was later led away from the main stream of Christianity and sought to purify the church of its Jewish element. He adopted Paul as his patron saint, since Paul was the most avid spokesman against the Jewish Law, and decided that only the Pauline Epistles (exclusive of the Pastorals) along with an emasculated form of Luke's Gospel should be accepted as authoritative. Whether Marcion was the first to collect Paul's epistles[5] or whether he simply took over a collection that had previously been made by the church[6] is debatable. In either instance, Marcion is important because he made the church conscious of the necessity to decide upon the limits of the books to be accepted as authoritative in order to protect itself from the influx of heresy.

Justyn Martyr, a learned Christian born in Palestine of Greek parents, directed himself against the errors of Marcion in his two famous apologies written after A.D. 160. Justyn appeals to the "memoirs" of the apostles, which he evidently places upon a par with the Old Testament prophets: "And on the day called Sunday, all who live in cities or in the country gather together to one place and the memoirs of the apostles, or the writings of the prophets are read, as long as time permits" (*Apology* I, LXVII.).

And these "memoirs" are defined as the apostolic recollections concerning Jesus Christ: "For the apostles, in the memoirs composed by them, which are called Gospels, have thus delivered unto us what was enjoined upon them" (*Apology* I, LXVI). Elsewhere Justyn seems to reflect not only the Gospels, but Acts, Romans, 1 Corinthians, Galatians, Ephesians, Colossians, 2 Thessalonians, Hebrews, 1 Peter, and the Didache.

Irenaeus, the noted churchman of Lyon in Gaul toward the end of the second century, had an influence that extended as far as Rome. Thus the writings he accepted would likely also have been recognized by the early church. He believes there should be four Gospels:

[5]Edwin C. Blackman, *Marcion and His Influence* (London: Society for Promotion of Christian Knowledge, 1948).

[6]John Knox, *Marcion and the New Testament* (Chicago: University of Chicago Press, 1942).

It is not possible that the Gospels can be either more or fewer in number than they are. For, since there are four zones of the world in which we live, and four principal winds, while the Church is scattered throughout all the world, and the "pillar and ground" of the Church is the Gospel and the spirit of life; it is fitting that she should have four pillars, breathing out immortality on every side, and vivifying men afresh. For it is evident that the Word . . . has given us the Gospel under four aspects, but bound together by one Spirit . . . John . . . Luke . . . Matthew . . . Mark (*Against Heresies,* III, XI, 8).

In addition to the Gospels, Irenaeus is known to have quoted from all of Paul's epistles except Philemon—from 1 Peter, 1 and 2 John, Hebrews, and extensively from Acts and Revelation.

Through the testimony of Clement, a leading churchman in Alexandria in the first quarter of the third century, it is learned that several sources other than those of the present New Testament were relied upon by the Alexandrian church. He cites Clement of Rome's epistle to Corinth as well as the epistle of Barnabas, which he attributes to the apostle by that name. Clement maintains that the heretics, who refuse the entirety of the "Scriptures" (Old Testament) and who do not "believe the voice of the Lord," must be withstood; and he openly acknowledges the four Gospels of the church as opposed to the so-called "Gospel of the Egyptians."

Successor to Clement of Alexandria was the outstanding biblical scholar, Origen, who headed the Alexandrian school until he moved to Caesarea in A.D. 230. Origen died in A.D. 255 as an outcome of the tortures inflicted upon him for his faith. From the voluminious writings of Origen himself, taken in conjunction with the words of Eusebius, the church historian (*ca.* A.D. 325), the following observations may be gathered concerning the possible boundaries of Origen's canon: (1) Origen accepted the four Gospels, "which alone are unquestionable in the church of God," and possibly Acts, since it was generally accepted along with Luke. (2) He acknowledged the acceptance of Paul's (thirteen) epistles, though he seems not to have alluded to Philemon in his own works. (3) First Peter, 1 John, and Revelation are stated to have a recognized status everywhere, and Origen himself accepts 2 and 3 John, though pointing out that these are questioned by some. (4) Although Hebrews is not by Paul, "the thoughts of the Epistle are admirable and not inferior to the acknowledged writings" (Eusebius, *EH,* VI, XXV, 12). (5) Both James and Jude are apostolic, while 2 Peter, which receives its first mention in the work of Origen, is questioned. (6) Finally,

Origen apparently equated the Shepherd of Hermes and the epistle of Barnabas with the other works mentioned, because he appeals to the authority of each.

In 1740, L. A. Muratori discovered the now famous Muratorian Canon in the Ambrosian Library of Milan. The author speaks with authority and most likely represents the official position of the Roman church toward the end of the second century. Although only the books listed below are included, the author seems to leave the door open for further inclusions, should they measure up to the apostolic standard. Noticeably omitted are Hebrews, 2 Peter, 3 John, and James. The first part of the canon is torn away and the enumeration begins with Luke.

> The third book of the Gospel, that according to Luke . . . the physician . . . The fourth Gospel is that of John, one of the disciples . . . Moreover the Acts of all the Apostles are comprised by Luke in one book. . . Paul . . . writes to no more than seven churches by name, in this order: the first to the Corinthians . . . Ephesians . . . Colossians . . . Galatians . . . Thessalonians . . . Romans . . . He wrote, besides these, one to Philemon, and one to Titus, and two to Timothy . . . The Epistle of Jude indeed, and two belonging to the above named John, are reckoned among the Catholic epistles . . . also the Apocalypse of John and that of Peter, though some amongst us will not have this latter read in the Church . . . it [Shepherd of Hermes] ought also to be read; but it cannot be made public in the Church to the people.

The fourth century.—Eusebius, writing from Caesarea, where he was bishop, describes the content of his canon:

> First then must be put the holy quaternion of the Gospels; following them the Acts of the Apostles. After this must be reckoned the epistles of Paul; next in order the extant former epistle of John, and likewise the epistle of Peter, must be maintained. After them is to be placed, if it really seem proper, the Apocalypse of John, concerning which we shall give the different opinions at the proper time. These then belong among the accepted writings. Among the disputed writings, which are nevertheless recognized by many, are extant the so-called epistle of James and that of Jude, also the second epistle of Peter, and those that are called the second and third of John, whether they belong to the evangelist or to another person of the same name . . . and besides, as I said, the Apocalypse of John, if it seem proper, which some, as I said, reject, but which others class among the accepted books (Eusebius, *EH,* III, XXV).

The earliest extant listing of the twenty-seven New Testament writings, as are currently accepted by the Christian church, comes from the thirty-ninth Festal Letter of Athanasius of Alexandria in the year 367. However, the canon of Athanasius likely gives only the judgment of the Alexandrian church and does not speak for the entire Christian world of that time. Athanasius concludes his remarks on the canon:

> These are the fountains of salvation . . . In these alone is provided the doctrine of godliness. Let no man add to these, neither let him take ought from these . . . and there are other books besides these . . . appointed by the Fathers to be read by those who newly join us, and who wish for instruction in the word of godliness . . . the Wisdom of Solomon, and the Wisdom of Sirach, and Esther, and Judith, and Tobit, and that which is called the Teaching of the Apostles, and the Shepherd. But the former, my brethren, are included in the Canon, the latter being [merely] read.

The procedure followed in this brief survey of the early witnesses to the New Testament canon has been to sound out a few of the major Christian centers as represented by some of their leading churchmen. Thus far no conciliar actions on the part of the church have transpired; each man has cited his own judgment in light of what he believes to be the tradition of the church in these matters. Whereas opinion has been rather unanimous with respect to the bulk of the New Testament writings (Gospels, Acts, Pauline epistles), opinion has been divided on some of the other writings (Revelation, Hebrews, 2 Peter, 2 and 3 John, James, Jude). At the Council of Carthage (A.D. 397), representing a significant segment of the church, a formal decision was made with respect to the New Testament canon. With Augustine present the Council of Carthage openly pronounced its sanction upon the twenty-seven writings, no more and no less, a decision previously reached by the Council of Hippo in A.D. 393.

Epilogue.—The ensuing centuries have tended to congeal rather than to challenge the vote of this council. Negative voices have spoken out from time to time, but no modification of the New Testament canon confirmed at Carthage has ever been formally recognized by the church. What of the future? For several reasons it remains extremely improbable that the traditional canon of the church will ever be officially altered, despite the insights that recently (or yet to be) discovered sources used by portions of the early church may contribute to the current life of the church. (1) Official conciliar action, such as would be recognized by all Protestant

57. Page from early manuscript of the Greek New Testament (Codex Alexandrinus)

Christianity, is impossible to imagine.[7] (2) The New Testament, as it stands, holds a status of sacredness for the average Christian and is too emotionally related to his life for him to permit a council to add to or to take from its contents. (3) By whatever process the twenty-seven writings came to be a part of the church's Scriptures, it has been and remains the conviction of the church that this choice was effected under the leadership of the Holy Spirit and cannot be altered.

---

[7] The situation may be somewhat different with the **Roman Catholic Church.**

11

Inspiration and Authority
of the New Testament

—THE WINE IS RED

Inspiration of the New Testament

It is rightly confessed by the Christian community that the New Testament is the inspired Word of God. But no unanimity exists with respect to the full implications of this confession. Among those who believe in the divine inspiration of the New Testament there are many diverse viewpoints regarding the relationship between the divine and human elements involved in this inspiration. Does the New Testament itself offer any witness that would prove valuable in defining what should be meant by the affirmation that it is the inspired Word of God? Expressed otherwise, does the New Testament define the nature of its inspiration and authority? Inasmuch as two Scripture passages are often cited in support of certain theories of inspiration, attention should first of all be directed 'o an examination of these passages.

2 Timothy 3:16.—At least two translations of this verse are possible:

All scripture is inspired by God and profitable for teaching, for reproof, for correction, and for training in righteousness (RSV).

Every scripture inspired of God is also profitable for teaching, for reproof, for correction, for instruction which is in righteousness (ASV).

Before deciding in favor of either of these translations several observations should be made.

(1) In keeping with acceptable Greek style, Paul has omitted the verb *is* which must be supplied by the translator. In both translations the verb *is* has been supplied, though to give altogether different meanings to the verse. The Revised Standard Version emphasizes the *divine origin* of the Scriptures, while the American Standard

Version assumes the divine origin of the Scriptures and places the emphasis upon the *profitable ministries* that may be exercised by a proper use of the Scriptures. It should be noted that both translations are faithful to the Greek text, but the more acceptable translation is the one that better suits the entire context of 2 Timothy 3.

(2) In the overall context in which this verse appears, Paul is not seeking to substantiate any particular theory of scripture. Accepting the inspiration of scripture, he is listing some of the ways that scripture may be used: for teaching, for correcting error, for instruction in Christian living, so that the man of God may be adequately equipped for his ministry.

(3) The Greek word *theopneustos,* translated by the phrase "inspired by God," is neutral as regards any particular theory of inspiration. It does not in any fashion hint at the way in which God chose to inspire the men who wrote the Scriptures.

(4) Paul does not define what he means by "scripture," though in light of the preceding verse he is evidently alluding to the Old Testament, for he reminds Timothy how "from childhood" he has been acquainted with the "sacred writings" (2 Tim. 3:15).

From this examination of 2 Timothy 3:16 the following conclusions are reached: (1) The second translation (ASV) of this verse is more probable in light of the context, even though both translations are possible on the basis of the Greek text. (2) No particular theory of inspiration may be supported upon the testimony of these words. (3) In no way does this verse speak concerning the inspiration and authority of the New Testament, since Paul's point of reference is the Old Testament and its value for the minister.

2 Peter 1:20-21.—"First of all you must understand this, that no prophecy of scripture is a matter of one's own interpretation, because no prophecy ever came by the impulse of man, but men moved by the Holy Spirit spoke from God" (RSV).

One of the main aims of this epistle was to refute the misinterpretations and misuses of the Scriptures on the part of heretical teachers. But what "prophecies" does the author have in mind? In 2 Peter 3:16 these false teachers are described as those who "twist to their own destruction [the epistles of Paul], as they do the other scriptures." Taking this passage into consideration, 2 Peter 1:20-21 presents several possibilities. This may be a reference to (1) Old Testament prophecies in which the church saw predictions concerning Christ, (2) written apostolic traditions relating to the person of Christ, or else (3) a further collection of New Testament writings equated in authority with and placed alongside of a collection of Paul's letters.

All indications from the survey of the history of the canon militate against (3), but the choice between (1) and (2) is difficult. Fortunately enough, the same general conclusions are valid, no matter which of these two alternatives one selects, and the conclusions may be listed as three. (1) Second Peter argues that all scripture has its origin within the community of faith. Consequently, scripture cannot be properly interpreted by those outside the fellowship of the church. From Peter's point of view this would have been a legitimate claim, whether he had in mind certain Christian traditions or the Old Testament, since the church believed itself to be the heirs of the oracles of God contained in the Old Testament. (2) No definition of scripture is offered; the boundaries of authority are not marked out. (3) The exact relationship between the divine and the human elements in the inspiration of scripture are not specified. Nor is there intimated the degree of freedom which God granted those men who, "moved by the Holy Spirit, spoke from God."

Unity and diversity in inspiration.—One must conclude from the foregoing discussion that these two passages, when examined closely, neither substantiate any particular theory of inspiration, nor do they define the nature of the authority residing in the New Testament. Furthermore, there seems to be no single passage or group of passages in the New Testament wherein can be found a definition of inspiration. All indications from the reading of the New Testament itself suggest that God chose to let the writers use whatever sources were at their command and express in their own words what they had experienced concerning the Word of Life.

How otherwise can one account for the diverse styles and varying writing abilities of the New Testament authors? If God did not allow the different writers to speak his message in their own words, why is it that the author of Hebrews writes in excellent Greek style, while the author of 2 Peter struggles with Greek like a college freshman? Any theory of inspiration must necessarily take into consideration the *totality* of the New Testament witness, recognizing both its unity and its diversity. There is unity because the same Spirit of God inspired each of these men in the writing of his work; there is *diversity* because God chose to relate himself to these witnesses in a way that would utilize their individual personalities or abilities.

This is the *miracle of inspiration,* that God used frail and sinful human beings as the means of conveying his message to other persons in need of the good news. In a manner beyond understanding or definition God revealed himself and his will to "men of old," and these men have left in writing God's message for all subsequent generations. The value of a belief in the inspiration of the New Testament (and of the Old Testament) is not that the Christian possesses a pet theory with which to indoctrinate persons of a different viewpoint, but that he has the Word of God which he is called upon to proclaim to the world!

Authority of the New Testament

In the previous chapter it was confirmed that the ultimate authority of the New Testament resides in its witness to the person of Jesus Christ. But in what manner does this witness relate to the present life of the church? And what must be the attitude of the individual believer toward the authority of the New Testament?

Authority in the life of the church.—In truth it may be said that the church and the New Testament are mutually dependent upon

58. Approximately seven verses from Greek New Testament

θείας. ᾿Ιωάννης μαρτυρεῖ περὶ αὐτοῦ καὶ κέκραγεν λέγων᾿· οὗτος ἦν ὃν εἶπον·᾿ ὁ ὀπίσω μου ἐρχόμενος ᵀ ἔμπροσθέν μου γέγονεν, ὅτι πρῶτός μου ἦν·ᵌ. ᴦὅτι ἐκ τοῦ πληρώματος αὐτοῦ ἡμεῖς πάντες ἐλάβομεν, καὶ χάριν ἀντὶ χάριτος· ὅτι ὁ νόμος διὰ Μωϋσέως ἐδόθη, ἡ χάρις καὶ ἡ ἀλήθεια διὰ ᾿Ιησοῦ Χριστοῦ ἐγένετο. Θεὸν οὐδεὶς ἑώρακεν πώποτε· ᴦμονογενὴς θεὸς᾿ ὁ ὢν εἰς τὸν κόλπον τοῦ πατρός, ἐκεῖνος ἐξηγήσατοᵀ.

Καὶ αὕτη ἐστὶν ἡ μαρτυρία τοῦ ᾿Ιωάννου, ὅτε ἀπέστειλαν ☐πρὸς αὐτὸν᾿ οἱ ᾿Ιουδαῖοι ἐξ ᾿Ιεροσολύμων ἱερεῖς καὶ Λευίτας ἵνα ἐρωτήσωσιν αὐτόν· σὺ τίς εἶ;ᛁκαὶ ὡμολόγησεν καὶ οὐκ ἠρνήσατο, καὶ ὡμολόγησεν ὅτι ἐγὼ οὐκ εἰμὶ ὁ χριστός. καὶ

one another. There would be no New Testament were it not for the church: the New Testament was written, proclaimed, collected, canonized, and translated by the church under the leadership of God's Spirit. On the other hand, the church could not exist apart from the New Testament. This fact can be readily illustrated through a discussion of a few of the many areas where the authority of the New Testament is inseparably bound to the life of the church.

(1) The New Testament is the only valid and authoritative witness to the Lord of the church. Any interpretation of the person of Jesus Christ must stand or fall upon the basis of its conformity to or departure from the portrayal of Christ given in the New Testament. In a most unique sense the documents of the New Testament are related to the event which they proclaim as no other source can ever be, for they are based upon the testimony of eye- and ear-witnesses who had known Christ in the days of his earthly life.

(2) The New Testament forms the "sounding board" from which is echoed the voice of God's Spirit. Many times the leadership of God's Spirit has been wrongly interpreted because of the failure to take into account the words of the New Testament. It is an axiom that the Spirit of God never leads contrary to the will of God as expressed in the pages of the New Testament. For this reason, the New Testament is an indispensable tool for the understanding of the Spirit's leadership in the life of the church.

(3) The New Testament is necessary for understanding the nature and mission of the church. Even though the Old Testament can aid in the understanding of God's mission for the church, the New Testament is the final authority in this matter. Only the New Testament gives an adequate understanding of what it means for the church to be the redeemed people of God and what the mission of God's people is in a world that does not acknowledge God.

(4) The New Testament contains the message of the church. The only message which the church has is given in the New Testament (and in its companion, the Old Testament), and it is only through the preaching of this message that people are genuinely drawn to God. Also it is only through the preaching of the Word of God that the church perpetuates itself in the world. Men may otherwise become members of an organization which is called "the church," but they do not become a part of the *true church* except through responding to the witness to God contained in the New

Testament. Surely then it is the obligation of the church to *accept* gratefully and *use* prayerfully the New Testament Scriptures.[1]

Authority and the individual believer.—It should go without saying that the authority of the New Testament should extend to the life of the individual believer in the same fashion that it extends to the life of the church. In the same areas that the New Testament holds authority for the church it is also authoritative for each Christian. But does this mean that the believer must accept as an authoritarian absolute the entirety of the New Testament, or is he permitted to raise questions concerning the content and significance of these twenty-seven writings? The answer lies within the realm of *faith.*

In faith the New Testament was written, and in faith one accepts the Lord whom it proclaims. Under the guidance of the Holy Spirit, and within the fellowship of the church, the believer can and *must* analyze reverently and evaluate honestly all that he professes in faith. There can never be a severance between genuine faith and an honest study of the New Testament. And an honest study of the New Testament requires that the believer utilize all the available tools of biblical research, realizing that these are designed to aid him in his understanding of and appreciation for the Scriptures. Prayer and a reverent study of the Scriptures are not foes, they are allies, which together lead one to "grow in the grace and knowledge of our Lord and Savior Jesus Christ" (2 Peter 3:18).[2]

---

[1]Filson, *op. cit.*, p. 131.

[2]See the excellent discussion of Frederick C. Grant, *How to Read the Bible* (New York: Collier Books, 1961), pp. 27-38.

Appendix

—THE DATE OF THE LAST SUPPER AND THE CRUCIFIXION ACCORDING TO THE SYNOPTIC TRADITION

This chart is intended to provide the reader with an overall glance into the last events of Jesus' ministry. Three factors should be noted. (1) *Nisan* (April-May) was the Jewish name of the month in which the Passover annually occurred; preparation was made on the fourteenth, and the meal itself was eaten on the fifteenth. (2) Jewish months were *lunar*, which meant that a designated day of the month annually fell on different days of the week. (3) The Jewish day began at *sunset* (about 6:00 P.M.) and continued until the following sunset.

  I. *Nisan 14* (According to the Synoptic tradition it began in the year of the crucifixion on Wednesday evening)—*Preparation for the Passover* (Mark 14:12-16; Matt. 26:17-19; Luke 22: 7-13) would have been completed before sunset on Thursday.
 IIa. *Nisan 15* (Began on Thursday evening)
    1. *Eating of the Passover* (Mark 14:22-25; Matt. 26:26-29; Luke 22:14-20)
    2. *Gethsemane* (Mark 14:32-42; Matt. 26:36-46; Luke 22: 40-46)
    3. *Arrest* (Mark 14:43-52; Matt. 20:47-56; Luke 22:47-54)
    4. *Trial Before the Priest—Peter's Denial* (Mark 14:53-72; Matt. 26:57-75; Luke 22:54-71)
 IIb. *Nisan 15* (Continued until *Friday* at sunset)
    1. *A Second Council of the Priests and Sanhedrin* (Mark 15:1; Matt. 27:1-2; Luke 22:66)
    2. *Trial Before Pilate* (Mark 15:2-5; Matt. 27:11-14; Luke 23:2-5)
    3. *Christ Before Herod Antipas* (Luke 23:6-11)
    4. *Sentence of Death* (Mark 15:6-15; Matt. 27:15-26; Luke 23:17-25)

5. *Crucifixion* (Mark 15:22-32; Matt. 27:33-44; Luke 23: 33-43)
   Took place the third hour (Mark 15:25), i.e., at 9:00 A.M.
6. *Death* (Mark 15:33-41; Matt. 27:45-56 and Luke 23: 44-49)
   (1) Darkness, sixth to ninth hour (Mark 15:33), i.e., from 12:00 noon until 3:00 P.M.
   (2) Death at the ninth hour (Mark 15:34), i.e., at 3:00 P.M.
7. *Burial* (Mark 15:42-47; Matt. 27:57-61; Luke 23:50-56)
   This took place late on Friday, Nisan 15, i.e. about 4:00 P.M. Mark explains it was *late on the day of preparation for the sabbath,* which explains the urgency of Joseph's actions (cf. John 19:31).

IIIa. *Nisan 16—The Sabbath Day* (Saturday) began at sunset following the burial.

IIIb. *Nisan 16* cont'd. *The Guard Placed at the Tomb* (Matt. 27: 62-66)

Selected Bibliography
for Supplementary Reading

An attempt has been made to list books on the basis of their probable availability in the libraries of colleges where courses in New Testament are offered. Although this list represents a variety of viewpoints, each book was written by a recognized scholar in the area of New Testament study. Except in a very few instances all of the books in this bibliography are usable by persons who have no knowledge of Greek.

I. The Current Status of New Testament Studies

Reginald H. Fuller, *The New Testament in Current Study* (New York: Charles Scribner's Sons, 1962).

William Klassen and Graydon F. Snyder, *Current Issues in New Testament Study* (New York: Harper and Brothers, 1962).

Stephen Neil, *The Interpretation of the New Testament 1861-1961* (London: Oxford University Press, 1964).

II. New Testament Introductions

The following books are concerned mainly with the literature of the New Testament from the viewpoint of authorship, date, purpose, and historical setting.

Morton Scott Enslin, *The Literature of the Christian Movement* (New York: Harper and Row, 1956).

Robert M. Grant, *A Historical Introduction to the New Testament* (New York: Harper and Row, 1963).

Edgar J. Goodspeed, *An Introduction to the New Testament* (Chicago: The University of Chicago Press, 1953).

Richard Heard, *An Introduction to the New Testament* (New York: Harper and Row, 1950).

Archibald M. Hunter, *Introducing the New Testament* (Philadelphia: The Westminster Press, 1957).

Werner Georg Kummel, *Introduction to the New Testament*, Trans. A. J. Mattill, Jr. (Nashville: Abingdon Press, 1966).

A. H. McNeile, *An Introduction to the Study of the New Testament* (Oxford: The Clarendon Press, 1953).

Samuel Sandmel, *A Jewish Understanding of the New Testament* (Cincinnati: Hebrew Union College Press, 1957).

III. Surveys of the New Testament

The following deal at various levels with the background, history, content, and thought of the New Testament.

Floyd V. Filson, *A New Testament History* (Philadelphia: The Westminster Press, 1964).

Howard Clark Kee, Franklin W. Young, and Karlfried Froehlich, *Understanding the New Testament* (2nd ed.; Englewood Cliffs: Prentice Hall, 1965).

Bruce M. Metzger, *The New Testament: Its Background, Growth, and Content* (New York: Abingdon Press, 1965).

James L. Price, *Interpreting the New Testament* (New York: Holt, Rinehart and Winston, 1961).

IV. New Testament Background

C. K. Barrett, *The New Testament Background: Selected Documents* (New York: Harper and Row, 1961).

Matthew Black, *The Scrolls and Christian Origins* (New York: Charles Scribner's Sons, 1961).

Joseph Bonsirven, *Palestinian Judaism in the Time of Jesus Christ,* trans. William Wolf (New York: Holt, Rinehart and Winston, Inc., 1964).

A. C. Bouquet, *Everyday Life in New Testament Times* (New York: Charles Scribner's Sons, 1954).

William Hugh Brownlee, *The Meaning of the Qumran Scrolls for the Bible* (New York: Oxford University Press, 1964).

F. F. Bruce, *Second Thoughts on the Dead Sea Scrolls* (Grand Rapids: Wm. B. Eerdmans Publishing Co., 1956).

Rudolf Bultmann, *Primitive Christianity,* trans. R. H. Fuller (New York: Meridian Books, 1956).

Frank M. Cross, Jr., *The Ancient Library of Qumran* (2nd ed.; Garden City: Doubleday and Co., 1961).

Werner Foerster, *From the Exile to Christ: A Historical Introduction to Palestinian Judaism,* trans. Gordon E. Harris (Philadelphia: Fortress Press, 1964).

Theodore H. Gaster, *The Scriptures of the Dead Sea Sect* (New York: Doubleday and Co., 1964).

Edgar J. Goodspeed, *The Story of the Apocrypha* (Chicago: University of Chicago Press, 1952).

Robert M. Grant (ed.), *Gnosticism* (New York: Harper and Brothers, 1961).

——————————, *Gnosticism and Early Christianity* (New York: Columbia University Press, 1959).

Frederick C. Grant, *Ancient Judaism and the New Testament* (New York: The Macmillan Co., 1959).

——————————, *Roman Hellenism and the New Testament* (New York: Charles Scribner's Sons, 1962).

Bruce M. Metzger, *An Introduction to the Apocrypha* (New York: Oxford University Press, 1957).

W. O. E. Oesterley, *A History of Israel* (Oxford: The Clarendon Press, 1951).

Steward Perowne, *The Later Herods* (Nashville: Abingdon Press, 1958).

R. H. Pfeiffer, *History of New Testament Times with an Introduction to the Apocrypha* (New York: Harper and Brothers, 1949).

D. S. Russell, *The Method and Message of Jewish Apocalyptic: The Old Testament Library* (Philadelphia: The Westminster Press, 1964).

Emil Schürer, *A History of the Jewish People in the Time of Jesus,* ed. Nahum N. Glatzer (New York: Schocken Books, 1961).

Norman H. Snaith, *The Jews from Cyrus to Herod* (Wallington, England: The Religious Education Press, Ltd., 1949).

Krister Stendahl (ed.) *The Scrolls and the New Testament* (New York: Harper and Brothers, 1957).

R. McL. Wilson, *The Gnostic Problem* (London: A. R. Mowbray and Co., 1958).

Solomon Zeitlin, *The Rise and Fall of the Judaean State, Vol. I* (Philadelphia: The Jewish Publication Society of America, 1962).

V. The Person, Message, and Ministry of Jesus

A. The following books are concerned primarily with the form of Jesus' message and its transmission.

Rudolf Bultmann, *The History of the Synoptic Tradition,* trans. John Marsh (New York: Harper and Row, 1963).

Rudolf Bultmann and Karl Kundsin, *Form Criticism,* trans. Frederick M. Grant (New York: Harper, 1962).

Martin Dibelius, *The Message of Jesus Christ,* trans. Frederick C. Grant (New York: Charles Scribner's Sons, 1939).

Edwyn Hoskins and Noel Davey, *The Riddle of the New Testament* (London: Faber and Faber, 1952).

Robert Henry Lightfoot, *History and Interpretation in the Gospels* (London: Hodder and Stoughton, 1935).

Alan Richardson, *The Miracle Stories of the Gospels* (London: SCM Press, 1941).

E. Basil Redlich, *Form Criticism* (London: Duckworth Press, 1948).

Vincent Taylor, *The Formation of the Gospel Tradition* (London: Macmillan and Co., 1953).

B. The following books are concerned primarily with an understanding of Jesus ministry, though in varying degrees each discusses certain aspects of his person and message.

Francis Wright Beare, *The Earliest Records of Jesus* (Nashville: Abingdon Press, 1962).

Dwight Marion Beck, *Through the Gospels to Jesus* (New York: Harper and Brothers, 1954).

Cecil John Cadoux, *The Historic Mission of Jesus* (New York: Harper and Brothers, n.d.).

Morton S. Enslin, *The Prophet from Nazareth* (New York: McGraw-Hill Book Co., 1961).

Maurice Goguel, *The Life of Jesus* (London: George Allen and Unwin Ltd., 1954).

Martin Dibelius, *Jesus,* trans. Charles B. Hedrick and Frederick C. Grant (Philadelphia: Westminster Press, 1949).

Archibald M. Hunter, *The Work and Words of Jesus* (Philadelphia: The Westminster Press, 1950).

Joseph Klausner, *Jesus of Nazareth: His Life, Times, and Teaching,* trans. Herbert Danby (New York: The Macmillan Co., 1925).

R. D. A. Major, T. W. Manson, G. J. Wright, *The Mission and Message of Jesus* (New York: E. P. Dutton and Co., 1938).

Vincent Taylor, *The Life and Ministry of Jesus* (New York: Abingdon, 1955).

H. E. W. Turner, *Jesus, Master and Lord* (London: A. R. Mowbray and Co., 1957).

C. The following books are concerned primarily with the interpretation of Jesus' message and teaching.

G. R. Beasley-Murray, *Jesus and the Future* (London: Macmillan and Co., 1954).

Günther Bornkamm, *Jesus of Nazareth,* trans. Irene and Fraser McLusky with James M. Robinson (New York: Harper and Brothers, 1960).

Rudolf Bultmann, *Jesus and the Word,* trans. L. P. Smith and E. Huntress (New York: Charles Scribner's Sons, 1958).

Martin Dibelius, *The Sermon on the Mount* (New York: Charles Scribner's Sons, 1940).

C. H. Dodd, *The Parables of the Kingdom* (London: Nisbet and Co., Ltd., 1956).

S. MacLean Gilmore, *The Gospel Jesus Preached* (Philadelphia: The Westminster Press, 1957).

Archibald M. Hunter, *Interpreting the Parables* (Philadelphia: The Westminster Press, 1960).

Joachim Jeremias, *The Parables of Jesus,* trans. S. H. Hooke (rev. ed.; New York: Charles Scribner's Sons, 1963).

Harvey K. McArthur, *Understanding the Sermon on the Mount* (New York: Harper and Brothers, 1960).

T. W. Manson, *The Teaching of Jesus* (Cambridge: The Cambridge University Press, 1951).

————, *The Sayings of Jesus* (London: SCM Press Ltd., 1949).

Hans Windisch, *The Meaning of the Sermon on the Mount,* trans. S. Maclean Gilmour (Philadelphia: The Westminster Press, 1951).

D. The following books are concerned primarily with an interpretation of Jesus' person and work.

George S. Duncan, *Jesus, Son of Man* (London: Nisbet and Co., Ltd., 1948).

William Manson, *Jesus the Messiah* (London: Hodder and Stoughton, 1956).

Rudolf Otto, *The Kingdom of God and the Son of Man,* trans. Floyd V. Filson and Bertram Lee-Woolf (London: Lutterworth Press, 1951).

Edward Schweizer, *Lordship and Discipleship* (Naperville, Ill.: Alec R. Allenson, 1960).

Vincent Taylor, *Jesus and His Sacrifice* (London: Macmillan and Co., 1955).

E. Commentaries on and Special Studies in the Synoptic Gospels

Ernest Best, *The Temptation and the Passion: The Markan Soteriology* (Cambridge: University Press, 1965).

Edward P. Blair, *Jesus in the Gospel of Matthew* (Nashville: Abingdon Press, 1960).

Gunther Bornkamm, Gerhard Barth, and Heinz Joachim Held, *Tradition and Interpretation in the Gospel of Matthew* (Philadelphia: Westminster Press, 1963).

Harvie Branscomb, *The Gospel of Mark: The Moffatt New Testament Commentary* (New York: Harper and Brothers, n.d.).

Robert G. Bratcher, and Eugene A. Nida, *A Translator's Handbook on the Gospel of Mark* (Leiden: E. J. Brill, 1961).

T. A. Burkhill, *Mysterious Revelation: An Examination of the Philosophy of Mark's Gospel* (Ithaca: Cornell University Press, 1963).

B. C. Butler, *The Originality of St. Matthew* (Cambridge: University Press, 1951).

Hans Conzelmann, *The Theology of St. Luke,* trans. Geoffrey Buswell (London: Faber and Faber, 1960).

W. D. Davies, *The Setting of the Sermon on the Mount* (Cambridge: University Press, 1964).

William R. Farmer, *The Synoptic Problem* (New York: The Macmillan Co., 1964).

Martin H. Franzmann, *Follow Me: Discipleship According to St. Matthew* (St. Louis: Concordia Publishing House, 1961).

S. MacLean Gilmour, "The Gospel According to St. Luke: Introduction and Exegesis," *The Interpreter's Bible,* VIII (Nashville: Abingdon Press, 1952), 3-434.

——————, "The Gospel of Matthew: Introduction and Exegesis," *The Interpreter's Bible,* VII (Nashville: Abingdon-Cokesbury Press, 1951), 1231-1625.

Frederick C. Grant, *The Gospels: Their Origin and Their Growth* (New York: Harper and Brothers, 1957).

——————, "The Gospel According to St. Mark: Introduction and Exegesis," *The Interpreter's Bible* (Nashville, Abingdon-Cokesbury Press, 1951), VII, 629-917.

——————, *The Gospel According to St. Mark: Harper's New Testa-*

ment Commentaries (New York: Harper and Row, 1960).

A. R. C. Leaney, *The Gospel According to St. Luke: Harper's New Testament Commentaries* (New York: Harper and Row, 1958).

R. H. Lightfoot, *The Gospel Message of St. Mark* (Oxford: Clarendon Press, 1950).

William Manson, *The Gospel of Luke: The Moffatt New Testament Commentary* (New York: Harper and Brothers, n.d.).

Theodore H. Robinson, *The Gospel of Matthew: The Moffatt New Testament Commentary* (New York: Harper and Brothers, n.d.).

B. H. Streeter, *The Four Gospels. A Study of Origins* (London: Macmillan and Co., 1951).

Charles H. Talbert, *Luke and the Gnostics* (Nashville: Abingdon Press, 1966).

F. The person and work of Jesus in light of the Gospel of John.

Rudolf Bultmann, "The Theology of the Gospel of John and the Johannine Epistles." *The Theology of the New Testament,* trans. Kendrick Grobel (New York: Charles Scribner's Sons, 1955), II, 1-92.

H. E. Dana, *The Ephesian Tradition: An Oral Source of the Fourth Gospel* (Kansas City: The Kansas City Seminary Press, 1940).

C. H. Dodd, *The Interpretation of the Fourth Gospel* (Cambridge: University Press, 1954).

───────────, *Historical Tradition in the Fourth Gospel* (Cambridge: University Press, 1963).

Edwyn Clement Hoskyns and Francis Noel Davey, *The Fourth Gospel* (London: Faber and Faber Ltd., 1961).

Wilbert Francis Howard, *The Fourth Gospel in Recent Criticism and Interpretation,* rev. C. K. Barrett (London: Epworth Press, 1955).

R. H. Lightfoot, *St. John's Gospel: A Commentary* (Oxford: Oxford University Press, 1961).

C. H. C. Macgregor, *The Gospel of John: The Moffatt New Testament Commentary* (New York: Harper and Brothers, n.d.).

E. F. Scott, *The Fourth Gospel: Its Purpose and Theology* (Edinburgh: T. and T. Clark, 1943).

T. C. Smith, *Jesus in the Gospel of John* (Nashville: Broadman Press, 1959).

R. H. Strachan, *The Fourth Gospel* (London: Student Christian Movement Press, Ltd., 1955).

William Temple, *Readings in St. John's Gospel,* First Series (London: Macmillan and Co., 1942), chaps. 1-12.

VI. Studies in the Acts of the Apostles and in the Life of the Early Church

F. F. Bruce, *Commentary on the Book of Acts: The New International Commentary on the New Testament* (Grand Rapids: Wm. B. Eerdmans Publishing Co., 1955).

Henry J. Cadbury, *The Book of Acts in History* (New York: Harper and Brothers, 1955).

G. B. Caird, *The Apostolic Age* (London: Gerald Duckworth and Co., 1955).

Oscar Cullmann, *Peter: Disciple, Apostle, Martyr,* trans. Floyd V. Filson (Philadelphia: The Westminster Press, 1953).

Martin Dibelius, *Studies in the Acts of the Apostles,* ed. Heinrich Greeven; trans. Mary Ling (New York: Charles Scribner's Sons, 1956).

C. H. Dodd, *The Apostolic Preaching and Its Developments* (New York: Harper, 1937).

Floyd V. Filson, *Three Crucial Decades: Studies in the Book of Acts* (Richmond: John Knox Press, 1963).

F. J. Foakes-Jackson, *The Acts of the Apostles: The Moffatt New Testament Commentary* (New York: Harper and Brothers, n.d.).

——————, and Kirsopp Lake (eds.), *The Beginnings of Christianity* (5 vols.; London: Macmillan and Co., 1920-33), especially vol. 4, a commentary on Acts and vol. 5, a series of essays on subjects related to the study of Acts.

William M. Ramsey, *Pictures of the Apostolic Church* (Grand Rapids: Baker Book House, 1959).

Frank Stagg, *The Book of Acts* (Nashville: Broadman Press, 1955).

C. S. C. Williams, *The Acts of the Apostles: Harper's New Testament Commentaries* (New York: Harper and Row, 1957).

VII. The Apostle Paul

A. The Life and Thought of the Apostle Paul

Elias Andrews, *The Meaning of Christ for Paul* (Nashville: Abingdon Press, 1949).

William Barclay, *The Mind of St. Paul* (New York: Harper and Brothers, 1958).

C. K. Barrett, *From First Adam to Last* (London: Adam and Charles Black, 1962).

Rudolf Bultmann, "The Theology of Paul," *The Theology of the New Testament,* trans. Kendrick Grobel (New York: Charles Scribner's Sons, 1951), I, 185-352.

Francis Wright Beare, *St. Paul and His Letters* (London: Adam and Charles Black, 1962).

L. Cerfaux, *The Church in the Theology of St. Paul,* trans. Geoffrey Webb and Adrain Walker (Freiburg: Herder and Herder, 1959).

Henry Daniel-Rops, *St. Paul: Apostle of Nations,* trans. Jex Martin (Chicago: Fides Publishers Association, 1953).

W. D. Davies, *Paul and Rabbinic Judaism* (London: S.P.C.K., 1958).

George S. Duncan, *St. Paul's Ephesian Ministry* (London: Hodder and Stoughton, 1929).

E. Earle Ellis, *Paul's Use of the Old Testament* (Edinburgh: Oliver and Boyd, 1957).

——————, *Paul and His Recent Interpreters* (Grand Rapids: Wm. B. Eerdmans Co., 1961).

A. M. Hunter, *Paul and His Predecessors* (London: SCM Press, Ltd., 1961).

Wilfred L. Knox, *St. Paul and the Church of the Gentiles* (Cambridge: University Press, 1961).

Emil G. Kraeling, *I Have Kept the Faith: The Life of the Apostle Paul* (New York: Rand-McNally and Co., 1965).

Henri Metzger, *St. Paul's Journey's in the Greek Orient*, trans. S. H. Hooke (London: S.C.M. Press, Ltd., 1955).

Arthur Darby Nock, *St. Paul* (New York: Harper and Row, 1963).

H. J. Schoeps, *Paul*, trans. Harold Knight (Philadelphia: Westminster Press, 1961).

Hugh J. Schonfield, *The Jew of Tarsus* (New York: The Macmillan Co., 1947).

Albert Schweitzer, *The Mysticism of Paul the Apostle*, trans. William Montgomery (New York: Henry Holt and Co., 1931).

James S. Stewart, *A Man in Christ* (New York: Harper and Brothers, n.d.).

Alfred Wikenhauser, *Pauline Mysticism* (Freiburg: Herder Druck, 1960).

B. Commentaries on the Pauline Epistles

C. H. Dodd, *The Epistles to the Romans: The Moffatt New Testament Commentary* (New York: Harper and Brothers, n.d.).

C. K. Barrett, *The Epistle to the Romans: Harper's New Testament Commentaries* (New York: Harper and Row, 1957).

Karl Barth, *The Epistle to the Romans*, trans. Edwyn C. Hoskyns (Oxford: University Press, 1933).

John Knox, "The Epistle to the Romans: Introduction and Exegesis," *The Interpreter's Bible* (Nashville: Abingdon Press, 1954), IX, 353-668.

John Murray, *The Epistle to the Romans: The New International Commentary on the New Testament* (Grand Rapids: Wm. B. Eerdmans Co., 1959), Vols. I and II.

Anders Nygren, *Commentary on Romans*, trans. Carl C. Rasmussen (London: S.C.M. Press Ltd., 1952).

Clarence Tucker Craig, "The First Epistle to the Corinthians: Introduction and Exegesis." *The Interpreter's Bible* (Nashville: Abingdon Press, 1953), X, 1-262.

Floyd V. Filson, "The Second Epistle to the Corinthians: Introduction and Exegesis," *The Interpreter's Bible* (Nashville: Abingdon Press, 1953), X, 263-425.

F. W. Grosheide, *The First Epistle to the Corinthians: The New International Commentary on the New Testament* (Grand Rapids: Wm. B. Eerdmans Co., 1953).

Jean Héring, *The First Epistle of Saint Paul to the Corinthians* (London: Epworth Press, 1964).

Philip Edguembe Hughes, *Paul's Second Epistle to the Corinthians: The New International Commentary on the New Testament* (Grand Rapids: Wm. B. Eerdmans Co., 1962).

James Moffatt, *The First Epistle of Paul to the Corinthians: The Moffatt New Testament Commentary* (New York: Harper and Brothers, n.d.).

R. H. Strachen, *The Second Epistle of Paul to the Corinthians: The Moffatt New Testament Commentary* (New York: Harper and Brothers, n.d.).

George S. Duncan, *The Epistle of Paul to the Galatians: The Moffatt New Testament Commentary* (New York: Harper and Brothers, n.d.).

Herman N. Ridderbos, *The Epistles of Paul to the Churches of Galatia: The New International Commentary on the New Testament* (Grand Rapids: Wm. B. Eerdmans Co., 1953).

R. T. Stamm, "The Epistle to the Galatians: Introduction and Exegeis," *The Interpreter's Bible* (Nashville: Abingdon Press, 1953), X, 427-593.

Frank W. Beare, "The Epistle to the Colossians: Introduction and Exegesis," *The Interpreter's Bible* (Nashville: Abingdon Press, 1955), XI, 131-241.

The Epistle to the Philippians: Harper's New Testament Commentaries (New York: Harper and Row, 1959).

"The Epistle to the Ephesians: Introduction and Exegesis," *The Interpreter's Bible* (Nashville: Abingdon Press, 1953), X, 597-749.

Edgar J. Goodspeed, *The Key to Ephesians* (Chicago: University of Chicago Press, 1956).

John Knox, "The Epistle to Philemon: Introduction and Exegesis," *The Interpreter's Bible* (Nashville: Abingdon Press, 1955), XI, 553-573.

——————, *Philemon Among the Letters of Paul* (London: Collins, 1960).

J. Hugh Michael, *The Epistle of Paul to the Philippians: The Moffatt New Testament Commentary* (New York: Harper and Brothers, n.d.).

C. L. Mitton, *The Epistle to the Ephesians: Its Authorship, Origin, and Purpose* (Oxford: Clarendon Press, 1951).

Dale Moody, *Christ and the Church: An Exposition of Ephesians with Special Application to Some Present Issues* (Grand Rapids: Wm. B. Eerdmans Co., 1963).

J. J. Miller, *The Epistle of Paul to the Philippians and to Philemon: The New International Commentary on the New Testament* (Grand Rapids: Wm. B. Eerdmans Co., 1955).

Ernest F. Scott, "The Epistle to the Philippians: Introduction and Exegesis," *The Interpreter's Bible* (Nashville: Abingdon Press, 1955), XI, 1-129.

——————, *The Epistles of Paul to the Colossians, to Philemon and to the Ephesians* (New York: Harper and Brothers, n.d.).

E. K. Simpson and F. F. Bruce, *The Epistles to the Ephesians and Colossians: The New International Commentary on the New Testament* (Grand Rapids: Wm. B. Eerdmans Co., 1957).

Ray Summers, *Ephesians: Pattern for Christian Living* (Nashville: Broadman Press, 1960).

J. W. Bailey, "The First and Second Epistles to the Thessalonians: Introduction and Exegesis." *The Interpreter's Bible* (Nashville: Abingdon Press, 1955), XI, 243-339.

Leon Morris, *The First and Second Epistles to the Thessalonians: The New International Commentary on the New Testament* (Grand Rapids: Wm. B. Eerdmans Co., 1959).

William Neil, *The Epistle of Paul to the Thessalonians: The Moffatt New Testament Commentary* (New York: Harper and Brothers, n.d.).

C. K. Barrett, *The Pastoral Epistles in the New English Bible, with Introduction and Commentary: The New Clarendon Bible* (New York: Oxford University Press, 1963).

Burton Scott Easton, *The Pastoral Epistles* (New York: Charles Scribner's Sons, 1947).

P. N. Harrison, *The Problem of the Pastoral Epistles* (Oxford: University Press, 1921).

J. N. D. Kelly, *The Pastoral Epistles: I Timothy, II Timothy, Titus—Harper's New Testament Commentaries* (New York: Harper and Row, 1963).

E. F. Scott, *The Pastoral Epistles: The Moffatt New Testament Commentary* (New York: Harper and Brothers, n.d.).

VIII. The Epistle to the Hebrews

F. F. Bruce, *The Epistle to the Hebrews: The New International Commentary on the New Testament* (Grand Rapids: Wm. B. Eerdmans Co., 1964).

William Manson, *The Epistle to the Hebrews* (London: Hodder and Stoughton, 1957).

H. W. Montefiore, *The Epistle to the Hebrews: Harper's New Testament Commentaries* (New York: Harper and Row, 1964).

A. C. Purdy, "The Epistle to the Hebrews: Introduction and Exegesis," *The Interpreter's Bible* (Nashville: Abingdon Press, 1955), XI, 575-763.

Theodore H. Robinson, *The Epistle to the Hebrews: The Moffatt New Testament Commentary* (New York: Harper and Brothers, n.d.).

E. F. Scott, *The Epistle to the Hebrews: Its Doctrine and Significance* (Edinburgh: T. and T. Clark, 1923).

IX. The General Epistles

C. H. Dodd, *The Johannine Epistles: The Moffatt New Testament Commentary* (New York: Harper and Brothers, n.d.).

B. S. Easton, "The Epistle of James; Introduction and Exegesis," *The Interpreter's Bible* (Nashville: Abingdon Press, 1957), XII, 1-74.

A. M. Hunter, "The First Epistle of Peter: Introduction and Exegesis,"

The Interpreter's Bible (Nashville: Abingdon Press, 1957), XII, 75-159.

James Moffatt. *The General Epistles: James, Peter and Judas—The Moffatt New Testament Commentary* (New York: Harper and Brothers, n.d.).

Alexander Ross, *The Epistles of James and John: The New International Commentary on the New Testament* (Grand Rapids: Wm. B. Eerdmans Co., 1954).

Amos N. Wilder, "The First, Second and Third Epistles of John: Introduction and Exegesis," *The Interpreter's Bible* (Nashville: Abingdon Press, 1957), XII, 207-313.

X. The Book of Revelation

John Wick Bowman, *The Drama of the Book of Revelation* (Philadelphia: The Westminster Press, n.d.).

Philip Carrington, *The Meaning of the Revelation* (London: Society for Promoting Christian Knowledge, 1937).

Austin Farrar, *The Revelation of St. John the Divine* (Oxford: Clarendon Press, 1964).

Martin Kiddle, *The Revelation of St. John: The Moffatt New Testament Commentary* (New York: Harper and Brothers, n.d.).

Edward A. McDowell, *The Meaning and Message of the Book of Revelation* (Nashville: Broadman Press, 1951).

Ernest F. Scott, *The Book of Revelation* (2nd ed. Naperville: Alec R. Allenson, Inc., 1949).

Ray Summers, *Worthy Is the Lamb: An Interpretation of Revelation* (Nashville: Broadman Press, 1951).

XI. The Theology and Christology of the New Testament

Thomas Boslooper, *The Virgin Birth* (Philadelphia: The Westminster Press, 1962).

Rudolf Bultmann, *The Theology of the New Testament,* trans. Kendrick Grobel (2 vols.; New York: Charles Scribner's Sons, 1951 and 1955).

Oscar Cullman. *The Christology of the New Testament,* trans. S. C. Guthrie and C. A. M. Hall (Philadelphia: The Westminster Press, 1959).

Reginald H. Fuller, *The Foundations of New Testament Christology* (New York: Charles Scribner's Sons, 1965).

Frederick C. Grant, *An Introduction to New Testament Thought* (Nashville: Abingdon Press, 1958).

H. A. A. Kennedy, *The Theology of the Epistles* (Naperville: Alec R. Allenson, 1956).

John Knox, *The Death of Christ: The Cross in the New Testament History and Faith* (Nashville: Abingdon Press, 1958).

Charles M. Laymon, *Christ in the New Testament* (Nashville: Abingdon Press, 1958).

A. M. Ramsey, *The Resurrection of Christ: An Essay in Biblical Theology* (Naperville: Alec R. Allenson, 1956).

Alan Richardson, *An Introduction to the Theology of the New Testament* (New York: Harper and Brothers, 1959).

Frank Stagg, *New Testament Theology* (Nashville: Broadman Press, 1962).

Ethelbert Stauffer, *New Testament Theology,* trans. John Marsh (New York: The Macmillan Co., 1956).

George Baker Stevens, *The Theology of the New Testament* (New York: Charles Scribner's Sons, 1914).

Vincent Taylor, *The Person of Christ in the New Testament* (New York: St. Martin's Press, 1958).

appearances after resurrection.
1. Women
2. Peter
3.   12
4. 500
5. James
6. apostles
7. Paul

Seven Signs of John
1. Water to wine
2. healing noblemans son
3. feeding multitude
4. walking on water
5. sight to man born blind
6. raising Lazarus
7. own death, burial + resurrection

Summary of Paul's messages
1. Christ appeared sig nifing fulfillment
   of scriptures + beginning of new age
2. Christ is Born of the seed of David.
3. died according to scriptures to deliver
   us from evil age
4. buried
5. rose on 3rd day ascending to scriptures
6. Presently Son of God on Gods Right Hand.
7. Future Judge + Redeemer in second coming